Barbara A. Drummond.

A
Marriage of
Inconvenience

A
Marriage of
Inconvenience

The Persecution
of Ruth and Seretse Khama

Michael Dutfield

UNWIN

HYMAN

LONDON   SYDNEY   WELLINGTON

First published in Great Britain by the Trade Division of
Unwin Hyman Limited, 1990

UNWIN HYMAN LIMITED
15–17 Broadwick Street
London W1V 1FP

Allen & Unwin Australia Pty Ltd
8 Napier Street, North Sydney, NSW 2060, Australia

Allen & Unwin New Zealand Pty Ltd with the Port Nicholson Press
Compusales Building, 75 Ghuznee Street, Wellington, New Zealand.

British Library Cataloguing in Publication Data

Dutfield, Michael
   A marriage of inconvenience: the persecution of Ruth and
Seretse Khama.
1. Great Britain. Khama, Ruth. Interpersonal
relationships with Khama, Sir Seretse, *1921–80*. South
Africa. Khama, Sir Seretse. 1980 interpersonal
relationships with Khama, Ruth
I. Title
941.085'092'4
ISBN 0–04–440495–6

Typeset in 11 on 12½ point Palatino by Columns of Reading.
Printed in Great Britain by Hartnoll Ltd, Bodmin, Cornwall.

To
Margaret my mother
and
Heather my wife

Contents

Preface   *page* ix

Introduction   xi

 1 London Love   1
 2 Children of the Kalahari   10
 3 The Bishop Decides   25
 4 Seeing Sense   35
 5 Stern Realities   40
 6 A Fire Burning   46
 7 Seachange   58
 8 Pula!   64
 9 The Perfect Chief   74
10 God's People   79
11 For the Greater Good   85
12 In the Interest of the Nation   97
13 No Alternative   107
14 'Mrs Jones' Flies Out   113
15 Loaded Dice   121
16 Cover-up   130
17 The Invitation   139
18 Money on the Table   146
19 Tricked!   156
20 Midsummer Madness   168
21 Shattered Faith   175
22 Sleepless Nights   188
23 Together at Last   198
24 Exile   202

Postscript   208

Bibliography   216

Index   218

List of Illustrations

Map of Bechuanaland, now the Republic of Botswana   *page* x

Between pages 114 *to* 115
1. Clement Attlee (*Topham*)
2. Patrick Gordon-Walker (*Topham*)
3. The Right Revd William Wand, Bishop of London (*Topham*)
4. Sir Evelyn Baring (*Topham*)
5. Philip Noel-Baker (*Topham*)
6. Ruth's sister Muriel and their Mother and Father (*Lady Khama*)
7. Tshekedi Khama (*Hulton Picture Library*)
8. Ruth and Seretse after their marriage (*Lady Khama*)
9. The marriage certificate
10. Seretse pleading his case at the Kgotla
11. Ruth waves at the plane at Mahalapye (*Lady Khama*)
12. Ruth meeting Seretse as he arrives for a weekend visit (*Lady Khama*)
13. Arriving in exile
14. Ian Khama as Paramount Chief (*Lady Khama*)
15. The twins Tshekedi and Tony with Jacqueline (*Lady Khama*)
16. Lady Ruth Khama (*Lady Khama*)

Preface

This is a work of fact. None of the characters is fictitious, none of the events imagined. It is a synthesis of the memories of those who were involved and of the hitherto secret documents left behind by powerful men now dead.

The better to engage the reader, the book is written in a narrative style. This has involved the creation of dialogue in direct speech. On every occasion, such creations are based on clear documentation or the vivid recollection of one of the participants.

The long speeches given by various tribesmen in the Kgotla meetings in Serowe, for example, are based on the detailed notes taken down by the resident missionary at the time, and translated and typed up by him every evening. Those notes and other relevant London Missionary Society documents are stored at the School of Oriental and African Studies, London University. The confrontations between Seretse Khama and various British government ministers are drawn directly from contemporaneous notes written by civil servants present at the meetings. Similarly, other discussions between officials and ministers, secret until now, reflect exactly the official records. Those documents, stored in the British Public Record Office, are listed in the Bibliography.

I hope that by adopting an accessible style based rigorously on documented evidence and vivid memory, the reader will enter into the drama and emotion of the events here depicted assured that what is read is as true to what actually happened as surviving testimony will allow.

M.J.D.
London, January 1990

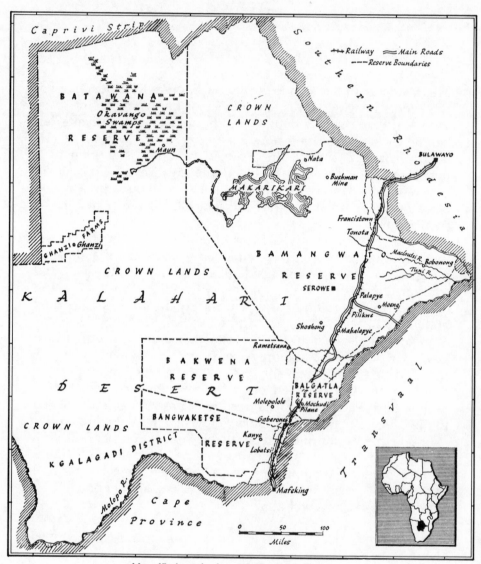

Map of Bechuanaland, now the Republic of Botswana.

Introduction

The door opened in a blaze of African sunlight and Lady Khama swept into the room. As slim as in the 40-year-old photographs I had seen, her hair still more blonde than grey, she greeted me brusquely and suggested we drive into town for morning coffee. It was a suggestion which sounded like an instruction. Parking near the central shopping area, we walked quickly through the glare and the heat to a hotel verandah. On either side of us people watched her, nodding a greeting when she caught their eye. The widow of the dead President commanded deep respect in Botswana. The waiter showed us to a shaded table and she ordered.

I had only a few hours in the country before catching my flight to London that afternoon and had managed to reroute my ticket on my way home from an assignment in neighbouring South Africa. She had agreed to meet me.

For four years I had been writing to her and reading the published reports of her life. I had been little more than a year old when her name had been in headlines from Britain to South Africa, India to the USA. Then, as Ruth Williams, a 24-year-old English girl, she had met Seretse Khama, an African prince and heir to the chieftainship of a tribe of more than 100,000. They had fallen in love and married, setting heads shaking and tongues wagging from the London of their courtship to the tribal capital on the edge of the Kalahari Desert which was his home. To begin with, that marriage between black and white had been no more welcome in the round, mud huts of Africa than in the smart restaurants of the West End.

But even the prejudice and bitter rejection they had both suffered then were nothing to what followed. Within a year of their wedding, the young couple had provoked an astonishing sequence of events that has never been explained. For reasons it never justified, the British government had embarked on what appeared to be a vendetta against them, robbing Seretse of his birthright and his people of their chief. In the process, he and Ruth had been forcibly separated at the very time when she needed him most. When, at last, the British drove them both into exile, the loyalty of blacks throughout the Empire was undermined and the moral basis of the whole government was shaken. Why had it happened? What had this young couple done to deserve such hostility? What had been their crime? Why should a marriage provoke such vindictiveness? Was it simply that he was black and she white? Was it because of pressure from South Africa whose policy of apartheid was even then enslaving 15 million blacks? If so, what hold did South Africa have over Britain to enforce her will? A hundred questions were asked at the time but had never been answered and the world had moved on.

Those answers, I knew, were only partly to be found in the person sitting opposite me sipping coffee. There were clues to be discovered in a string of villages along the south-eastern edge of the Kalahari with names like Palapye, Mahalapye, Mmadinare and Shoshong. Above all I would have to go to Serowe, a village of a thousand huts squatting at the foot of a hill where the desert sands peter out into scrubland grass and thorn bushes. There I would find many of the old tribal elders, the 'royal uncles', still alive – tall, lean men, some in their eighties, others even older, all burnt black by the sun.

They would retell what Seretse had done, how news had come to their huts and to their cattle-posts that he had married a white woman on the other side of the world. They would remember how the tribe had been split almost in two at the prospect of a white queen; how, finally, he had brought her to them, and how her loyalty to Seretse and to them had made them love her. And they would remember what the British had done. Sitting round open fires in the dusk, they would feel again the passions of those days. Though some of them were too bent to stand, they would wave their arms, flash their eyes, and shout out their memories. But it would be back in Britain, in piles of government documents, unseen for forty years, that the story of the twisting and turning, the lies and the hypocrisy, the cruelty and the deceit would unravel. Most of the men revealed in the papers before me, Cabinet ministers, senior civil servants, diplomats of high distinction, were honest enough, true to themselves and their duty in the normal course of things. But the problem of Ruth and Seretse seemed to offer them no solution that was honourable. While what appeared to be some of the nation's most vital interests were threatened, the dilemma could not be solved, without a sacrifice. A price had to be paid and Ruth and Seretse must pay it.

In other sources too, in private papers, in the records of missionary societies and in the memories of those few participants still living, the story slowly came together. And at the centre of it all was Ruth. She had been the cause of it all, a young slip of a girl shaking the security of national governments. Without her, the story could not be told. But she was wary of me. When she had swept into the room earlier that morning, she had intimidated me with her firm, no-nonsense manner, delivering instructions and opinions in a firm Home Counties voice, self-confident and self-assured. But even before we had emptied our coffee cups, I began to see a different, more vulnerable woman. Would I cheapen and sensationalise what had happened? She had suffered enough in the past from those who had. Why should she trust me when others had let her down?

She took me to the airport, out of the capital and through the dusty scrubland, the sun hammering down on her car as she drove along the ruler-straight road. I said goodbye and flew back to London.

We wrote to one another many times before we met again. Gradually, she began to change her mind. Perhaps she was persuaded by the prospect of revealing the scale of the British government's deceit for the first time. After more than forty years there would be some satisfaction, surely, in letting others know how she had been misused. Perhaps, too, she was prompted by her pride in the love that had kept her husband and her united in defiance of all that could be thrown against them.

Perhaps also, in a much smaller way, she had been persuaded by the memories evoked by a music cassette which I had posted to her. She told me that she had played it regularly as she drove through her adopted country's harsh but beautiful landscape. It was the music of a black American singing group which she hadn't heard for years. Perhaps the songs of the Ink Spots took her back to that warm, humid night in London more than forty years before.

1

London Love

On the evening of 1 September 1947, Seretse Khama waited with Ruth Williams and several hundred other young people outside the Casino Theatre in London's West End. Although he had met this young English girl three months earlier, this was their first date.

The evening was warm and humid. It had been the hottest summer since 1941 and the city was sticky and uncomfortable. Seretse had found it particularly exhausting. Although he had been brought up on the edges of the Kalahari, the heat in Serowe had been a dry heat, fanned by desert winds. Standing in Old Compton Street surrounded by crowds jostling against him, Seretse felt oppressed by the humidity.

Since seven o'clock that evening the streets around the theatre had been packed. Lines of people now stretched from the theatre doors across Old Compton Street and into Shaftesbury Avenue. The pavements were full all the way down Charing Cross Road as far as Leicester Square underground station.

At last the queues began to move. As Ruth and Seretse shuffled slowly towards the theatre entrance, the crowd's excitement began to mount. If you were young and in London that late summer evening there was no better place to be than the London Casino theatre. The Ink Spots were in town and this was the opening night of their British tour. Since coming together in 1939, the black American quartet had become the most popular singing group on both sides of the Atlantic. With their roots in jazz and the blues, they were part of a developing tradition in American music which would, in the 1950s, become Rock 'n Roll.

When Seretse had asked her if she wanted to go to the Ink Spots' concert, Ruth had agreed at once. They were most definitely an attraction as was, she had to admit, this tall, athletic African. Inside the theatre it was cooler, a relief for Seretse in his sports jacket and grey flannels. Ruth was

1

unflustered in a dress of navy blue and white, her blonde hair, worn to the shoulder, revealing touches of red in the theatre houselights. She was an attractively slim girl of nearly 23 with green eyes, in one of which was an unforgettable hazel cast.

The Ink Spots were marvellous. Billy Kenny, with his distinctive falsetto, led the group through all their hits: 'If I Didn't Care', 'Can You Look Me in the Eyes?', 'Do I Worry?' and, with Orville Jones supplying the base line, their most famous hit of all, 'Whispering Grass'. As one music critic, who was also there that evening, said: 'It made me proud of the English language. They caressed every syllable, gave every nuance its full tone value.'

It was almost eleven o'clock before Ruth and Seretse were back in Old Compton Street again. The crowds, content now and tired, melted quickly into the city. Seretse, with Ruth on his arm, walked slowly down Charing Cross Road and into Trafalgar Square. They walked past the towering stone façade of South Africa House before turning left into The Strand.

The evening had been fun. There had been no tension between them, no awkwardness. Seretse had complained of the heat which Ruth had found very funny. Seretse then found it funny too; the hottest man in the place was an African. It would be difficult to imagine two people from more different worlds. He had been born into the royal family of a tribe, the name of which most Britons couldn't even pronounce, in a country most had never heard of. The dusty lanes of Serowe were a world away from London's West End, even the sparse, ration-card London of 1947. The tribe had wanted their future chief to be educated like a white man so that he would be better able to protect them from the white man's ambitions. That was what had brought him to London to study law. Had it been otherwise, he and Ruth would have remained continents apart.

Ruth's comfortable middle-class childhood had been upturned in 1940 when Hitler's Luftwaffe demolished the family home in suburban Blackheath. They had found another home in neighbouring Lewisham and Ruth, her elder sister Muriel, and her mother and father had moved there. At 17, she had left school to join the Women's Auxiliary Air Force, the WAAF. Her job had been to drive crash ambulances at airfields in the south of England, racing across the grass as crippled aircraft, often with their crews badly wounded, staggered home. She had found making close friends a painful business in wartime. Too often, death intervened. Far better, she had decided, to skate across the surface of friendship rather than dive too deep.

After the war she had joined a firm of Lloyd's insurance underwriters as a confidential clerk working on the North American desk. After six years of war, she, like many of her age, was hungry for some fun, to float a little while, meet different people, play the field.

Crossing the road, she and Seretse walked into Charing Cross station to find Muriel waiting as planned beneath the clock. The two girls still lived with their parents in east Lewisham and had arranged to travel home together on the train to Blackheath. It was Muriel who had brought Ruth and Seretse together. Some years earlier, Muriel had joined her local Congregational church. The Congregationalists had firm links with the London Missionary Society, that towering Victorian institution which had sent Robert Moffat, John Mackenzie, David Livingstone and others to shine the light of Christianity in the heathen darkness of Africa.

The society took a great interest in the welfare of all African students who were studying in London. Through the Congregational Church, the society tried to arrange social visits for the students among the families of church members. In return, the students, at their hostel in the Edgware Road not far from Marble Arch, organised social evenings once a month. Muriel had dragged Ruth along to one of those because she felt certain that she would get on well with Seretse. Their mutual love of jazz, she was sure, would spark an instant friendship. At that first meeting, aware that they were expected to get along, Ruth and Seretse ignored one another. And yet Ruth had gone less unwillingly the second time. That evening, she and Seretse had even danced a little. On the third occasion, he had suggested the Ink Spots.

As the three chatted on the platform waiting for the train to leave, a small group of young men started to take a great interest in the two girls. It was a scene that would be repeated many times in the next few months. Ruth could never explain why, but in London at that time white girls talking to a black man were frequently thought to be no better than prostitutes. Perhaps it was because much of Britain's small black population after the war lived in dockland areas, traditionally the places where prostitutes often worked.

Whatever the reason, it was obvious to Ruth, Seretse and

Muriel that the young men planned to join the girls in whatever railway compartment they chose and pester them on the short journey to Blackheath. Although it was the last train of the night, Seretse felt he must go with the two sisters to Blackheath and make sure they were safe. He would then make his way back to central London as best he could.

Seretse had a long – and, by then, cold – journey home that night. Catching a ride with the odd taxi driver finishing his shift, finding a last bus going in roughly the right direction, and then walking the rest, Seretse finally made it back to the Edgware Road.

In the weeks that followed, Ruth and Seretse began to meet regularly. Ruth was a keen ice-skater and a member of the Queen's Ice Skating Club in Queensway, Bayswater. One night she took Seretse along. He tried hard but ice-skating does not come easily to those brought up near the sands of the Kalahari. He was hopeless and both agreed there was little point in persevering. But he often went to meet Ruth there. Athough not a member, the club allowed him to wait for Ruth in the members' bar. Seretse made friends easily. His manner was quiet and humorous, his voice soft.

Yet Ruth and Seretse, like most of us, moved largely in a world of strangers. Many people resented the sight of these two young people obviously enjoying one another's company. On buses, people would glare at them and mutter comments just too softly to be heard; in restaurants, head waiters would try to steer them to tables behind pillars and out of sight.

Ruth did not easily adjust to this pattern of prejudice. Although she knew the purpose of the hostility was to shame her, she found the whole thing preposterous. How could a country, she wondered, which had just fought a war against a racist enemy and which had welcomed friends of all colours to fight at its side, resent her being with Seretse? What had the war taught these people?

She had been offended by people's prejudices since she had joined the Services at the age of 17. At RAF Friston, an emergency landing field near Eastbourne on the south coast, she had been amazed by people on the base telling anti-Jewish jokes. How could an airman fly off to Germany and risk death fighting the Nazis and all they stood for and then fly back to England apparently still sharing Nazi beliefs? Even worse for Ruth had been the attitude towards some of the Jamaican

4

ground crews at the airfield and she felt ashamed at the way some of her countrymen spoke to these men. She did not know whether they genuinely felt racially superior or were just reflecting the accepted opinions of the day. Nevertheless, the hurt suffered by black people from such remarks and attitudes was obvious.

Ruth felt that prejudice was like a disease and it was only right to point this out to people when she noticed they were suffering from it. Yet it would be wrong to imagine that she felt herself to be on some sort of crusade. True, her attitude had made her unpopular with some people but there were still plenty of friends to be found if you were an attractive teenage girl on an RAF base. It was just that prejudice offended her natural sense of justice.

By the end of 1947, Ruth and Seretse were seeing one another three or four times a week. Jazz concerts, ice-skating, walks in the park or just chatting with Seretse's fellow students at the hostel – they floated along, happy in one another's company but never talking of the future.

One evening a rumour ran round the hostel that a white girl was pregnant by one of the African students.

'I wonder what colour the baby will be?' said Ruth.

Seretse leant towards her pulling at his sleeve. 'About halfway between you and me, I should think,' he said, pressing his dark, shiny forearm against hers.

Ruth had not told either of her parents about Seretse. Her father, George, to whom she had always been very close, would, she knew, have been angry and hurt. He had spent six years in the British Army in India and had been invalided out at the end of the First World War. During that period he had acquired very fixed opinions about the roles of black and white in the world. Born into an age when Britain ruled huge parts of the globe, George Williams regarded the differences between the races as fundamental and obvious. Any relationship other than that of ruler to ruled seemed to him absurd.

After the war, George had married his fiancée, Dorothy, had become a wholesale buyer and seller of coffee and tea and had provided a comfortable life for his wife and two daughters. It was a close-knit family with George playing the role of patriarch and upholder of stern establishment values. Dorothy, home-loving and gentle, supplied the balm of kindness and reconciliation whenever her husband's strict beliefs rubbed roughly against her growing daughters' aspirations. She it was who brought George to something like acceptance of Muriel's decision to leave the Anglican Church, of which the whole family were committed members, and join the Congregationalists. When he later learned of her involvement with welfare work for African students, he said he had no objection as long as she didn't bring any of them home with her.

Ruth had no doubts, therefore, that her developing relationship with Seretse would be anathema to her father. With Muriel's connivance it was always possible to concoct some explanation of where she had been and with whom. Dorothy, however, perhaps more sensitive to her daughter's moods, soon realised that Ruth was becoming seriously involved with somebody. Accepting that she must have some good reason for not telling her parents about it, she said nothing to her husband.

In the spring of 1948, she finally told Ruth that she would like to meet the man who meant so much to her daughter. That weekend it was arranged that Seretse would entertain Ruth and her mother to afternoon tea at the hostel. Dorothy Williams was charmed by Seretse's courtesy as he escorted them to the hostel and helped them to tea. After he had taken them back to their bus stop and seen them safely on their way, she told Ruth what a delightful young man she had found Seretse to be. She was not keen, however, on the relationship going any further. The pressure of society's disapproval of such a match might, she feared, prove overwhelming. In the hope that Ruth's obvious affection for Seretse might eventually trickle away, she felt there was as yet no need to tell her husband.

But it was not to be. In the summer of 1948, a year after they had first met, Seretse proposed. He said he wanted no answer then but that she must carefully consider what would be involved if she were to accept. He was a chief, he said, and he must go back to serve his tribe. If they were to marry, his uncle, the regent, would be very angry that he had married without his permission. He might even try to stop Seretse taking over as chief. If he was banned from the throne, he would still ask the tribe to take him back in some other capacity. Serowe was where his people and his duty were and he would never be happy living anywhere else.

If Ruth were to go back with him, he explained, she must be prepared for a very different life. Bechuanaland was a poor country, most of the people barely scratching a living from the dusty soil. The few white traders in the area would include people who would be bitterly opposed to a mixed marriage. The shops were few and entertainment was limited. The land of the Bamangwato was a very long way away from all that she knew. Also, as was obvious, the marriage would be bitterly opposed by her father. If she married him, she would be hurting both her parents deeply. They might refuse to talk to her for years – her father, indeed, might never be reconciled. He asked Ruth to think carefully about all this for if they were to be married, it must be forever.

Ruth had been suppressing the truth about her feelings for Seretse for months. Ever since the war she had affected an attitude of studied flippancy. Nothing in life should be taken too seriously; have fun and don't get involved was the philosophy she offered to any who asked. She had refused to face the problem of what she would do when he left to return to Africa. To accept that she loved him would mean dealing with all the problems that would follow.

For two weeks after Seretse's proposal she tried to push what he had said from her mind. Finally – she thought he had completely forgotten – he asked her if she had considered all he had said and whether or not she would marry him.

'Yes,' she replied.

'Well, so what's your answer?' he asked.

'Yes, of course, yes.'

It was a decision that she would always believe she had taken at that moment. Until then she had refused to admit to herself how she felt for all the reasons that Seretse had explained – not least a great reluctance to hurt her parents.

At that moment they both sat down, Ruth's pulse quickening as her decision took her breath away. Quietly, she and Seretse discussed the opposition that would confront them, both in Serowe and in London. They must be sure that their love was strong. If they were to break up at the first blow they would look ridiculous in front of everybody. They had to stand firm against all those who would part them. Ruth understood, too, that she must be ready to go to Serowe to serve the Bamangwato as the wife of their chief.

The first problem to be overcome was clearly that of Ruth's parents. For several days she put it off. Then she told Seretse that she would tell them that evening. Getting in from work at six o'clock, she went straight into the family sitting room. Her father was reading the newspaper, her mother sewing. Dorothy Williams told her daughter later that the moment she saw Ruth's face she knew what was coming. Ruth told them both that she was planning to be married, probably within a month. The man she loved was an African, a kind, gentle loving man who was a chief in his own country. She would have to go back with him so that he could rule his tribe, saying she was sorry for the hurt she knew she was causing them.

Ruth's father was as angry as she feared he would be. A mixed marriage was a disaster for all those involved and a tragedy for any children, he told her. Ruth would be excluded from black and white communities alike. If she was set on this ridiculous match, then she could stay in her home until the morning of her wedding day and then she must get out. He would never give her his blessing because what she was doing was wrong and shameful. Dorothy was much gentler. She asked her to consider all the things that her father had said and to give up this affair which would come to no good. She could not argue with her husband's ruling and begged Ruth to think again.

For the next four weeks, Ruth spent as little time as possible at home. Leaving early and not returning till late at night, she hardly saw her father and when they did meet, he refused to speak to her. Seretse called her at Lloyd's the next day and she told him everything that had happened.

It was Lloyd's that presented her with her next problem. The head of her department, a Mr Priestly, had been very kind to Ruth ever since she had joined the firm. He would often take her and the other juniors out for a drink after work and they were happy and relaxed in his company. But when he heard that Ruth was marrying a black man he sat her down and lectured her severely on how ridiculous she was being. He said that he was very angry with her.

The next day he told her he wanted to transfer her immediately to the firm's New York office. She said it was impossible as she was getting married. He offered her a choice: either she accepted the transfer or she was sacked. She refused and left at the end of the week.

Meanwhile, Seretse was looking for somewhere for them to live after the wedding but it was proving difficult. Answering advertisements in the evening paper, he would make an appointment to see a place. When he called, he would almost always find the flat had just been let. If not, then the advertised rent had been a misprint and the real rate was much higher, beyond his means.

Eventually, Ruth began telephoning the landlords after they had told Seretse that the flats had been taken. Frequently, of course, she would find they were still available. At last, Seretse found a place – number 10, Campden Hill Gardens, just off Notting Hill Gate in West London. On the second floor he rented a flat which had a sitting room with a bed in it, a tiny bathroom and an even smaller kitchen. Around the corner from his flat, Seretse found the local church. St George's was a lofty, rather ugly Victorian basilica squeezed between the neighbouring houses with its entrance almost on the pavement. Inside he found the vicar of Campden Hill, the Revd Dr Leonard Patterson. A bookish academic more interested in botany than his parishioners, the Revd Patterson was remote from his flock. Still, he received Seretse well enough and arranged for a special marriage licence to be issued. It would cost £2 10s and the date for the wedding was set for 2 October.

On 12 September, Seretse finally plucked up courage and sat down to write to his uncle, Tshekedi. For twenty-five years he had ruled as regent, waiting for his nephew to finish his education. He had taken the place of Seretse's dead father as well as any man could. As a sign of Seretse's gratitude, the young man always called him 'father'. Now, Seretse wrote, he was getting married in three weeks.

I realise that this matter will not please you because the tribe will not like it as the person I am marrying is a white woman. I do not know what the people will say when they hear of this. In spite of what they might do or say I shall return home whenever you say to serve them in any capacity. I realise that it was my duty to have asked your consent before I had done this thing but I know you would refuse and it would be difficult for me to disregard your advice and that is why I notified you when it was all done. Please forgive me. The woman that I am marrying is having a very trying time at home but I know that she will be received by you in a friendly way. Please don't try to stop me, father, as I want to go through with it.

Sealing the letter, Seretse sent it airmail to Serowe.

9

2
Children of the Kalahari

Nobody knows when the first people came to the land which, by 1947, was known as the British Protectorate of Bechuanaland. They were almost certainly distant ancestors of the Bushmen or, as the Bamangwato call them, the 'Basarwa'. Small, wiry people with yellowish rather than dark brown skins, the Basarwa came to live in and around the Kalahari in the Late Stone Age, about 35,000 years ago.

There they learned their secrets of survival, finding food, moisture and shelter. Isolated from every outside influence, they evolved into a highly efficient society of hunter-gatherers with mystical beliefs forged in the desert heat. For them, time stood still; but for those beyond their borders it was marching on.

At about the time of the Norman Conquest of Britain, upheavals in central Africa caused mass migrations southwards. By the thirteenth century, the first of several waves of tribesmen began moving down into southern Africa, claiming territory that eventually spread from Atlantic to Indian Ocean seaboards. Those Basarwa who could fled deeper into the desert where the newcomers had no desire to follow. Those Bushmen who stayed behind became their slaves.

The people who conquered Bechuanaland were called the Tswana and were the direct ancestors of Seretse and his people. Taller and stronger than the Bushmen with dark brown skins and classic negroid features, the Tswana were herdsmen and farmers who built large villages, staked out their territory and defended it. The southern Tswana spread down into what would become the northern Cape and the western Transvaal, while the northerners installed themselves on the southern and eastern fringes of the Kalahari. There, before the scrubland bush and thorn trees gave way to desert sands, they built villages, planted their crops and prayed for rain. The women kept mainly to the simple round, mud-walled huts, raising children and crops. The men spent weeks, sometimes months, away herding their cattle over huge areas as the animals foraged for food among the rough brown grass. Sometime in the 1700s, the Tswana split into three with the birth, according to tribal legend, of three sons to the Tswana chief Malope-a-Masilo.

The three boys were called Kwena, Ngwaketse and Ngwato, each born from a different wife of the great chief Masilo. The last wife, the mother of Ngwato, had great difficulty conceiving and the chief had given her, as an ironic present, a strip of poor, gristly beef – in Tswana, an *ngwato* – as a symbol of her barrenness. When, at last, she did present a baby to her chief, she named him Ngwato as a living reminder to her husband of his coldness.

With the death of Masilo, his three sons – young men now – quarrelled over the succession and in the war that followed Ngwato was forced to run for his life. Hiding in the long grass, he watched his enemies approach him. As they were almost upon him, a small deer – in Tswana, a *phuti* – suddenly broke cover. Convinced that nobody could be hiding in the bushes if the phuti had lain undisturbed until their arrival, the enemies moved off. When they had gone, Ngwato was able to rejoin his followers and together they moved to the north and established their own territory, calling themselves the Bamangwato, meaning 'the people of Ngwato'. To this day, the phuti is the tribal emblem and hunting or killing the deer is forbidden.

In the south, the two remaining brothers lived in uneasy alliance founding the Bakwena and Bangwaketse tribes, marking out adjoining territories.

Throughout the latter half of the eighteenth century, all the different tribes of southern Africa lived in uneasy coexistence. Each with their herds to protect and settled village life to foster, many tribes began to develop a very sensible way of resolving differences, one which caused the minimum of bloodshed and disruption. Often, if two tribes were in dispute, the two armies would line up opposite one another, parading their warriors and their arms. By mutual consent, victory would go to the more splendid often without a blow being struck.

Towards the end of the eighteenth century, a man was born who soon changed such picturesque customs. On the Indian Ocean side of southern Africa and far from the land of the Bamangwato, the princess of a small and insignificant tribe called the eLangeni was seduced by the chief of a neighbouring tribe. His name was Senzangakona and he led an equally insignificant clan called the Zulu – which meant 'the Heavens' – who occupied about ten square miles of lush pastoral land along the Indian Ocean coast. The princess – her name was Nandi – became pregnant and her relatives sent word to Senzangakona that he should accept her as his wife. But the Zulus replied curtly that Nandi was probably the victim of a local intestinal beetle called iShaka notorious for menstrual disorders. Seven months later, a messenger from the eLangeni called again on the chief of the Zulus requesting that he collect Nandi and her newly-born son as soon as was convenient. The boy, wryly named Shaka by his mother, grew up to succeed his father as chief of the Zulus.

Shaka had a lust for power and he devised a very simple means of acquiring it. He developed a short stabbing spear and trained his fellow Zulus in its use. Instead of carrying long hunting spears into their ritual displays of power, Shaka trained his men to use their shields to knock aside the weapons of their opponents before sinking their own assegais, blade and shaft, deep into their enemies' ribs. The assegai, not plumes and feathers, would now decide the victor.

Soon his men had butchered the warriors of a score of different tribes, capturing their cattle and their women. Other tribes came to him offering allegiance in return for their lives. Shaka incorporated these men into his *impis* – vast, highly disciplined regiments of warriors who marched as masters across the African plains. In front of their advance, other tribes scattered, fearing what they called the *mFecane*, the 'crushing'. By the 1830s, the effects were being felt as far away as the land of the Bamangwato and dozens of smaller tribes fled to them, begging their protection. It was not long before the Bamangwato and their allies numbered almost 100,000 and far outnumbered their two sister tribes, the Bakwena and the Bangwaketse. But even a thousand miles was not enough to escape the mFecane. Soon it was to come to the very doorstep of the Bamangwato.

The power and wealth of the Zulu empire was creating its own internal tensions. One of Shaka's cruellest and most able captains was called Mzilikasi and he led his own clan, the Matabele. One day Shaka sent Mzilikasi to confiscate the herds of a disobedient chief. The Matabele leader, ambitious for power himself, decided to challenge Shaka. He captured the cattle as ordered but then refused to hand them over to the Zulu emperor. Shaka acted immediately to punish such insolence, sending his impis against Mzilikasi who fled to the north-west with his army. Rampaging and butchering as he went, Mzilikasi finally crossed the Limpopo River establishing himself in what is today south-western Zimbabwe, deposing and enslaving the resident Mashonas.

From there, Mzilikasi launched raids against the Bamangwato, stealing cattle and women and killing all those who came against him. The Bamangwato chief, Sekgoma, descended through more than half a dozen generations from the legendary Ngwato, feared that soon the Bamangwato, too, would fall under the Matabele heel. To add to his troubles, Sekgoma was beginning to feel threatened by other tribes – tribes of white men. In the late seventeenth and early eighteenth centuries, Dutch seamen trading with the East Indies had established a colony on the southern tip of Africa – the 'Cape of Good Hope' – to provide fresh meat and vegetables for their merchant ships. The colonists had found little local opposition to their presence, only yellow-skinned tribes calling themselves San and Khoikhoi, distant cousins of the Bushmen and no serious military threat.

Seduced by the beauty of the landscape, the kindliness of the climate and the fertility of the soil, the Dutch had moved further into the hinterland and soon began farming for themselves. Staunch and severe in their Protestantism, they were later joined by co-religionists from Germany and by Huguenots fleeing the religious persecution of the Roman Catholic King of France.

Fierce and independent, these people soon became a nation of their own. They called themselves Afrikaners after their adoptive continent and began speaking a new language, Afrikaans, a mixture of old Dutch and words coined to describe their new surroundings. Within a hundred years they were scattered across the southern tip of Africa living on lonely farms, their rifles and Bibles for protection. Fiercely proud to have survived on their wits and courage, they were developing a growing conviction that, like the people of whom they read in their Old Testaments, they too were somehow a chosen people, charged with bringing the light of Christianity to the godless darkness of Africa.

At the beginning of the last century, the Afrikaners, secure in their own beliefs and completely ignorant of the tribal upheavals a few hundred miles to the north of them, were suddenly conquered by the greatest power on earth. The British Empire, in the form of His Majesty's Royal Navy, decided the Cape was of too strategic an importance to be left in foreign hands. Consequently, a squadron of warships sailed into Table Bay annexing Cape Town and all the territories of the Afrikaners in the name of His Majesty, the terminally insane King George III. Within a decade, the British had imposed their own system of administration, had made English the only official language of government, court and school, and were imposing taxes.

Large numbers of Afrikaners could not accept the loss of their birthright. These men and women, with their children and their possessions packed into ox wagons, chose the unknown dangers of the African interior rather than suffer British rule. This division between those who left and those who stayed behind was to prove a trauma for the Afrikaner nation. Ever after, those who left, the 'Voortrekkers' as they were called, would believe themselves to be the true guardians of the Afrikaners' sacred identity. Many would always regard those who stayed behind – and their descendants – as somehow compromised. Throughout the rest of their history, this division, real or imagined, would recur.

In the 1830s, long lines of ox wagons began trekking north away from the British. They quickly realised that they were marching from the embrace of one empire straight into the arms of another. With the British at their backs, they now faced the Zulus and their new commander, the usurper Dingaan, who had just murdered Shaka. In 1838, the year after Queen Victoria's accession, and after losing many men in skirmishes with the Zulus, the Voortrekkers at last won a great victory. On the banks of the Ncome River, deep in Zulu territory, 10,000 warriors attacked a Voortrekker force of around 800. After six hours of fighting, 3,000 Zulus had died before the Afrikaner guns, the blood of the slaughtered impis turning the river red. For the Afrikaners, the battle which they christened Blood River was another sign from God that they were truly a chosen people with a sacred mission to fulfil. That belief grew stronger through the years and neither the might of the British nor of the Zulus would shake it.

Further persecution was to follow. First, the Voortrekkers fought their way over the Drakensberg Mountains and down to the Indian Ocean coast. There they declared the independent republic of Natal. Then, within months, the British sailed in again and annexed it. Back into their ox wagons and once more over the precipitous mountain range, the Voortrekkers struck

14

out again for the interior, founding first the Republic of the Orange Free State and then of the Transvaal. By now the British were calling them 'Boers', the Afrikaans for 'farmers', but these independent 'Boer Republics' were to bring the Afrikaners no peace. First diamonds were discovered at Kimberley in the Free State and then gold in undreamed of quantities was found at Johannesburg in the Transvaal. Such riches ensured they would never be free of the British who arrived in tens of thousands to mine the earth of its treasures. Constantly pushing on to the north, further into Africa's interior, the Boers with their ox wagons continued their search for somewhere to be free. Soon they were deep in the country of the Tswanas.

So, by the 1850s, Sekgoma, Chief of the Bamangwato, not only had the voracious Mzilikasi threatening his north-eastern flank, but Boers approaching from the south. For ten years they had been arriving in increasing numbers searching for farmland and stealing it from the southern Tswanas. Now more were arriving and threatening to steal the Bamangwato's.

Fortunately for Sekgoma and the Bamangwato, there was one final ingredient in this volatile southern African mix. With the British Empire had come British missionaries. Robert Moffat and his son-in-law, David Livingstone, had been sent by the London Missionary Society to spread the Word of God. In the case of the Bamangwato, these unarmed evangelists arrived several years ahead of the Boers.

David Livingstone had been one of the first white men to visit Chief Sekgoma. In 1842, he arrived at the then Bamangwato capital of Shoshong but although Sekgoma was intrigued by the religious messages that Livingstone brought, he remained unconverted. Sekgoma, however, had a son, Khama. The young man had been born in 1837 and grew up to be a tall, brave and athletic prince. By the time Khama was in his 20s, Sekgoma, although still adamantly pagan, had allowed a group of German Lutherans to establish a small mission in Shoshong. Khama responded strongly to their Christian teaching and, on 6 May 1862, he was baptised with his wife, Mmabessie.

The Lutherans were followed by the London Missionary Society's John Mackenzie who built a mission school at Shoshong at which Khama helped to teach. Khama's Christian zeal soon caused conflict with his father, the chief. He publicly refused to support the traditional tribal customs of polygamy, witchcraft and initiation rites for those reaching puberty.

15

He put aside the traditional tribal skins and began to wear European clothes. At the same time, through his courage and ability as a military commander, Khama was becoming the de facto chief of the tribe. As the Matabele raids became more severe, Khama finally led bands of Bamangwato warriors against them. In 1863, he won a fierce battle. Five of Mzilikasi's sons were in the raiding party and Khama and his men killed three of them. Of the two surviving sons, one, Lobengula, who would eventually succeed Mzilikasi as chief, was shot in the neck by a bullet which he carried until his death. The Matabele returned to their own lands and Mzilikasi was forced to admit that while he thought the Bamangwato were dogs, Khama was a man.

Another source of friction between father and son was that Sekgoma, together with an increasing number of Bamangwato, was in the habit of getting drunk on liquor sold by the white traders who were starting to appear in the area. One such trader, while trying to sell Sekgoma a horse, offered the chief such large quantities of brandy that the old man became drunk and fell over. Khama immediately stopped the negotiations, ordered servants to pick up Sekgoma and swore that when he became chief he would ban the sales of all liquor.

Finally, the old man's patience with his son and his strange new ways snapped. Civil war broke out in the tribe and at least three times Sekgoma tried to have Khama killed. Each time, Khama defended himself and his followers but refused to retaliate. Not until the old man died in 1875 did Khama install himself as chief.

As soon as he took over, Khama made most of his Christian beliefs into tribal law. Witchcraft, the more savage forms of corporal punishment, polygamy, initiation rites and the sale of any intoxicating drink were all banned. Every morning he sat in the Kgotla ground to settle the disputes the tribesmen brought to him. Every morning, the proceedings began with Christian prayer. Meanwhile, the Bamangwato remained pressed by enemies on almost every side. Although the British army was finally subduing the Zulus in a long series of bloody battles, the Matabele were as yet beyond their reach. Furthermore, the ambitions of the Afrikaners for land and of the British entrepreneurs for anything they could get their hands on were increasing. Cecil Rhodes and his British South Africa Company nursed dreams of Union Jacks from the Cape to Cairo. Bechuanaland formed a corridor to the north between the Boer

Republic of the Transvaal and the impassability of the Kalahari Desert. There were also rumours of gold in Khama's land.

With the advice of his missionaries – Mackenzie was almost his constant companion – Khama was able to distinguish between the ambitions of the Boers and men like Cecil Rhodes, on the one hand, and the concerns of the British government in London, on the other. In 1876, together with the chief of the Bakwena, he appealed to Queen Victoria for protection from the Matabele, the Boers and the likes of Cecil Rhodes. The appeal was ignored but less than a decade later international politics worked to his advantage. Bismarck dreamed of a German Empire in Africa and announced the annexation of South-West Africa – present day Namibia – threatening to form alliances with the Boer republics and squeeze out the British. This time, London was delighted to accept Khama's invitation and in 1885 a British major-general with seventy mounted troopers drove all the Boer intruders from Khama's land and rode into Shoshong. The lands of the Bamangwato and that of their two sister tribes, the Bakwena and the Bangwaketse, were declared a protectorate of the British Crown. The chiefs, it was agreed, would continue to rule their people according to tribal customs – as long as these did not offend the Christian sensitivities of the British – and London would protect them from their enemies, black and white.

However, the Bamangwato were far from safe. More and more the British allowed influence to pass into the hands of Cecil Rhodes and his British South Africa Company. Rhodes wanted mining rights in Bechuanaland and was growing impatient with Khama's opposition. Rhodes was a powerful figure in southern African politics and a key player for the British in their approaching confrontation with the Boers. In London, officials were listening closely to his complaints and by 1895 they were openly suggesting that the time had come to transfer the protectorate to Rhodes' British South Africa Company. Almost immediately Khama, together with Chief Sebele of the Bakwena and Chief Bathoen of the Bangwaketse, sailed for England to appeal to Queen Victoria in person.

Khama was already well known in England. The London Missionary Society was a powerful influence in government and at court and Khama was one of their greatest successes. His adherence to Victorian Christian values and in particular his complaint that wherever Rhodes and his company went they filled trading stores with liquor, evoked widespread public

17

sympathy from the moment he landed in Britain. His appearance and manner, tall and dignified, quiet and intelligent, impressed those who met him. The Colonial Secretary, Joseph Chamberlain, had initially felt that Bechuanaland should be handed over to Rhodes but the effectiveness of Khama's British campaign made him think again. Also in that year of 1895 Rhodes' stock in Whitehall suddenly plummeted. He financed and planned an armed raid into the Boer Republic of the Transvaal, hoping that it would trigger a general uprising of all the British working in the gold-mines around Johannesburg. But the attempt was ill-conceived and badly managed. No uprising occurred and the armed band, led by Dr Leander Starr Jameson, was easily captured.

Finally, after the three chiefs had been in London for nearly two months, they were granted an audience with the Queen herself, the Empress Victoria, in Windsor Castle. Victoria, whom the chiefs respectfully called Mosadinyana, 'the little woman', was much impressed by the three Africans. They gave her leopard skins and she gave each of them a Bible, inscribing Khama's: 'The secret of Khama's greatness'.

So it was decided. Bechuanaland was to remain free of Rhodes and the chiefs were to go on ruling their people as before. Apart from a narrow strip of land on which a railway to the north would be built and some farmland on the Transvaal border to act as a buffer to the Boers, no whites would be allowed to settle in the protectorate.

It had been a great achievement by the three chiefs and they returned home well satisfied. Mighty forces, however, were still at work in southern Africa. In October 1899, the imperial ambitions of the British and the determination of the Boers to be free of them finally exploded into war. The Afrikaners left their farms and took to their horses, forming well-armed and highly mobile guerrilla bands which ambushed British contingents and then melted into the veld. Unable to devise a military strategy to defeat them, the British commander, Lord Kitchener, decided to cut off the Boers' sources of supply. After their raids, the Boer commandos would return to their farms where their wives would replenish their stocks of food and ammunition and prepare fresh mounts for them. Kitchener felt victory was impossible under such circumstances.

He therefore decided to establish camps in which the Boers' wives and children could be 'concentrated'. The farms could then be burned to the ground and the cattle rounded up, thus denying the Boers the means for carrying on the war. The British, however, proved incapable of organising and supplying the camps. Standards of hygiene were appalling and supplies of fresh food and water completely inadequate. Diseases swept through the 'concentration camps' and more than 26,000 Afrikaner women and children, weakened by hunger, died. The shameful strategy brought the war to an end and the Boers to heel but they never forgave the horror of it all. While every Afrikaner was revolted at what had happened, once again it was the northerners, the sons of the Voortrekkers, who had borne the brunt of the British oppression. They would never forget.

Meanwhile, in what was now called the Bamangwato Reserve, an area almost the size of Wales, Khama ruled his people in relative peace. The Boers were now defeated and Cecil Rhodes had successfully disinherited Lobengula and his Matabele in 'Rhodesia', the newly created country to the north. Even the German ambitions in South-West Africa would shortly be destroyed by the First World War. Khama found the burden of the British administration an easy one to bear. The local officials, following a policy of benign neglect, were only too pleased to allow the chiefs to rule the tribes as before.

Only one threat remained. On 31 May 1910, the South African Act of Union came into being. The various old republics and colonies now came together to form a self-governing dominion within the British Empire. The status of Bechuanaland, and that of two other British protectorates in southern Africa, those of Swaziland and Basutholand, were left ambiguous. Although for the time being they would continue to be administered directly from London as separate territories, officials in both London and Pretoria felt they were too poor and unskilled ever to make it alone with such a powerful neighbour on their borders. Incorporation into South Africa seemed inevitable. The British therefore neglected Bechuanaland since they felt it would eventually become South Africa's problem. As the policies of discrimination increased in South Africa, fear of incorporation shaped the policies of every Bechuana chief.

In the meantime, Khama was facing problems at home. Following the tradition of his family, he was growing angry with his son, Sekgoma. First, the boy had married a woman of whom Khama disapproved and then, while ruling during his father's absence in England in 1895, Sekgoma had passed laws which

Khama decided were unchristian. Other disputes between father and son led to Sekgoma's exile in 1900. At the root of this row, as with so many others, was the Bamangwato belief that a son should submit completely to the will of his father. That so many successful rulers – including above all Khama himself – had felt unable to do this was always forgotten.

The old man's anger continued until his eightieth birthday when he allowed his son to come home after seventeen years in exile to the new Bamangwato capital at Serowe. There, in 1921, Sekgoma and his wife, Tebogo, had a son, Seretse – meaning 'wet earth', a precious thing in Bechuanaland. Seretse's 84-year-old grandfather, the great chief Khama, carried the infant into the Kgotla ground, the tribal assembly area which acted as both Parliament and High Court, and told the tribe to acclaim their future chief.

Two years later, the old man was dead. His son, Seretse's father, ruled as Chief Sekgoma II. But within two years, sickly and advanced in years himself, Sekgoma too was dead. While the tribe all recognised Sekgoma's 4-year-old son Seretse as the rightful heir, they looked for someone to rule as regent until the baby came of age. Their choice was Tshekedi, Khama's second son, a young man of 20 who was away at college in South Africa. He arrived back in Serowe to find himself in the middle of several violently quarrelling factions. Bamangwato politics continued to be as stormy as they had always been. Tshekedi even survived a murder attempt – in which he was slightly wounded – before establishing himself as the undisputed ruler of the tribe. During the years that followed, Tshekedi became one of the most important Africans on the continent. His single-minded determination to do what he felt was right for the tribe – and his belief that no one knew better than he what was right for them – brought him into continual conflict with the British. Among the first arguments concerned Tshekedi's refusal to allow any Christian denomination other than the London Missionary Society to practise in the reserve. This was partly out of respect for the beliefs of his father and for the support the missionaries had afforded down through the years, but also for the pragmatic reason that he believed different churches would divide the people, further complicating tribal affairs. The British put great pressure on Tshekedi to let the Anglicans in – the official denomination of the British crown – but the young man would not budge.

That dispute was soon followed by another. In 1929, the British tried to force him to grant mining concessions to British companies. Tshekedi was frightened that if great mineral wealth was found the tribe would suffer. While at first sight it might seem of benefit to his people, in reality it would mean a great influx of white people who would quickly become too powerful to control. The next step, the young man knew, would be the subjugation of his people which every black man in South Africa was already experiencing. As the pressure grew, the young chief followed his father's example and went to London to press his case in person. Once again, with the help of the London Missionary Society, the Bamangwato campaign was expertly handled. Tshekedi won major changes to the original proposal including the power to control who would be allowed to enter the reserve to work on the mines. In the event, the areas surveyed produced nothing of value and the threat receded.

In 1930, a new British Resident Commissioner, Lieutenant-Colonel Charles Rey, appeared in Bechuanaland. Almost immediately he began drafting changes to the constitution governing the Bamangwato and their sister tribes which, from Tshekedi's point of view, seemed to be taking the protectorate closer to the South African system. For years the rights of black people in South Africa had been increasingly eroded and their power to control their own affairs whittled away. Rey's proposals seemed to Tshekedi to be an attempt to impose the same sort of system in Bechuanaland by robbing the Tswana of many of their rights as well.

Tshekedi told Rey that this was against the letter and the spirit of what had been agreed between his father and Joseph Chamberlain, in 1895, and that he would resist it with all his power. For eighteen months Tshekedi blocked every effort by Rey to introduce the new proposals. It was then that a crisis occurred that not only gave Rey a chance to undercut Tshekedi but also exposed the true relationship between the British and their allegedly self-governing subjects.

For a number of years, Tshekedi had been complaining to the British authorities in Serowe about white men seducing young Bamangwato girls. The complaints had never been acted upon. Then, in August 1933, a young white man called Phineas McKintosh struck a tribesman after a quarrel about the young black girl who was living with McKintosh at the time. Tshekedi decided to take matters into his own hands for once, particularly as this was not the first complaint against this young white man. He ordered McKintosh to be brought before the Kgotla.

After hearing all the evidence, he sentenced McKintosh to be flogged. In so doing he had the support of the whole tribe, most of the white residents of Serowe and even McKintosh was to say later that he felt he deserved it.

For Rey this was a heaven-sent opportunity to rid himself of Tshekedi. He immediately telegraphed Admiral Evans, the Acting High Commissioner, then in charge of the British Fleet in Simonstown, the naval base just outside Cape Town. Evans ordered 200 marines, fully armed and with three naval howitzers, to board a train for the Bamangwato Reserve. Arriving at the nearest railway station to Serowe, they then marched the final forty miles arriving in full naval splendour in the dusty capital. At a ceremony which all the senior tribesmen were made to attend, Admiral Evans publicly dismissed Tshekedi from his position as chief as punishment for exceeding his authority by punishing a white man. The navy then solemnly marched back to its ships.

For many people in Britain, this was the first any of them had heard of the Bamangwato. The farcical nature of what the British had done, together with a general sense that moral right was on the side of Tshekedi, made for strong stories in his support in the press. The public outcry was great and shortly afterwards Tshekedi was quietly reinstated, his position among the British greatly enhanced by the whole débâcle. He immediately resumed the fight against Rey's constitutional reforms, first, unsuccessfully suing him and then threatening to take the matter to the Privy Council in London. Finally, in 1937, Rey left the protectorate and his replacement had no stomach to continue the fight. Tshekedi had won.

This then was the situation in which the young Seretse grew up in Serowe. In many ways the protectorates were unique in the Empire. They had never been colonised in the traditional way. There weren't large numbers of white settlers owning vast tracts of land that had formerly belonged to the native population. Indeed, for most of the Bamangwato, life went on as it always had. The chief, advised by a small number of councillors, ruled the tribe through a system of village headmen. In each village there was a local kgotla, an assembly of all the senior men in the locality, which tried to settle affairs at village level. Those cases of more importance were referred to the Serowe Kgotla where Tshekedi himself presided. The majority of tribesmen would hardly ever come into contact with white officialdom. The British in turn wanted a quiet life. The policy of neglect continued as the belief persisted that eventually the protectorate would be incorporated into South Africa and hardly any investment took place. The British, through the chiefs, imposed a tax which went to support the administration itself and sponsor modest development projects. By the 1940s for example, a typical year's revenue from the whole protectorate was only £486,400 with an expenditure that year of some £475,000. The administration itself, headed by a resident commissioner, was stationed outside the protectorate, in Mafeking, across the South African border. All roads were untarred and deeply rutted, the best communication being by rail which ran from Mafeking north-east through Bechuanaland to Bulawayo in Rhodesia. Along this line, like dusty buttons strung on steel wire, tiny settlements had sprung up, some as refuelling stops for the trains and maintenance centres for the track, others as goods depots handling the protectorate's modest import and export needs. In each of the main centres, white tradesmen had set up general stores selling agricultural and household goods and making a modest living. Within the tribal areas themselves, each trader was there on the sufferance of the chief and the local British official, the District Commissioner. If a trader fell foul of either, he had to get out.

If life was hard for the Bamangwato, it was often no less so for the whites. Young Len Tarr, son of a farmer who had moved up to Bechuanaland from South Africa, arrived at Mahalapye, one of the train halts in the Bamangwato Reserve, in 1933. He had come to try to start a small creamery to process the tiny amounts of milk which the local cattle produced during the brief rainy season. It was a project of which Tshekedi approved. Setting up camp under a camelthorn tree, Len worked busily away for six months. Then he decided to make the two-day journey to Serowe to see Tshekedi.

'I have been here now in your land for six months, Chief,' Len said when he was eventually shown in to the great man's presence. 'Do you think you could allow me to build a house as I have been living under a tree all this time?'

Hardly looking up, Tshekedi replied: 'It is not our custom to allow visitors to build houses.'

His audience at an end, Len returned to his camelthorn tree at Mahalapye and continued working at his creamery. More than a year later he tried again. This time, rather grudgingly, Tshekedi told him to tell the local headman in Mahalapye which plot of land he wanted and then to get on and build his house. This Len did and more than fifty years later he was still living there.

Yet the anomaly of it all was that the few hotels along the railway line were 'whites only', barred even to Tshekedi himself. The British, while encouraging local blacks to join the administration, paid them rates of pay often half those given to whites for performing the same jobs. No matter how highly qualified a black might be, he would always find a white man above him. Racial discrimination was a matter of custom and practice in the protectorate. Across the border, in South Africa, it was increasingly becoming legislative fact. And always, constantly hanging over the heads of the Bamangwato, was the threat that the protection of the British crown would one day be removed and they would be thrown to the South Africans, falling under the same yokes of prejudice and discrimination that millions of their fellows already suffered.

In such difficult times, it was no wonder that Tshekedi and the tribe wanted the very best education for their young chief-to-be. With the help, once more, of the London Missionary Society, Seretse was sent, in late 1945, to Balliol College, Oxford, to study politics, philosophy and economics. After a year there, he had transferred to the Inner Temple in London to study law. While there he had met and fallen in love with Ruth. Now they were to be married and, on 20 September 1947, Tshekedi opened the airmail letter from Seretse telling him so.

3

The Bishop Decides

'. . . the person I am marrying is a white woman.' Tshekedi read Seretse's words and could scarcely believe what he saw. His nephew's news had come as a complete surprise. They had been as close as father and son ever since Sekgoma's death. They had written to one another regularly since Seretse's arrival in England and Tshekedi had known the young man had been lonely when he first arrived. Since then, he had been glad to hear that he was developing a circle of friends but had been given no inkling that anything as preposterous as this was being planned. When Tshekedi had recovered from the initial shock he began to analyse why he felt so angry. To begin with, it seemed to the regent, Seretse was turning his back on the duties and obligations to which he had been born. In Bamangwato custom, to marry without your father's permission was a serious offence. If you were the chief-to-be, to marry without the tribe's permission struck at the foundations of government. In the hotbed of tribal politics, the marriage of the chief was a principal instrument in forging alliances, breaking up power blocs and helping to ensure the future unity of the tribe. The Bamangwato had a right to decide who their future queen would be. European monarchs had never been able to marry just as they pleased. Only ten years earlier Edward VIII had been forced to give up the British throne because his bride had been unacceptable. The king, whether in Serowe or Buckingham Palace, was not as other men. He enjoyed great privilege but shouldered great responsibility.

Nevertheless, it had to be said, Bamangwato chiefs had married without consent before and the tribe had somehow survived. What no chief had done before, what no chief had even thought about doing before was to marry a white woman. How could the tribe accept such a queen? What would she know of their customs, their language? How could she play the part of the chief's wife without such knowledge? Even more seriously, what would be the position of any children they might have? Those of mixed race, or 'Coloureds' as they were called in southern Africa, were the victims of prejudice by many in both white and black societies. Would the Bamangwato agree to the prospect of one day being ruled by a Coloured? Would the tribe split and scatter causing riots and strife, giving the South Africans the excuse they needed to march in and occupy Bechuanaland? What would the white government of South Africa think anyway of such a mixed marriage? 'Please don't try to stop me, father, I want to go through with it,' Seretse had written. Tshekedi would see about that. He was a decisive man who had grown used to being obeyed after more than twenty years as regent. He would soon bring this infatuated young man to heel.

The very next day, 21 September 1948, Tshekedi acted. He informed the senior British official in Serowe, the District Commissioner for the Bamangwato Reserve, what Seretse was planning. The British government must do everything to stop this marriage, he said. The consequences for the tribe if the marriage went ahead were extremely dangerous. He could not guarantee peace, he could not even promise that the tribe would stay together. He told the District Commissioner that London must know immediately that if Seretse married a white woman it would prove the biggest test of British rule in the whole history of the protectorate.

From the District Commissioner's house Tshekedi went to Serowe's tiny Post Office. It was run by the Postmaster, Joe Burgess, with the help of young Audrey Blackbeard, the daughter of Gwen who ran the little village school for the children of the white traders. Walking into the small brick and corrugated iron building, Tshekedi told Burgess he wanted to send an urgent telegram to his lawyers in Cape Town.

Along the single telegraph wire, held on flimsy poles above the brown scrub of Bechuanaland, Tshekedi's instructions ran. To the railway line at Palapye and then south, for 250 miles following the track all the way to Mafeking. From there, the orders of the Regent Chief of the Bamangwato travelled a further 800 miles to the centre of Cape Town, to the grand offices in Temple Chambers of Douglas Buchanan, King's Counsel and barrister-at-law. Douglas Buchanan, one of South Africa's most distinguished advocates, had first met Tshekedi in 1929. He had by then already begun to specialise in African tribal law and the

London Missionary Society had introduced him to the young Bamangwato regent. The son of a judge and the grandson of a missionary, Buchanan had studied at St John's College, Cambridge, and at London's Inner Temple. As a young boy in Cape Town he had seen the old chief, Khama, leaving the docks for his trip to see Queen Victoria and he had been intrigued to meet the old man's son. Now in his early 60s, Buchanan was a distinguished and authoritative figure in Cape Town society.

Receiving Tshekedi's cable, Buchanan immediately began composing telegrams of his own. The first was to his brother, John, a London solicitor.

> Chief authorises me to urge you to take every possible and impossible step to prevent Seretse, 10 Campden Hill Gardens, Notting Hill Gate, marrying English girl on 2 October. Consult Dominions Office re immediate priority air transport for Seretse to Africa. Suggest caution parson who called banns. If Congregational contact London Missionary Society, if Church of England contact Archbishop. Consider extraditing Seretse . . . Inform girl's parents of ostracism and misery awaiting her. Such marriage possible cause Seretse's deposition.

Buchanan next cabled the London headquarters of the London Missionary Society addressing the telegram to Ronald Orchard, the society's Africa Secretary. He urged the society to do all they could to prevent the marriage, warning once more of the misery awaiting the girl and the disastrous consequences for Seretse's prospects of becoming chief.

Buchanan then cabled Sir Reginald Coupland of All Souls College, Oxford, asking for his help. Coupland had taken Seretse under his wing when the young man, lost and lonely, had first arrived at the university. Buchanan pointed out the disastrous consequences of what Seretse was about to do and urged Coupland to do his best to talk him out of it. Finally, Buchanan asked his secretary to telephone the British High Commission, just around the corner from his office, and make an appointment for him to see the High Commissioner himself, Sir Evelyn Baring, on a matter of great urgency.

Back in Serowe, Tshekedi was growing distraught. The night after he had cabled Buchanan he had sat up all night with the senior members of the royal family discussing the crisis. All, without exception, agreed that such a marriage would be a disaster for both Seretse and the tribe. Tshekedi, they said, must do all in his power to prevent it. The following morning messages were sent out from Serowe to the outlying villages and the isolated cattle-posts telling the men of the Bamangwato to assemble in the Serowe Kgotla ground as soon as possible.

Later that day, Buchanan telegrammed Tshekedi suggesting that he prepare to fly to London to talk to Seretse personally. Tshekedi was now on the point of nervous collapse and his doctor warned him against any such trip. Instead, he sent a cable direct to his nephew:

> Your proposal more serious and difficult than you realise. It is surest way of disrupting Bamangwato tribe. You seem to have forgotten that your home is in South Africa not England. Have made arrangements for your immediate return. Get ready to leave at moment's notice. I shall only discuss your proposal personally after your arrival here. I repeat your proposal more serious and difficult than you realise.

Back in Cape Town, Buchanan was ushered in to the imposing offices of His Majesty's High Commissioner to South Africa and the Protectorates of Bechuanaland, Basutholand and Swaziland. Sir Evelyn Baring, tall and patrician, greeted him and waved him to a chair. Baring's job was twofold: on the one hand, he was London's representative to the government of the self-ruled dominion of the Union of South Africa; on the other, he was the administrator general of the three protectorates bordering the Union. Each protectorate had its own staff of District Commissioners and junior officials all reporting to a Resident Commissioner. The three Resident Commissioners then reported direct to Baring who alone spoke to London. Similarly, London only spoke to the protectorates through Baring.

A report of Tshekedi's interview with the District Commissioner in Serowe had already reached Baring via Mafeking so he was aware of what had happened. Buchanan then showed him all the cables that he had sent and then added his own opinion to Tshekedi's that the most serious repercussions would follow any marriage between Seretse and a white woman. Baring took both men's warnings very seriously and after Buchanan had left he sent a cyphered telegram to the Permanent Secretary of State at the Commonwealth Relations Office in Whitehall. Sir Eric Machtig, the department's most senior civil servant, was the closest adviser to the Secretary of State himself, Philip Noel-Baker. Baring's telegram to Machtig informed him of the marriage and briefly sketched in why he felt it to be so dangerous. 'Most grateful for any help you can give since marriage would be disastrous for Bamangwato tribe and Seretse personally,' Baring wrote.

In London, Ruth had been to Fenwick's in Bond Street to buy an outfit for her wedding. She had now given up all hope that her parents would become reconciled to the marriage and since that meant she would have no father to give her away, she felt she couldn't wear white. The dress she chose was turquoise. Also in Fenwick's she found a pillbox hat of exactly the same shade. Back home in Lewisham, she began to pack her things. Her father was determined to carry out his threat to bar her from the house once she was married.

She and Seretse had also decided to advance the date of the wedding by a week. Perhaps they were beginning to sense the massive forces of opposition gathering against them. Anyway, the Revd Patterson, vicar of Campden Hill, agreed that he would marry them on Saturday, 25 September at 1.30 p.m.

By the previous day, Friday the 24th, those forces had quickly organised themselves. Buchanan's brother John had contacted both the Commonwealth Relations Office and the Colonial Office.* The man he contacted at the Colonial Office was John Keith, the Chief Welfare Officer and the Director of Colonial Scholars. Keith's first suggestion was that Tshekedi should stop paying Seretse's allowance immediately.

Buchanan also contacted Ronald Orchard at the London Missionary Society. Orchard, having received Douglas Buchanan's telegram from Cape Town, was trying to find Dr Roger Pilkington, a director of the LMS who had entertained Seretse in his home on a number of occasions during the

---

* There was frequently confusion about these two great departments of state. The Colonial Office had responsibility for all the administered colonies of the Empire whereas the CRO, which until 1947 had been called the Dominions Office, dealt with the self-governing dominions within the Empire, namely, Canada, New Zealand, Australia and South Africa. With the coming of independence for India and the emerging concept of a Commonwealth club of equal nations, the name had been changed to the Commonwealth Relations Office. The anomaly was that the protectorates were not self-governing and should, therefore, have fallen under the Colonial Office. However, because they were the responsibility of the High Commissioner to South Africa who reported to the CRO, it was administratively simpler for the CRO to look after them as well. This only increased the suspicion in the minds of Tshekedi and others that it was but a matter of time before the British handed them over to South Africa.

previous two years. Orchard also roped in the Revd A. J. Haile, the LMS Regional Director in southern Africa who was in London on leave. Buchanan and the three LMS men, with Keith doing what he could in the Colonial Office, now set out to ensure that Seretse Khama would never marry Ruth Williams.

As soon as he heard the news from Orchard, Pilkington telephoned Seretse at his tiny flat in Campden Hill Gardens. Seretse told him first of all that he and Ruth were determined to marry and nobody could talk them out of it. Then he dropped the bombshell that they had brought the wedding day forward by a week. Within twenty-four hours, he told Pilkington, he and Ruth would be man and wife. Before he rang off, Seretse agreed to meet Pilkington and his wife later that evening to discuss the whole matter once more before it was too late.

Alerting the others to this new urgency, Pilkington then telephoned Ruth's parents in Lewisham. They were as much against the marriage as anybody else, they told him, but they had lost all influence over their 24-year-old daughter. Pilkington also managed to speak to Ruth who refused to say anything to him beyond agreeing to read a message which he would send round to the house by taxi the following morning.

Pilkington's last call of the day before going to see Seretse was a visit to the Revd Patterson. The bookish vicar of Campden Hill was becoming very upset at the sudden dramatic turn of events and seemed to resent the pressure Pilkington tried to put on him. 'Unfortunately the clergyman turned out to be extremely unreliable,' Pilkington was to write to Tshekedi two days later, 'and is what is described in the Gospel as "a reed shaken by the wind". We had a great deal of trouble on the following day because of his constant changes of mind.'

It was very late on that Friday evening when Dr Pilkington and his wife arrived at Seretse's flat. It was to be much later when they left. Pilkington tried until four o'clock the following morning to persuade Seretse to give up Ruth. Pilkington told him he was behaving disgracefully and it was cowardice to get married in this way before facing up to the tribe. He told him he would be guaranteeing a life of misery and ostracism for his wife if he took her to Bechuanaland, and if he remained in England he would be turning his back on all the responsibilities to which he had been born.

By the time he left, the new day already lightening the sky,

Pilkington was convinced he had persuaded Seretse at least to postpone his wedding.

After less than four hours sleep, Pilkington met Orchard, Haile and Buchanan to discuss their strategy for the day. Buchanan reported that John Keith at the Colonial Office had been searching the records most of the night to try to find precedents on which to declare the marriage illegal. He hadn't come up with much. A tea-planter from Ceylon had apparently had difficulty getting his marriage recognised in Scotland. A group of foresters from British Honduras, his researchers told him, had had similar problems. Keith admitted that this did not seem to offer much hope but he would keep looking.

Pilkington then sat down to write the message he had promised to send to Ruth in Lewisham before she moved out in preparation for her wedding:

> I have a cable stating that the tribe is strongly opposed to Seretse's marriage to a European. In view of this and of Seretse's position of responsibility amongst his people, I strongly urge that you should take no action until Seretse has consulted his people about the matter. I would be glad to put you in touch with a man who knows the Bechuana well and could explain their views to you. Please let me know when you could meet him and others with recent messages from the tribe.

A junior from the LMS, drafted in for the day to help, was then dispatched with the message in a taxi to Ruth's home. An hour later he returned. Ruth, surrounded by suitcases and wearing a very smart turquoise dress with matching hat, had accepted the sealed envelope from him, he reported. Noticing that she had put the letter aside unopened, he asked if he should wait for a reply. She said there would be none and showed him to the door. The men agreed it was going to be a difficult day. At about the same time, Ruth, suitcases and all, was arriving at Seretse's flat. Muriel had agreed to come with her to act as a witness at the wedding. Already waiting at the flat was John Zimmerman, a friend of Seretse's from Oxford, who had volunteered to be the second witness. The four were due to leave the flat at one o'clock for the short walk to St George's church, well in time for the 1.30 p.m. ceremony. At five minutes to one the telephone rang. It was Patterson to say that Pilkington, Haile and Orchard had been to see him. They had threatened to wait in the church and object at that point in the service when Patterson would ask if anybody knew of any reason why the two people before him should not be joined in holy matrimony. Patterson felt this would be extremely embarrassing for everybody and wondered whether or not they should all agree to postpone the wedding. What was more, he said, the men had hinted that if the marriage went ahead, he, Patterson, would get into serious trouble with the Foreign Office. He hadn't the faintest idea what they had meant, he said, but it did sound rather serious. All things considered, he felt it would be unwise to go ahead.

The three LMS men were at that moment standing at the back of St George's ready to carry out their threat should the wedding party arrive. Buchanan had been left by a telephone keeping in touch with Keith at the Colonial Office and his opposite number at the CRO. There was just the chance, they supposed, that Keith would come up with something better than the inconclusive fate of Honduran lumberjacks.

Seretse and Ruth, meanwhile, had gone round to the vicarage to see Patterson. What right had he, they asked, to refuse to marry them? They were free people in a supposedly free country. Patterson said he now felt obliged to refer the matter to the Bishop of London. If they, Ruth and Seretse, could get the bishop's permission, then the vicar would marry them with the greatest pleasure – 'I will tie the knot', were his words – and he reminded them that it was possible to be married up until six o'clock in the evening. The bishop at that moment, Patterson went on, was not half a mile away at the bottom of Kensington Church Street leading an ordination ceremony for a new vicar at St Mary Abbot's Church.

Ruth knew St Mary Abbot's well. It was a large, beautiful church on Kensington High Street with a long, cloistered approach to the main entrance. She had wanted to be married there but Seretse's flat fell just outside the parish and they would have had to wait a long time for permission.

Ruth and Seretse went back to his flat to tell Muriel and John Zimmerman that they must now go and plead their cause with the Bishop of London.

Back in St George's, the LMS trio waited until 1.45 p.m. and then went to a callbox to telephone Patterson to discover what had happened. Once again, as Pilkington would later complain, the vicar had been a reed bending in the wind. Their only chance now, the men reasoned, was to get to the Bishop of London first. Hailing a taxi, they drove down Kensington Church Street to St Mary Abbot's. There they found that the congregation was still assembling and that the bishop had not yet arrived. They waited to one side of the cloister's entrance where they could see all who arrived.

As they took up their position, Ruth, Seretse and their two witnesses left his flat and began their journey down Kensington Church Street. They arrived to find the local clergy and the choir forming up in procession in the cloisters awaiting the arrival of the bishop. The last of the parishioners were filing into the body of the church and they followed on behind. As she walked along the cloisters to the church, Muriel, a few steps behind Seretse and her sister, saw Ronald Orchard, a man whom she knew well from her social work at the LMS, standing on the pavement. It seemed to her that he had just left the church. Beyond thinking to herself that it was a strange coincidence she gave it no more thought and followed the others into the nave. As they settled into their pews, the Bishop of London, the Right Revd William Wand, arrived. As he prepared to line up in the cloisters for the stately procession into St Mary Abbot's, the three men boldly approached him. Murmuring their apologies, they told him they had a matter of the utmost importance to discuss. For five minutes they talked while the procession waited in the cloisters. They told him that the consequences of the marriage would be very serious and that the tribe's refusal to consent might even represent a legal barrier. Nothing should be done, they advised, without consultations with the Commonwealth Relations Office. Inside the church, Ruth and Seretse waited for their chance, unaware it had already gone.

After the ceremony was over, they approached Bishop Wand. To Ruth he seemed cold and aloof and, surprisingly, to be already aware of their case. He really could not give his permission for them to marry, he said, until he had consulted with Africa. If they didn't mind, he must ask them now to run along as he had much business to attend to.

More slowly now, Ruth and Seretse, their witnesses trailing behind, walked back up the hill to St George's and the Revd Patterson. As they arrived, the vicar told them he had just been telephoned by Bishop Wand's secretary and warned that on no account must he marry them until the British government agreed. Under those instructions, Patterson said, he was sorry but he had no choice. Ruth burst into tears. It had been a long day for her. She had moved out of her home, breaking her ties with her parents; all day she had tried to marry the man she loved; she had been refused marriage by the Church of England, HER church, not Seretse's, who, if he belonged to any, was a Congregationalist through his country's links with the London Missionary Society.

Now, late on a Saturday afternoon, standing in her turquoise dress outside the church where she thought she would be wed, she broke down. She supposed, she said, that the Church now expected her to go and live in sin with the man she loved since she had nowhere else to go. The vicar said he was sure that Mrs Patterson would be delighted to offer her a bed for the night. The couple declined. Walking through Notting Hill Gate and on to the Bayswater Road, they found a hotel where Ruth checked in alone for the night.

Meanwhile, John Buchanan finally got a telephone call from John Keith at the Colonial Office. He said that when he had heard that the church wedding had been postponed he had come up with rather a good idea. He would ask the Home Office to circulate every Register Office in the country with the story that if the couple applied to them to be married they should first check with Bechuanaland to make sure that Seretse wasn't already married. He was sure that such checks would take a very long time indeed. As soon as he could, he would contact the Commonwealth Relations Office so they could make a joint approach to the Home Office. He had also got a message to Seretse making an appointment for him at his office on Monday morning. Perhaps after the events of the day, Keith said, the young man might have come to his senses anyway and would give up the idea of the marriage voluntarily.

4
Seeing Sense

On the following morning, Sunday, with the immediate crisis averted, John Buchanan, Pilkington and the others were able to draw breath. They had taken great hope from what Bishop Wand had reported to them the previous evening. He had heard Seretse say to Ruth at the end of their fruitless discussions at St Mary Abbot's: 'I think we need to go away and rethink the whole affair.'

Pilkington felt strongly that Ruth had been bullying Seretse into an immediate marriage. He was convinced that he had persuaded Seretse in the early hours of Saturday morning to postpone the wedding but that Ruth had changed Seretse's mind again when she had arrived. The others agreed that she was the dominant force in the relationship and that, if left alone, Seretse could probably be talked out of the whole ridiculous affair. It may well be, they thought, that Seretse, more rational than Ruth and with a lawyer's mind, was already beginning to realise what he was letting himself in for. Anyway, even if they were still determined to go ahead, it would be impossible for them to marry in an Anglican church now that the bishop had done what was required. John Keith was still doing his best at the Colonial Office to find legal obstacles to place in their way and his plan to plant false stories at the Register Offices seemed a good one. It was also a good sign that Seretse had agreed to meet Keith at his office on Monday morning. All was far from lost.

Pilkington's assessment of Seretse was in fact very wide of the mark. His quiet manner and unemotional reaction to events disguised a strength of purpose at least equal to that of the woman he was trying to marry. When she had arrived at Seretse's flat the previous morning, she had found his resolve unshaken. The pledge they had made to one another at the time of his proposal, that they would stand firm together against all attempts to break them up, was growing stronger as the opposition mounted. But whereas Ruth had a will like an arrow, fired directly at its target, Seretse could see the value of retreat in order to advance on another front. Brought up in the byzantine world of Bamangwato politics and now with more than a year of legal studies behind him, Seretse was a difficult man to thwart. Even now his apparently chance aside to Ruth about the need for a 'rethink', overheard by Bishop Wand and faithfully relayed to the others, was doing its work. Already it had taken the edge off his pursuers' sense of urgency.

Pilkington, meanwhile, was writing to Tshekedi about the events of the previous day. Although never having met Ruth, he felt able to describe her to the chief-regent.

She does not care at all either for the tribe or for Seretse as far as his position with the tribe is concerned. Actually this surprises me because I believe that she is not altogether a bad kind of girl but that she started this business off out of a kind of emotional reaction to the Colour Bar in Africa . . . She and her sister were in the habit of visiting the colonial students' hostel out of a genuine interest in Coloured people and their affairs. I can well understand her falling in love with Seretse – particularly if she had some kind of resistance in her home environment. I think it quite likely that she felt she would overcome the tribe's resistance by her own personality and that she would help him to lead his country onward. But, at the same time, her unwillingness even to listen to representations from his country seemed to indicate the kind of selfishness which however is not at all unusual in young people on the verge of marriage.

John Buchanan also sat down that Sunday to write his own letter. He was reporting to brother Douglas in Cape Town and though he, too, had yet to meet Ruth, his opinions about her were already formed.

By all reports she is a respectable, not very intelligent girl, inspired possibly by a sort of proselytising zeal to improve relations between the Native and the White. If this is true . . . she will possibly be more difficult to deal with than if it had been the case of a chorus girl or suchlike, when money would have talked possibly. I gathered it was Pilkington's view that neither Seretse nor the girl would be the least affected by money or economic outlook.

Apart from all else, it would be a tragedy for both Seretse and the girl to get married. If Seretse takes the line 'the world lost' and threw up the chieftainship and South Africa and tried to live here, what possible future has he? How could he earn his living? How long could such a marriage last in this country (where just as I know so well in Northern Rhodesia, there is in theory no Colour Bar but in practice!!!)? Looking further ahead, what possible hope have any children of such a marriage?

The following morning, Monday, 27 September, Seretse Khama left his flat and walked down the hill to the Kensington Register Office. There he applied for a special licence to marry and was told to come back, with his bride, in two days time at 9 a.m. He then went to the Bayswater Road to collect Ruth from her hotel. Climbing on to an underground train, they travelled as far as they could go, to Cockfosters at the very end of the line. They would now stay out of everybody's way until they were safely married. Seretse had no intention of keeping his appointment with John Keith at the Colonial Office. Instead, he would spend his day in the country with Ruth.

In the meantime, a messenger from Fulham Palace was delivering a note from Bishop Wand to Ronald Orchard at the London Missionary Society. 'Dear Sir,' the bishop wrote, 'I am very grateful for your communication of 25 September. I saw Dr Patterson and I write to let you know that the matter is now being dealt with by the Colonial Office.'

Orchard was delighted. If Bishop Wand had seen Patterson in person then there would definitely be no more trouble from that quarter. Even more welcome was the news that the bishop had been talking to the Colonial Office. Clearly, the least known about the details the better, but if such a senior member of the Anglican Church had reached an understanding about the matter with the British government then the odds really were stacking up against Ruth and Seretse.

Orchard immediately wrote his reply:

My dear Lord Bishop,
I am very grateful for the action that you took on Saturday last and I regret the urgency of the situation compelled such a

hurried and unceremonious reference to you. I am sure that the Colonial Office, in consultation with the Office of Commonwealth Relations which is concerned with the Bechuanaland Protectorate, can best deal with the matter, and I am glad it has been referred to them. In the meantime we must give what help we can of a pastoral kind to those concerned.
Faithfully Yours,
R. K. Orchard.

On Monday afternoon, John Buchanan heard from Keith at the Colonial Office that Seretse had failed to show up for their appointment. Buchanan wrote immediately to Campden Hill Gardens asking Seretse to contact him urgently. Keith also had no more news about his plans for circulating the false story to the Register Offices. The necessity of winning the cooperation of first the Commonwealth Relations Office and then the Home Office was proving time consuming.

The following day Ruth and Seretse spent the day in Brighton, walking along the seashore. At eight o'clock the next morning, Wednesday, 29 September, Seretse collected his bride from her Bayswater Hotel. Fearing that the turquoise dress had brought her bad luck, Ruth was now dressed in a severe black suit with matching hat and shoes. In a state of high anxiety, fearing that some lawyer, bishop or missionary would jump out on her at every street corner, she made her way with Seretse to Kensington Register Office. Meeting their witnesses, Muriel and John Zimmerman, outside, they all went in and sat in the waiting room. Their appointment had been for 9 a.m. but the hour came and went and still they were not called. Soon other couples began arriving and Ruth began to fear the worst. Finally, after nearly thirty minutes, the door to the waiting room opened and an official asked if he could see Seretse alone for a moment. A wave of despair washed over Ruth as she watched Seretse follow the man out of the room. Somehow, the all-seeing, all-knowing opposition had triumphed again. In spite of all she had given up, her family, her home, her career, she was still to be denied what she wanted most.

But not so. Seretse was taken to see the Registrar, who explained, with some embarrassment, that when he had filled in the application forms on the following day he had written 'Native Chief' in the space marked 'father's occupation'. For the last thirty minutes the Registrar and his staff had been arguing about whether such a title constituted an occupation. Seretse explained that as chief, his father had been the tribe's 'administrator'. The Registrar accepted this and Ruth and the witnesses were called in. Ruth was now so nervous that her voice had gone and several times during the ceremony the Registrar had to wait while she struggled to answer his questions. Finally, and to her utter relief, he pronounced them man and wife.

All fear, all anxiety now left Ruth. No longer did she care who might be waiting on every corner, they could do nothing now. She and Seretse went back to her hotel, collected her things and moved them into the tiny flat in Notting Hill Gate. Seretse, noticing John Buchanan's note from the previous day, telegrammed him saying: 'Have married Ruth. Do you still want to see me?' From there it was off to a celebratory lunch and then preparations for the party they were planning for all Seretse's friends that evening. Tiny though the flat was, Ruth and Seretse estimated they must have entertained representatives from almost every black country in the British Empire that night. All Seretse's friends from the colonial students' hostel, young men from Africa, the Caribbean and Asia, came to congratulate them and wish them well. At the end of the evening Ruth felt tired and happy. Only the rift with her parents, the break with those to whom she had been so close and whom she loved so much, cast a sadness on her day.

She had not spoken to them since leaving home the previous Saturday. They knew what had been happening, of course, because Muriel was still living at home. Perhaps time would close the gap between them.

During the evening a telegram had arrived from Tshekedi in Serowe.

You are apparently taking no notice of my strong objections to your marrying an English girl. I ask you to pay attention to what Commonwealth Office advises you. Your obstinacy can only result in serious consequences for yourself. Have asked Commonwealth Office to arrange your immediate return. On no condition can we agree to your marrying an English girl.

5

Stern Realities

News spread quickly to Serowe that Seretse was married. Muriel had mentioned it to a member of her church who immediately told Orchard at LMS headquarters. When he telephoned John Buchanan he found that the solicitor had already received Seretse's telegram and was cabling the news to brother Douglas in Cape Town.

As Ruth and Seretse woke up in their tiny flat in Notting Hill Gate, Douglas Buchanan was already sending his telegram the thousand miles and more to Joe Burgess's Post Office in Serowe. All that was needed then was a brave messenger to walk the hundred yards to the chief-regent's bungalow.

John Buchanan also told the Commonwealth Relations Office who sent an immediate telegram to the High Commissioner, Sir Evelyn Baring, in Cape Town. Sir Eric Machtig, the Permanent Secretary at the CRO, was on leave but his assistants had spent the weekend trying to contact Sir Reginald Coupland of All Souls College, Oxford. He had befriended Seretse at Oxford and, it was hoped, could try to dissuade him from his marriage. Coupland had agreed to help but now Machtig's officials informed him that the wedding had already happened. 'It is indeed a sorry mess,' they wrote. 'Now the matter is one primarily for Tshekedi and the tribe.' Coupland replied: 'It will be a miracle if the marriage turns out happily in the end for either of them or for their children. It's a real tragedy, or so it seems.'

Tshekedi was in despair when he learnt of the marriage and blamed the British for letting it happen. Surely they could have found some way of stopping it? Didn't they realise the seriousness of what Seretse had done? Even if, and this was most unlikely, the tribe were to accept a white woman as their queen, they could never possibly accept the offspring of such a marriage. Those of mixed race – or Coloureds as they were called – were generally regarded as inferiors and unacceptable as heirs to the chieftainship.

The best hope now seemed to lie in threatening to disqualify Seretse from the chieftainship as long as he was married to this woman. If only Tshekedi could talk to him face to face then perhaps he would see what he was putting at risk. The regent's senior counsellors agreed that Tshekedi should use all his influence to persuade Seretse to come to Serowe to talk to the tribe. On no account should his wife come and, if necessary, the British should be asked to refuse her a passport. Once they had Seretse in Serowe on his own, they would be able to make him see things clearly. He might even prefer to stay and not bother going back for this woman who was causing so much trouble. They also agreed to stop his allowance making it more difficult for him to stay in London. Tshekedi told Douglas Buchanan in Cape Town what had been decided and then cabled Seretse:

> Formal signing of document in England does not constitute your marriage. As far as we are concerned no marriage exists. Apparently you took my advice for a threat. We accept nothing short of dissolution of that marriage. Our decision firm, welfare of tribe paramount in this case.

Back in Notting Hill Gate, Seretse had realised that his uncle would almost certainly stop his allowance. When he had finally gone to see John Keith after the marriage he had complained that he had no money at all and would have to live off Ruth's savings. It was his duty and his intention to support his new wife. If the allowance was stopped then he would have to consider suing Tshekedi for the value of his father's cattle herds.

Back in Serowe, Tshekedi was waiting for Seretse to agree to come home. In the meantime, he thought, there was little to lose from a more direct approach. He asked Douglas Buchanan to tell his brother John to offer Ruth money if she would divorce Seretse and forget all about him. John did not relish the prospect of this at all but he did invite the newlyweds to lunch at his home. Before they had finished their soup, he knew that such an offer would be deeply insulting and would probably result in the breaking of all contact between the two sides. He decided to say nothing about money beyond passing on Tshekedi's decision to stop Seretse's allowance.

On 5 October, a week after the wedding, Douglas Buchanan wrote to Ronald Orchard at the LMS. He wanted to thank the missionary society for all the efforts they had made in trying to stop the wedding and also to make sure that they knew what he and Tshekedi were planning. It was vital that Seretse return to Serowe as soon as possible and on no account must Ruth go with him.

> At the moment, we here think it would be advisable for the British authorities to refuse the wife a passport . . . I personally do not know what will be the tribe's decision but they naturally look to the young chief's wife as being the mother of the future and Chief Tshekedi and I cannot believe they will regard with equanimity the idea of a 'Coloured' man as their future chief.
> Even if it has not been possible to prevent the marriage, under all the circumstances and when the parties come to a fuller realisation of what is involved, a divorce by reason of desertion might still be the best solution should Seretse return to southern Africa and leave his wife in England. Naturally, arrangements would have to be made for her maintenance but I imagine the tribe would be only too willing to get out of an unsatisfactory position by some such means. I feel certain they will not want to depose Seretse if, from their point of view, there is any possible way of preventing the present wife's issue coming to the chieftainship.

Buchanan then wrote to the High Commissioner, Sir Evelyn Baring. He told him that Tshekedi wanted the British to stop Ruth getting a passport should she try to accompany her husband to Serowe. Buchanan was given no written reply but Baring's legal staff told him later that day that, however undesirable it might be, they could find no legal grounds for stopping Ruth travelling to Bechuanaland.

At the same time, Tshekedi was also writing to thank Orchard at the LMS for all their efforts to stop the wedding:

> In future, when the stern realities of life make themselves apparent to Seretse he will not say that he got where he is for lack of suitable advice. I see most troublous times ahead of me as far as the tribe is concerned and with regard to Seretse a very gloomy future indeed.

Orchard now felt it was time that Tshekedi understood more

clearly the two people he was dealing with. He thought that both Tshekedi and Buchanan were underestimating the depth of feeling and the bond of loyalty that had developed between Ruth and Seretse. On 14 October, he wrote a long letter to Serowe.

From information I have been able to gather it is clear that Seretse's wife is not in any sense an adventuress. She does not, of course, understand at all clearly the consequences of her action in marrying Seretse and has not been prepared to discuss it with anyone who could help her to see the real position. She has, I understand, gone into it despite opposition (including that of her parents) first because she appears to be genuinely in love and secondly with some vaguely idealistic idea of helping Seretse in his work.

Perhaps it would not be unfair or liable to misunderstanding if I also said that Seretse seems to have been quite determined to go forward with the marriage at all costs. But I think he has kept that determination in a separate part of his mind from the part in which he knows his responsibilities to his people and has never allowed himself really to think of the two things together. Consequently, the determination to get married, being nearer and more obvious here than his tribal responsibilities, has got the upper hand . . . We will have you and your people and Seretse very much in our thoughts and prayers as you now try to discover what is the right way to deal with this disturbing position. May God guide you all.

Seretse had now come to believe that there was no way forward until he had been to Serowe and faced the tribe. But he was very suspicious that once in Serowe, Tshekedi and the British would find some way to stop him coming back or Ruth coming out to join him. He therefore telegrammed Tshekedi: 'Tribe and you important to me. Suspension of allowance being felt. Suggest passage for two. Dissolution of marriage unacceptable.'

On Saturday 16 October, the story of Ruth, Seretse and the tribe finally hit the British press. The *Daily Mirror*, on its front page, sported a picture of Ruth and Seretse with the headline: 'Ruler-to-be Weds Office Girl, Is Called Home to Explain.' The story explained how the heir to the chieftainship of the Bamangwato had 'secretly' married a white English girl. 'He has been ordered by his uncle to return home for talks of "grave importance".'

Far from being ordered home, Seretse was keen to go but only if he could get a guarantee that he would be able to come back to London. Finally, John Keith at the Colonial Office convinced him that the authorities could not stop him coming back whenever he wished. Consequently, unable to afford two air tickets and feeling that, on balance, it was better that he face the tribe alone, he prepared to fly to Bechuanaland. His main concern was that there were now reporters regularly camped outside the flat in Campden Hill Gardens and Ruth was already growing nervous of them. 'White Bride Causes a Tribal Crisis' proclaimed the *Daily Mail*, reporting that Evelyn Baring was flying home to London to report on the 'delicate situation that has arisen'. In fact Baring's trip had been scheduled several months earlier and Tshekedi's problems were not high on his list of priorities. The British policy of indirect rule, allowing the tribes to run their own affairs as long as they did not embarrass the British, upset their neighbours or cost London any money, still applied. The 'marriage crisis' was Tshekedi's affair and he could get on with it.

From now on, the interest of Fleet Street in the affairs of the Bamangwato would be an important feature as the story developed. For the editors of the more popular papers in particular it seemed to offer their readers many different things. First of all, there was the fascination of a black man marrying a white woman. The vast majority of English people rarely met blacks. Even those who had just returned from the war had had little chance to meet black people socially. Those blacks from the Empire who were fighting with the British were frequently in separate regiments, often in the Pioneer Corps doing the vital but unglamorous work of digging ditches and laying drains. Britain's native black population was still small and restricted to well-defined inner city areas. It would not be until the 1950s that black people would become a common feature of British life when the British government openly recruited in the Caribbean for thousands of black families to come to England to work on the buses, the London Underground trains and in the nation's hospitals. Blacks, in 1948, were, in most people's eyes, both inferior and slightly mysterious. They were certainly not the sort of people that white girls should marry. And yet there was another, even more compelling layer to the story. Britain with its ration cards and queues was an austere and unglamorous place after the war. The economy was shattered, the nation's debts were huge and she had responsibilities around the globe that she could not possibly fulfil. But the nation was proud of its Empire and had been brought up since childhood on the imperial romanticism of writers like Rudyard Kipling and Rider Haggard. Haggard in particular had told stories of mysterious Africa, vast and timeless, peopled with strange and frightening tribes worshipping cruel gods and observing lurid rites. With the novelist's hero, Sir Allan Quatermain, Britain's schoolchildren had travelled across searing deserts, climbed cloud-topped mountains and seen sights beyond belief. In one famous novel, *She*, a beautiful white woman had commanded a vast tribe, exacting total obedience from them on pain of instant execution.

Now, in drab England, with bacon, butter, petrol – even, until 1948, bread – and much else rationed, where a woman could hardly buy a pair of nylons, here was a story to make the blood race. Would the tribe accept a white queen? When the papers learnt that Seretse was flying to Serowe, local correspondents in southern Africa were alerted to find out what would happen.

6

A Fire Burning

For the previous four weeks news of the threat to the chieftainship had been filtering slowly through the Bamangwato Reserve. At that time of year, most of the tribesmen were spread across vast areas of scrubland and bush moving their herds in search of pasture. From Serowe, Tshekedi now sent messengers to every part, summoning the men to a Kgotla meeting to discuss the gathering crisis.

Many of them were at their cattle-posts, encampments deep in the bush built around natural wells or boreholes, where they and their sons tended anything up to 500 cattle. It was at his cattle-post that Radipophu Sekgoma, a cousin of Tshekedi, first heard the news. As a member of the royal family, as one of the royal uncles of Seretse, Radipophu belonged to that inner circle of tribal counsellors who advised the regent. Now when he heard that young Seretse wanted to marry a white girl, he didn't believe it. So deep was his conviction that such a thing could not be that, today, more than forty years later, he still wags his head ruefully at the memory of how wrong he was. Nevertheless, whether he believed it or not, he had still to answer the summons of the regent. Issuing instructions to his sons for the care of the cattle, he set off for Serowe. Across the scrubland, from similarly remote encampments, other men began the trek to the capital, bewildered by the news.

Radipophu's cattle-post was at an isolated spot called Lephephe, well to the south of Serowe. Astride his horse, he rode slowly north through the brown scrub. October is the hottest month in Bechuanaland. It is the end of the dry season, the sun is high in the sky as the southern hemisphere's midsummer approaches and the cooling summer rain clouds are still to arrive. The temperature often rises well into the nineties with scarcely a breath of wind. Twice on the way Radipophu camped for the night, tethering his horse to a thorn tree and bedding down next to an open fire as the welcome cool of the evening turned into the sharp chill of night. His memories today, clearly recalled through the intervening years, tell of the opinions and attitudes with which many of the Bamangwato were to face the impending crisis.

In 1948 he had been 46, mature in his years and his judgement. Eight years earlier, with many other Bamangwato, he had volunteered to join the levies of troops being raised in all parts of the British Empire to fight the Germans. He had never been out of the protectorate before but within months he was fighting with the British Eighth Army against Rommel's Afrika Korps in the Libyan Desert. Although only a member of the humble Pioneer Corps, digging trenches and ditches, latrines and rubbish pits, Radipophu and his fellow Bamangwato had come under fire. Crossing to Sicily, they had helped fight the Germans the length of Italy before returning to Bechuanaland.

When Radipophu had returned to Serowe in 1946, Tshekedi had put him in charge of an age regiment. This custom went back to the Bamangwato's warrior days. Every six years or so, those young men aged between roughly 17 and 23 would be formed into a regiment under the leadership of a boy of the same age from the royal family. The formation of the regiment signified its readiness for military service and the group would always fight as a unit thereafter. They would remain members of their regiment for the rest of their lives, retaining a special loyalty toward their fellows. The custom had never died – though when the war against the Matabele ended it became largely ceremonial – and was still a sign that a young man had reached manhood. In the 1920s and 1930s, Tshekedi had revived the active role of the regiments calling them out to fulfil public duties, building clinics or dams, improving roads or clearing new areas for housing. As the men returned from fighting for the British, Tshekedi had begun mobilising them again for his ambitious social projects delayed by the war. Radipophu, because of his age and status as a royal uncle, had been given a regiment to build a primary school in Serowe. The work done he had resumed his cattle rearing, a tribesman like many others, albeit one of special status as cousin to the regent and uncle to the heir. On the morning of the third day of his journey, he saw the low, rounded Serowe Hill and by noon he had arrived in the capital. Going directly to the Kgotla ground, he found hundreds of men in excited debate.

Tshekedi had just received word from Douglas Buchanan that

Seretse was married. As Radipophu arrived, the regent was passing the news on to the men gathered in the Kgotla ground. Most of the men Radipophu spoke to that day were against what Seretse had done. Tshekedi and those of the royal uncles who were in Serowe at the time had been furious when they heard that Seretse had gone ahead with the marriage. Most of the tribe were taking their cue from them. Seretse was risking the cohesion and identity of the tribe by thinking only of himself. Who was this woman and who ever heard of a Mongwato (the singular of Bamangwato) marrying a white? What did she know about the duties of a chief's wife? Who were her parents, anyway, and what claims might they have on the tribe and its wealth? And if the Bamangwato did accept her, must they then agree to a Coloured as their future chief? Radipophu listened and felt inclined to agree.

But there were a few in Serowe that day who had already taken Seretse's side. The members of Seretse's age regiment, for instance, were unhappy with the tone the older men were setting. As yet they kept their own counsel because, for the time being at least, Tshekedi's anger was carrying all before it. Indeed, so great had been the regent's wrath that one of his closest aides had known for a whole day that Seretse was married but had said nothing. Goareng Mosinyi, a cousin of Seretse's and one of his closest friends, worked in Tshekedi's office in charge of the tribe's accounts. He and Seretse had been schoolboys together at the mission schools in South Africa where Tshekedi had sent them. Later, Goareng, a couple of years older than Seretse, had returned to Serowe to join the army levies the British were raising. Tshekedi however, having already seen so many able men leave for the war, insisted that Goareng stay and work for him. Seretse and Goareng had written constantly to one another and had been close companions whenever Seretse had been in Serowe. They were part of that new generation of Bamangwato, better educated than their elders, and looking forward to a time when the colonial era would end, when the whites would no longer rule. The day before Radipophu had ridden in, Goareng had received a one word telegram from London – 'Married'. Now he watched Tshekedi and the royal uncles and bided his time. Throughout October the Kgotla was in almost constant session. New arrivals from the cattle-posts went straight there to learn the latest news. When they went home they were interrogated by their wives.

Bamangwato custom barred women from the Kgotla meetings but, as concerned as the men about the future of the tribe, they held a hundred tiny Kgotlas on street corners every day.

Tshekedi himself was convinced that the tribe felt as he did. He was also sure, particularly after receiving Orchard's letter from the LMS, that Seretse would see sense once he got to Serowe. He reported to Buchanan in Cape Town that there was a 'fixed decision that a Bamangwato English queen is totally unacceptable'.

> From telegrams and a letter so far received I am convinced that Seretse is not alive to this situation. He appears to have convinced himself that, the marriage being accomplished, everybody will acquiesce but in this he is wrong . . . You have known me long enough to believe that I could not easily let the welfare of the tribe go and their status which I have suffered so much to maintain just be blown to pieces by a single thoughtless action of my nephew. You know, too, how I had built high hopes on this lad.

Finally, at the end of October, the tribe was told that Seretse was coming to Serowe to explain himself. Tshekedi was also happy to announce that the white woman would be staying in London. The regent knew that his niece, Seretse's younger sister, Naledi, was very concerned about her brother. She too had been sent away to mission school in South Africa and Tshekedi agreed that she could meet Seretse's London flight and accompany him to Serowe. In the late 1940s and early 1950s there were two ways of flying from England to southern Africa. The more luxurious way and the one which everyone preferred if they had the time and the money was by BOAC Solent Flying Boat. The Solent, a huge, four-engined aircraft which had been developed from the wartime Sunderland, lifted off from Southampton early in the morning. The twenty-five or so passengers reclined in luxury in the wide and lofty cabin while stewards served refreshments. That evening, the aeroplane touched down in the sea off the coast of Sicily where the passengers disembarked for a night in a local hotel. The next day, the flight continued through Alexandria and then up the Nile to a second night in a hotel at Luxor. Day three saw the passengers flying to Lake Victoria in Uganda for a night in Entebbe before reaching the majestic spectacle of Victoria Falls on the Zambesi River and another hotel. On the fifth and final day, the passengers, pampered and relaxed, touched down on the Vaal Dam, some thirty miles south of Johannesburg in South Africa. The alternative route was much more of an endurance test. South African Airways flew a DC4 Skymaster which left London's Heathrow Airport at 8 a.m. Landing to refuel at Tripoli in Libya, Khartoum in the Sudan and near Nairobi in Kenya, the passengers arrived exhausted at Johannesburg Airport at 7 p.m. on the following day. The advantages were that it was cheaper and much quicker.

It was from this flight that Naledi met Seretse at the end of October. From there, the two of them boarded a South African Railways train seating themselves in the carriages reserved for blacks. These were always the ones at the front since they were the ones most likely to be affected by the smoke and ash from the steam locomotive which pulled the train. From Johannesburg, the railway travelled west through the western Transvaal, passing through Mafeking before turning north and then north-east into Bechuanaland. At Palapye, thirty miles from Serowe, they were met by a car sent by Tshekedi to bring them home. Tshekedi had arranged, as always, for Seretse to stay with him in his European-style bungalow behind the Kgotla ground. When the car bringing Seretse arrived there, the two men greeted one another like strangers. Since before he could remember, Seretse had regarded Tshekedi as his father. Back in January 1926, standing rigidly to attention in a Scottish kilt, a custom inherited from the LMS's many Scottish missionaries, the 4-year-old Seretse had watched Tshekedi's inauguration as regent and heard him pledge himself to defend the tribe for Seretse's sake. In 1936, when he was only 15, he had been asked by Tshekedi to be best man at his marriage to his first wife, Bagakgametse Sekgoma. When that marriage had ended in divorce, the regent again asked his nephew to be his best man when he married Ella Moshoela, the love of his life. At every important point in his early life, Seretse had known that Tshekedi would be there, advising, helping, listening. Now they could scarcely talk to one another.

Tshekedi had invited the two chiefs of the protectorate's other major tribes to join the Bamangwato for these crucial discussions. Kgari of the Bakwena and Bathoen of the Bangwaketse were old friends of Tshekedi and agreed with his angry disapproval of his nephew. Seretse soon found the atmosphere in Tshekedi's house, with, as he felt, all three men ganged up against him, too much to bear and he moved out. The rift between uncle and nephew deepened.

A day or so after Seretse's arrival a Kgotla was held to welcome him back. Tshekedi told the tribe that they were facing a crisis but that if they did not all agree with the decisions that he felt must be taken, then he would leave the reserve and live with another tribe. Tshekedi said he wanted what was best for the Bamangwato but if they did not want him then he would go. In reply, Seretse told the tribe that he didn't want to lose either Tshekedi or Ruth.

The sight of Seretse standing amongst them affected many in the tribe in a way they had not expected. The Bamangwato had a deep respect for their chiefs almost like the European medieval belief in the divine right of kings. The history of the tribes of southern Africa had been a bloody one particularly since Shaka had revolutionised their warfare. Tribes had preyed upon one another, slaughtering the men, enslaving their women, destroying their villages. Whole tribes were swallowed up by stronger opponents. Frequently, it seemed, the destinies of nations had been decided by a few great men. Shaka, Dingaan, Mzilikasi and Lobengula had built empires out of the ruins of weaker tribes. Whether or not a tribe survived seemed to depend on the strength of its chief. Seretse's great grandfather, Sekgoma I, had been a rock in the shifting sands of the 1830s and had made the Bamangwato so strong that other tribes had come to them seeking protection. Seretse's grandfather, Khama, remained one of the most famous chiefs in southern African history, not only for his defeat of the Matabele but for withstanding the assaults of Briton and Afrikaaner alike. In spite of all the turmoils, the Bamangwato had not 'scattered', that most poignant of all African fears when the cohesion of the tribe is broken, when the village and its society is shattered by the enemy, and the people run for their lives. This had not happened to the Bamangwato and it was due to the House of Khama.

The young man who stood before them, for all his sins, carried the torch of Khama. Before Seretse arrived, one young man, Mokatcha Mokadi, had felt very much as the royal uncles had felt. He had joined in the talk that the grandson of Khama must choose between the tribe and the woman. But when, he remembered forty years later, he looked into the young prince's eyes that day, he had said to himself: 'This is the true chief. No other will do.' It is impossible to say how the tribe was divided that day. Some like Mokadi were converted to Seretse's cause the moment they saw him standing among them. Others, in particular the older men like Radipophu, found it harder to accept what Seretse had done. Closer in age and sentiment to Tshekedi, they still followed the regent. Yet others, those close to Seretse like Goareng Mosinyi, waited for the tide to turn.

On 13 November 1948, the most important of the royal uncles and cousins assembled to consider the marriage. Seretse began by telling them he would never give up his wife but that he should not be disqualified from the chieftainship because of it. His grandfather, Khama, had married without the consent of the royal family and his son, Sekgoma, Seretse's father, had married in the very teeth of his father's opposition. Even Ella, Tshekedi's wife, had been frowned on by the tribe. The uncles replied that when Khama had married Semane, the great chief's fourth wife and the one whom the royal family disliked, he already had a son and the succession was safe. The example of Tshekedi, they argued, was irrelevant since neither he nor his offspring could be chief. There were fifteen people at the meeting and, at the end, only one gave Seretse his support. The next day they held another meeting. This time there were sixteen people there but again only one vote went to Seretse.

On 15 November, 3,000 men assembled for the full Kgotla meeting. Most men carried little wooden folding stools for experience had told them that Kgotlas could be lengthy affairs. It was the custom – and the strength – of the Bamangwato that any man could have his say for as long as he liked. Both at local level and here in the capital, those with a grievance or a passionately held point of view could stand up before his peers and speak his mind. It had proved an invaluable safety valve, a way of releasing tension before it could build up. The humblest man present could criticise the proposal of a chief and never be thought disloyal or treacherous. Through endless, patient discussion the Bamangwato had learnt their own special kind of tolerance and good government. Although the Kgotla could not make a decision or pass a law – only the chief could do that – the wise ruler was he who listened to what the Kgotla told him and acted accordingly.

The disadvantage was that the Kgotla could go on for many days. As well as carrying his little stool, the right-thinking Mongwato also, if the gathering was small, took his place in the shadows cast by the two huge makala trees that dominated the Kgotla ground. There he and his fellows would sit in the pools of shade, moving every half hour or so as the shadows shifted.

That day, however, there was no such luxury to be had. Three thousand men more than filled the Kgotla and most would have to suffer the sun all day. The Kgotla ground itself measured some 60 yards by 40 yards, an oval space marked out by white-painted stones set in the dust. At the head of the Kgotla the stones were reinforced by a semi-circular pallisade of 4-foot stakes, in front of which stood a raised platform.

At seven o'clock, Seretse and Tshekedi took their places on the platform. At the front of the Kgotla, just below the platform, the LMS's resident missionary in Serowe, the Revd Alan Seager, prepared to take down all that was said.

Seretse began by saying that he knew the custom of the tribe. A man should marry with his father's permission, he said. A chief should marry with the permission of the whole tribe. He asked them all to forgive him because he had done neither. But, he went on, he could never give up his wife. He loved her and would never leave her. He wanted to be their chief but they would have to accept him with his wife. He repeated what he had said to the royal uncles earlier that both Khama and Tshekedi had married without the tribe's consent and that had not disqualified either of them from leading their people. Sekgoma had even been driven into exile by his father because of his marriage but still he had returned to become chief.

At different points in the crowd, men stood to have their say. Both Khama and Sekgoma had done as Seretse said but both times there had been disruption and bloodshed. The way to achieve peace was for the chief to marry with the tribe's consent. Some men said that they should prevent Seretse from leaving and ask the British to stop the wife from coming to Serowe. That, they argued, would put an end to the matter. If Tshekedi didn't agree, they said, it would be very suspicious. It would prove what some were already suggesting which was that Tshekedi was happy to get rid of Seretse so as to keep the chieftainship for himself. At this point, the regent stood up to reply that Seretse had agreed to come to Serowe on the understanding, given by Tshekedi and others, that he would be free to return to London whenever he liked. He had made those promises to the British authorities and they too had said that Seretse could not be stopped from going back to England. After much argument on this point, it was finally agreed that if Seretse should go back to England, then he went of his own accord and nobody was driving him away.

The meeting adjourned at noon reconvening that afternoon from three until five. The next day it met for five hours in the morning leaving the afternoon free to allow the tribesmen to attend to their own affairs. Wednesday was another full day session with the tribe refusing to draw the logical conclusion of the argument: they wanted Seretse to stay but not his wife; Seretse would not part with her; therefore Seretse could not be chief. Nobody seemed able to say it.

Finally, on Thursday, 18 November, Tshekedi invited Chief Bathoen of the Bangwaketse to speak. Not being a Mongwato, Bathoen was freer to speak than many of those present. Some would reflect later that, being as close as he was to Tshekedi, he was actually about to say all the things that the regent wanted to say but could not. He began by calling Seretse a coward for not saying outright that he did not want to be chief and that all his assertions of love for the Bamangwato were just words. He also accused him of encouraging opposition within the tribe against Tshekedi and he finished by urging him to be a man and admit the truth. He then asked Tshekedi to adjourn the Kgotla until the next day to give Seretse time to consider his reply.

At 7 a.m. on Friday, Seretse stood up before the tribe to do just that.

It has been said that I am a coward and that I ought to say outright that I do not want the chieftainship, that my heart is not with you or with this country. But I cannot say that; it is not in my thoughts and it is not so. I cannot say it just so that you will think that I am a man. You are angry with me because I will not leave my wife, a woman that you do not want. I cannot force you to accept her. I have admitted that I took her against your will and you have told me that you will not allow her to come here. You have the power to do that. If the power had been mine she would already be here. I love my country and my people and I have told you that even though there is this disagreement I still want to be your chief. You say that because of her I cannot be your chief.

Were I to part from her now and become chief and then take her up again tomorrow you would not then tell me that I must leave the tribe. Then I would be on the throne and could do as I pleased. But I have not cheated you. I have given you this chance to rule me. If I were already chief you would have to be silent. You all say you do not want the woman. I have told you, I tell you now, I cannot leave her, I cannot leave her.

Bathoen stood up to speak.

You say we refuse this woman because you are not yet chief, and that if you were we would all have to accept it. You are wrong. If you were marrying this woman when you were already the chief we should all leave this place and you would have nobody to rule. These people do not belong to you, they belong to a chief whom they can love and respect. If the people left you, you would be chief of the poles in the market place – nothing else.

Tshekedi then rose to close the meeting, thanking Bathoen and the chiefs of the other sister tribes for helping the Bamangwato in the talks.

A fire is burning here and you have come to pour water on it, so I thank you. I have looked after this place since I was a child. I have been tried by many things and have had the responsibility of a big tribe more divided than any other in the protectorate. I have done this for twenty years. You, Seretse, come here ruined by others, not by me. Although you speak as you do you are not my equal and you are not as experienced as I am. I will not say if I love the tribe – my actions speak it. If I had found the Bamangwato divided with a large number in favour of your marriage then I would have known what to do. I should have said that I refuse to accept her, I have no white blood in me, but, all the same, if the tribe wants it, I will not split the tribe and I will say goodbye. Nobody has suggested that I go but if I did and you became chief then you would scatter the tribe.

I tell you, Seretse, that you are wrong to marry this woman. I do not want this woman. If you marry her, then you marry her elsewhere. Would there be such a gathering as this if an ordinary person had married a white woman? No, we should merely have laughed at him. I am not the judge of this. You, the Bamangwato refuse this woman, just as I do, I am acting according to your words.

I am not afraid of this marriage. The missionaries have opposed it and it was not celebrated in our church. The white race ruling us respects our customs but Seretse doesn't. The government has power to refuse a chief. He can be sent a letter saying he is causing a dangerous disturbance in the tribe and he must go. We say that if this woman comes she will divide the tribe. Therefore, she cannot come to this country. Of those who have spoken at this Kgotla, seventy-eight have spoken against this marriage and only seven spoke in favour. I ask the government to refuse her entry.

Our law is not yet written. We had hoped that Seretse would be the one to write it. Instead he has poured earth on it. If he stays here, I am glad; if he wants to go, I must give him the money for his journey. We shall remain. The tribe may scatter after I have left it but not while I am here.

The Kgotla over, most of the men began to drift back to their cattle-posts. Many went with a sense of unease. Somehow the words of Tshekedi and Bathoen didn't quite square with the way they felt. It was true that very few people had spoken in favour of the marriage but Tshekedi was a powerful man with powerful friends. One did not cross him lightly. Nevertheless, Radipophu and others began to think to themselves that opposing the marriage was one thing, deposing the rightful heir to the throne was something else.

Seretse sensed the mood in the tribe and so did those, like Goareng Mosinyi, who were close to him. There was a growing suspicion in the tribe, justified or not it was impossible to tell, that Tshekedi, and, speaking on his behalf, Bathoen, had been arguing not so much against the marriage but about the chieftainship. A few people began to wonder for the first time whether Tshekedi was using the marriage crisis to disinherit Seretse and make sure that he, Tshekedi, retained the throne. It is possible that Tshekedi and some of the royal uncles closest to him also sensed the slowly changing mood of the tribe. In the days that followed the Kgotla, Tshekedi and his friends would suddenly arrive in a lorry at night in a Serowe suburb and call an impromptu meeting to discuss the crisis. Goaletsa Tshukudu, a distant cousin of Tshekedi and not one of the inner council of advisers, lived in a part of Serowe called Ditharapa on the road to Palapye. One evening, as he was sitting outside his hut smoking a pipe, he heard a lorry arrive and Tshekedi and others calling for a meeting. As the men gathered around the lorry in the gloom, Tshekedi harangued them on the dangers of allowing Seretse's white wife ever to come to Serowe. The implications for the tribe would be immense. Their customs and identity would be lost, the Bamangwato would split and scatter.

After Tshekedi and the lorry had left, Tshukudu went in search of Seretse to tell him what his uncle was doing. The young man received the report as he had received many others. The regent, it seemed, was rattled. As November turned into December, many people came to Seretse secretly telling him they did not agree with what Tshekedi had done and that they feared that he wanted the chieftainship for himself. With all communication between him and the regent now broken, Seretse watched as the Bamangwato started, slowly, to shift towards him.

His lieutenants were also now feeling optimistic. Many members of Seretse's age regiment began coming to them saying they supported Seretse. At first sight, the will of the tribe seemed the same as it had been at the November Kgotla. Beneath the surface, there was the start of a seachange.

Finally, in late December, Seretse asked Tshekedi to call a Kgotla so that he might say goodbye to the tribe. Tshekedi agreed but when the Kgotla began he announced that only members of age regiments above Seretse's would be allowed to speak. The issues at stake were too serious for young men to influence the discussions, he said. Only those of mature judgement should speak. It was clear that the regent had felt the groundswell too and knew where the younger men stood. This time there were more voices in favour of the marriage but nothing like a majority. It was agreed that Seretse would return in six months to see if the position had changed.

Seretse was now convinced that tribal opinion was swinging inexorably in his favour. Leaving Goareng Mosinyi to press his case, he caught the train for Johannesburg and the plane that would fly him home to Ruth.

7
Seachange

Fleet Street had found its first foray to Serowe a little daunting. The inaccessibility of the place, the difficulty of filing stories to London once there, and the apparently interminable Bamangwato meetings made the protectorate unattractive to reporters and editors alike.

However, using local stringers, the papers did manage to carry some garbled accounts of what was going on. Chief Bathoen's remarks about Seretse being chief of the poles in the market place if he brought Ruth to Serowe were widely reported, as were Seretse's declarations of love for his wife. There had also been other reports that the tribe would be willing to accept Ruth but only if she worked in the fields digging potatoes alongside the other wives.

When Seretse arrived back at London Airport on 6 January, reporters and photographers were there in force. Ruth, wearing her favourite black suit with a large silver brooch on the lapel, had arrived early to meet the South African Airways Skymaster. As Seretse appeared she rushed up to him and they both embraced as the flash bulbs popped. In their fourteen weeks of marriage they had been apart for ten. It also looked as if Seretse had now sacrificed all hope of becoming chief. Nevertheless, the reporters noted, the marriage looked as strong as ever. The *Daily Mail* made Seretse's return front-page news with a big picture showing the laughing couple arm in arm at the airport. The *Daily Mirror* gave the arrival similar coverage and Seretse was asked by both papers about the potato story. 'It isn't true to suggest that she will have to dig potatoes. We don't grow them. She won't have to dig anything,' he replied.

The couple's first task on Seretse's return was to find somewhere other than their Notting Hill Gate bedsitting room. This time luck was with them, for the landlady of a ground-floor flat in Finsbury Park, north London, said she had read about them in the newspapers and that they seemed a delightful couple. With a big kitchen, a separate bedroom and a garden, the new flat looked like luxury to Ruth and they moved in at the beginning of February.

Ruth was also talking to her parents again. Soon after Seretse had gone to Serowe at the end of October, her mother had come to see her. She had told Ruth's father what she was doing and also asked if he would object to Ruth visiting the family home in Lewisham while he was away. He said he didn't and regular visits to her mother helped alleviate the loneliness Ruth felt while Seretse was in Serowe. Just before Christmas her father made sure that he came home unexpectedly at a time when he knew Ruth would be there. Father and daughter were reconciled although he still could not bring himself to meet Seretse or allow him in the house.

Through the spring of 1949 and into the early summer, Seretse continued with his law studies and was kept regularly in touch with the shifts in tribal opinion by close friends and relatives. Press interest subsided and the only news from southern Africa concerned the policies of the new South African government which was turning its philosophy of 'apartheid' – the separation of the races – into law. That spring it became a criminal offence in South Africa for blacks and whites to marry one another or have sexual intercourse.

In Serowe, Tshekedi began to feel that control was slipping slowly but inexorably from his grasp and there seemed to be nothing he could do about it. There was no doubt that the tribe had always respected Tshekedi more than they had loved him. He had assumed the regency at a difficult time when many factions in the royal family were squabbling and threatening the unity of the tribe. He had even had to survive a murder attempt. Prompt and stern action had been necessary to restore order and Tshekedi had continued in that vein. No one doubted his commitment to the tribe but he drove others as hard as he drove himself, using his authority to force people to work on development schemes for long periods without pay and frequently imposing new taxes on the people to pay for them.

The darker, dictatorial side to Tshekedi's nature had shown itself at the outbreak of the Second World War. As the call had gone out through the Empire that the mother country needed her subjects' help, British officials had assumed that the military levies raised in Bechuanaland should be incorporated into those being formed in South Africa. Tshekedi immediately resisted this. Bamangwato had fought alongside white South African troops in Europe in the First World War and had been so embittered by the racial hostility and abuse to which they had been subjected that many refused to accept the medals offered by the British at the war's end. More importantly than that, Tshekedi saw merging troops from Bechuanaland with those from the Union as another move to blur the distinctions between the protectorate and the Union. He told the British that his people would be proud to make their own contribution to the war effort. The Bamangwato had nothing to offer but themselves, Tshekedi told the Resident Commissioner, Arden-Clark, in Mafeking, 'but we are placing ourselves entirely at the disposal of His Majesty the King'.

To make good this boast, it was essential that the Bamangwato and the other tribes in Bechuanaland raise large numbers of troops for the war, thus proving their independence and, Tshekedi hoped, earning the recognition and gratitude of Britain.

While some tribesmen saw the wisdom of this, others didn't. Royal uncles like Radipophu Sekgoma who were close to Tshekedi and could understand his reasoning were quick to volunteer. For others it was more difficult. Tshekedi agreed to provide the British with seven companies of 365 volunteers each – more than two and a half thousand men – and in 1942 he agreed to supply another 2,000. For men in remote villages struggling to provide for their families and themselves in a harsh terrain and harsher climate, the war in Europe seemed largely irrelevant. If they were sent away, who would care for the cattle and protect the village, they wondered. Many men went into hiding or even fled across the border to South Africa but Tshekedi and the other chiefs would not be denied. Eventually, the quotas were filled, sometimes at gunpoint, and the men shipped off to the war in North Africa and Europe. Those who were left behind were told to spend long hours away from their own crops growing grain on the chief's land which would go towards the 'war effort'. Since most who remained were the young, the old and the infirm, the result was that their own crops were neglected and huge amounts of maize had to be imported from South Africa to feed them.

Tshekedi and the other chiefs also began imposing a string of wartime taxes. At the same time, they were unable to stop some of the local white traders taking advantage of shortages to push up prices and make huge profits on the goods they sold.

Meanwhile, many of the Bamangwato at the warfront were suffering from racial discrimination. One Bamangwato company complained that the body of one of their men had been dug up from a white graveyard and buried elsewhere. Out of the more than 10,000 men from the protectorate as a whole, more than 200 tribesmen died and more than 600 were wounded or disabled.

Tshekedi was sure that the effort and sacrifice had been worthwhile. The protectorate's contribution to the war had increased the sense of its separate identity in British eyes and helped to distance it from South Africa. With the threat of incorporation into the Union ever present, any achievements in that direction were invaluable. But the war did nothing to increase the Bamangwato's affection for their stern-minded regent. His single-minded determination to do what he thought was best was too often left unexplained to the tribe who saw their objections overridden and discounted.

No sooner had the war ended than Tshekedi forced the tribe into his next project. He had long dreamed of building a technical school for the Bamangwato where they could learn the latest techniques of animal husbandry, agriculture, building skills and the rest. He had chosen, for no very clear reason, a site in an inaccessible valley called Moeng fifty miles east of Palapye. From 1946 onwards he imposed taxes on the tribe to raise money for the college and forced age regiments to leave their lands and cattle to work, unpaid, for long gruelling months building a road to the site and then erecting the buildings themselves. By 1949, the work was still not finished and Moeng College for many in the tribe was a pit into which they poured their time and effort and got nothing back.

Now, as the people mulled over the Seretse crisis, Tshekedi found he had no reservoir of tribal affection from which to draw. The rumours that he had objected to the marriage because he wanted to keep the chieftainship for himself persisted and the younger men told all who would listen that it was time for a more democratic chief who would respect the wishes of the tribe.

In reaction to this, Tshekedi did all he could to try to keep Ruth out of Serowe. When the British told him in April that they could not stop her coming to the protectorate, Tshekedi went personally to see the High Commissioner, Sir Evelyn Baring, to protest. He told Baring he could not guarantee peace if she came and pointed out that there were not nearly enough police in Serowe to restore order if riots started. Baring replied that the British could do nothing until *after* trouble started. In desperation, Tshekedi then wrote to Ronald Orchard at the LMS in London, asking him to organise a delegation to the Secretary of State for Commonwealth Relations to try to get Ruth banned. Orchard thought the proposal pointless but he agreed to show willing because, as he confided to a colleague, 'to do nothing would be interpreted as meaning we were not concerned with a matter so vital to the tribe and would weaken any influence that we have over them'.

By now, Orchard was also realising that Tshekedi's cause might be lost. The LMS southern African director, A. J. Haile, was now back at his base in Bulawayo in Southern Rhodesia after his attempts to stop Ruth and Seretse's marriage the previous September. In May, he wrote to Orchard recording his impressions over the previous few months of the mood of the Bamangwato. In March, Chief Kgari of the Bakwena, like Bathoen, a close confidant of Tshekedi's, had admitted to Haile that there had been a considerable swing in Seretse's favour. He said that even at the Kgotla called to say goodbye to Seretse in December he had seen from their faces that many people already supported the young man but were afraid to speak out.

Other visitors to Haile said they were sure that the majority of the tribe now supported the younger man and were prepared to accept his wife. As Haile pointed out in his letter to Orchard, this represented a potential problem for the London Missionary Society: 'There is a big popular wave of enthusiasm to get Seretse back and Tshekedi's stock is low. The old aristocrats support Tshekedi and they are found in considerable numbers within the church so it behoves us not to be tied to them too tightly. I don't possibly see how we can support any move towards separating a man from his lawful wedded wife.'

The changing mood of the tribe was also well known in the ground-floor flat at 34, Adolphus Road, Finsbury Park. Seretse's friends had kept him closely in touch with the developing situation and by June it was obvious that the time had come to go back. Seretse was confident that the mood of the tribe was with him but Tshekedi was still the man on the throne, the majority of the uncles would still support him, and after more than twenty years in power his prestige and authority were considerable. Nevertheless, he hoped that within weeks he would be cabling Ruth to fly to the protectorate to join him.

8

Pula!

In early June, Tshekedi suddenly received a cable from Seretse saying that he was in Mafeking. There had been no contact between the two since the previous January although the regent had been expecting him to arrive. Everybody realised a final Kgotla to decide the issue was unavoidable. Seretse had also failed to notify the British and they only knew of his arrival when he walked into the administration's headquarters in Mafeking.

Tshekedi caught the train to Mafeking and a short, bitter meeting between the two men took place in the administration offices. Seretse told his uncle that he now believed he was trying to wrest his right to the chieftainship from him and that was also the opinion of most of the tribe. Tshekedi denied it, repeating his belief that Seretse as chief, married to a white English woman, would scatter the tribe and it was his duty as regent to do all he could to prevent it. Tshekedi then went back to Serowe to start arrangements for what both believed would be the final showdown.

On 14 June, Seretse caught the night train, arriving at Palapye the following morning. He was met at the tiny station by another of his uncles, Phetu Sekgoma. Phetu had now openly declared himself as a supporter of the young man and, as the most senior Mongwato to do so, was now the unofficial leader of Seretse's faction. The two men drove in Phetu's lorry to Serowe where the older man had arranged somewhere for Seretse to stay. On previous visits, Tshekedi had always made one of his own cars available to Seretse but the rift between the two men was so great now that they could hardly speak to one another.

That afternoon, Tshekedi announced in the Kgotla that Seretse had arrived. There had just been a very unseasonal shower and the regent said he hoped the rain was a symbol of peace and a good omen that the tribe would deal with the matter of the marriage in a peaceful way. He then read out a telegram from the High Commissioner in South Africa, Sir Evelyn Baring, urging the tribe to put its true interests first and hoping that there would be no violence.

Tshekedi then told the tribe he had been aware of numerous secret meetings during Seretse's last visit and now, he said, these must stop. The place to speak was openly in the Kgotla and 'these secret meetings are hostile to the tribe and I forbid them'. When it came to conspiracies, Tshekedi obviously now felt he was outgunned.

Britain's District Commissioner in Serowe, Mr Lawrenson, then addressed the tribe reinforcing the ban on secret meetings. He pointed out that he had called Major Langley, the head of the protectorate's police force, to Serowe with extra policemen and any attempt to hold unofficial meetings would be stopped by force. 'The police are impartial and they are here to preserve peace and order. Anybody who tries to disturb the peace will be dealt with instantly,' Lawrenson warned. 'This issue is one for the tribe to decide and the British government will be impartial. I hope that you will come to your decisions speedily, thoroughly and peacefully.'

Tshekedi then announced he had sent word to the outlying villages and cattle-posts that the time for the deciding Kgotla had come. It would start, he said, on the following Monday 20 June, to give enough time for the tribe to assemble.

For the next four days, the two camps consolidated their forces. The main talk in the streets and around the cooking fires was the truth or otherwise of Tshekedi's desire to oust Seretse from the chieftainship. It seemed to many impossible that a man who had lavished care and affection on his nephew for twenty-five years could suddenly decide to do him such wrong. At the same time, others pointed out that it was difficult to give up power, especially the almost dictatorial control that the regent had established over the Bamangwato.

There was general satisfaction that the British had reinforced Serowe's tiny police force. Everybody knew well that the issue of chieftainship roused the passions of the tribe and tempers could quickly be lost. On the other hand, nobody doubted Lawrenson's assertion that apart from keeping the peace, the British would not interfere. Since Khama had met Queen Victoria, the principle of indirect rule had been firmly established. The tribe chose the chief and the British were happy to let them do it. The appointment had to be confirmed by the

High Commissioner and by the Secretary of State in London, but that had always been merely a formality. Who were the British to tell the tribe who their chief should be? After all, the British wanted a quiet life and imposing an unwanted chief on 100,000 people was hardly the way to have one.

Throughout the weekend, the tribesmen arrived in the capital and by the Monday morning there were more than 4,000 crammed into the Kgotla. Once again, Tshekedi had invited his close friend, Bathoen, and also the chiefs of the other tribes. Lawrenson was now joined by Vivian Ellenberger, the Government Secretary in Mafeking and one of the most senior officials in the protectorate. He had himself been District Commissioner in Serowe twice before and knew Bamangwato politics well. He was there as the personal representative of Sir Evelyn Baring, the High Commissioner. At the back of the Kgotla ground stood Major Langley and a large contingent of police armed with tear gas. Once again, the LMS's resident missionary, Alan Seager, was there to record what was said.

Tshekedi and Seretse mounted the platform and the regent began by welcoming everybody and asked Ellenberger to address the meeting. The Government Secretary stood up and turned to face the thousands squatting silently in the sun. Whether deliberately or not, Ellenberger immediately annoyed the regent by greeting Chief Tshekedi and *Chief* Seretse. After all, it could be argued, the whole point of the Kgotla was to decide whether Seretse *was* the chief. The Government Secretary, meanwhile, was pressing on. From the time when Khama had asked Queen Victoria to extend her protection to the Bamangwato, he said, the British had recognised the importance of the chieftainship and the right of the tribe to make their own decisions regarding the succession. 'The issue before you is straightforward. It would be better if the discussions were not prolonged but let the final decision be just, final and as far as possible unanimous. Common sense and sound judgement come from calm minds. Have a thought for the future as well as to the present and remember that the good name of the Bamangwato is in your hands.'

During that first day, Tshekedi and Seretse debated like two boxers warily sizing each other up, each wary of providing the other with an opening. The regent complained at Seretse's sudden arrival saying that he should have given proper notice of his coming. Seretse replied that he was a free man and did not have to get anybody's permission to visit his own country. He had heard no complaint from the British authorities about his coming. 'I have come here to await the decision of the Bamangwato; if they refuse me I will go, if they accept me I will come with my wife. It has been suggested that I should keep my wife overseas or that I should leave her. I refuse to leave her. You must have us both or refuse us both.'

On the second day, the debate was thrown open to the tribe. First to speak, because of their seniority, were the royal uncles. Manyaphiri Ikitseng recalled how the royal family had met before the November Kgotla and had almost unanimously disagreed with the marriage. At the Kgotla meeting itself the tribe had been equally unanimous in their condemnation.

> We were united but when we dismissed we found ourselves divided. We began to be afraid of each other. What was it that divided us? It was the rumours that Tshekedi wanted the chieftainship for himself, so now we are discussing that. But we should not be. It is the woman that is the problem, not Tshekedi, and it is the woman we should be discussing. Even now I am against the marriage. Seretse has asked for our forgiveness for not consulting the tribe but he has refused to give up the marriage.

Next on his feet was the most senior royal uncle of all. Old, blind Phetu Mphoeng had installed Sekgoma as chief when the great Khama died. Three years later, on the death of Sekgoma, he had installed Tshekedi as regent. In a weak voice, those around him straining to hear, Phetu declared that the beginning of all the difficulty had been the woman. The uncles had already told Seretse that he had broken the law of the tribe. 'I am amazed that discussions have begun again. Seretse is the heir, the son of Sekgoma, we all know that, but a chief's son should obey. He does not install himself, he is installed by the people. So I still refuse to accept him. To do otherwise would be to change the tribe.'

The next speaker was Goaletsa Tshukudu, the man who, the previous November, had been the first to inform Seretse of the secret night meetings that Tshekedi was holding. He now swung the whole debate around. He told how recently he had seen Tshekedi touring the cattle-posts declaring that the stray cattle and the elephant tusks were his personal property.

Traditionally, stray oxen belonged to the chief as did the tribe's collection of ivory. As far as Tshukudu was concerned, that meant only one thing: Tshekedi liked being chief and he intended to stay chief. 'It has never been the tribe that has refused a chief, it has always been the relatives of the chief. It is Tshekedi and his friends who say Seretse cannot rule, the tribe does not say so. We know who is driving out the chief, it is Tshekedi and his friends. The woman is only an excuse. I agree to the woman. Let the tribe and the British install Seretse.'

A rumble of assent ran round the Kgotla ground. Now it had been said. Tshekedi wanted the wealth and the power for himself. He wanted to break the line of descent from Khama and he wanted to do it not because he cared for the tribe but because he cared for himself.

The next speaker, Olweleng Ntsaga, joined in the attack on Tshekedi by reading to the Kgotla a letter he had received from one of the outlying villages. It had been written by a man called Ramarula Mathodi who was sitting a few yards from him. 'Sekgoma's child has no fault,' the letter said. 'The case is no longer about the woman, Tshekedi is fighting for the Chieftainship. He has held two secret meetings in my village calling on the people to help him. We have been afraid and have said nothing so as not to get into trouble. We have been paid by him with money meant for the building of the school so that we will take his side in this case. I say, save the child of Sekgoma, he is not at fault. Tshekedi is a thief and a cheat.' The Kgotla positively growled its anger as the letter was handed over to Lawrenson for safe-keeping. Mathodi, named as the author of the letter, then stood up to deny it saying it was a forgery and that he had never written any such thing. Whether the letter was a fake or whether Mathodi's courage failed him when his damning allegations were read to the tribe has not been recorded. Whatever the truth, he was followed by two more of the uncles who mounted a passionate defence of the regent declaring that his love for Seretse was well known but that the younger man had shown himself unworthy of it. 'Does a chief take a wife in the bush, like a migrant worker?' asked one contemptuously. Tempers were flaring now and Major Langley and his policemen shifted uneasily at the back of the Kgotla ground.

Seretse then complained that Tshekedi had ordered that only a few from each side should speak. 'I say that anybody should be allowed to speak, according to our usual custom.'

'I made this arrangement because of the weightiness of the matter we are discussing,' Tshekedi replied. 'I want arguments brought forth and answered and I want only responsible people to speak.'

Seretse appealed to the tribe. 'I ask that those who wish to speak be allowed to do so. I have said that I will not part with my wife; some of you have said you will accept me but not my wife. But I want a decision: what is it that you want? Is it agreed that I come with her or not?'

Tshekedi, however, as regent and chairman of the Kgotla, would not be moved. 'I am afraid that we will just have repetition of the same points and that there will be no progress in the argument. It will end up that you will have drunks shouting against me instead of reasonable speakers.'

The next man to his feet accused Seretse of arrogance. 'We have refused this woman. If you will not listen to us then you will not inherit us. I cannot accept this white woman and Seretse will not rule me. Because it began with this white woman, we are forced to refuse Seretse the Chieftainship.'

The following speaker declared he had never refused to accept Seretse's wife. 'I hear men calling for Seretse to divorce her. Divorce is when two people fail to agree, people are not ordered to divorce. The throne is his and the woman is his. If he leaves her, where should she go? Khama said people should be allowed to marry whomever they want.'

Although Tshekedi continued to ensure that supporters and opponents spoke in roughly equal numbers, the crowd had begun to hiss and complain at those who spoke against the marriage. The regent intervened: 'I am not discussing Seretse's position as heir, it is well known. Whenever a speaker says anything against the woman, you all make a threatening noise. Had these been the old times, guns would have spoken instead of mouths. As for the accusation that I regard the stray oxen and the elephant tusks as mine, they are as long as I hold my position. Afterwards, they will no longer be mine. I had expected my time as ruler to end but this marriage has interfered. I cannot hand over the Chieftainship while Seretse is in the wrong.' With that, Tshekedi adjourned the meeting and strode off the platform. Slowly, in small groups, the crowd drifted back into the village mulling over what had been heard. As night fell over Serowe, the tribe, around a thousand cooking fires, debated the crisis and the tide of support for the regent continued to ebb.

The next day the Kgotla resumed. Tshekedi was now finding it difficult to call on a speaker to support him every time someone spoke in favour of Seretse and 'the woman'. By the end of the day there was a growing sense of frustration in the crowd that the regent was resisting the inevitable, that a minority of speakers were being represented as equal to the overwhelming majority who clearly wanted to accept Seretse, wife and all. On the Wednesday night, the tribe went back to its cooking fires disgruntled and annoyed.

Ellenberger, the Government Secretary, had noticed the change in mood. As the Kgotla opened on Thursday morning, he asked if he might speak: 'I asked you on Monday to remain calm and dignified. I have, however, noticed a change and seen emotions rising. Men are apt to lose control of themselves when they become excited. When self-control goes something else takes its place. I say again to you, keep a hold of yourselves, stay calm. If you do not, I shall not hesitate to have the meeting closed.' With a nod to Major Langley and his police, Ellenberger resumed his place.

Tshekedi was now clearly anxious to be done with this Kgotla. He launched into a long speech against those whom he said had been conspiring against him since the November and December Kgotlas, spreading false rumours and filling Seretse's ear with poison so that now 'he will not talk to me, will not come to my house or eat there'. Turning to look at his nephew, he said: 'These people want to destroy the House of Khama by separating me from you. The House of Khama is Seretse's house. I want you to beget a black chief for me, not a white one.'

Clearly distressed, Tshekedi went on: 'I had wanted to give Seretse the chieftainship peacefully, properly, without disturbance. I will call on those of his uncles who think as I do, who grieve as I do, to stand up.' Nine of the royal uncles rose to their feet. 'Seretse looks on us all as his enemies, because we refuse to recognise this marriage. My last word is this: there are many senior men in the tribe thinking as I do. Shall we all be exiled?'

Seretse then walked to the front of the platform, seeing the thousands stretched before him. 'Those of my relatives who refuse to accept my wife have been asked to stand. I knew the opinions of some of them already, some I did not as they had been silent. I ask you all: if I refuse to part from the woman, does that mean I shall not be chief?

'They say that I hate them because they refused the woman. But is there one of them on whom I have looked unkindly? If any have come to me to shake my hand, have I refused them? If they say I hate them, it comes from their own hearts, not from me. I would not act badly to anybody for refusing the woman. But if I am sent away, will those who have wanted her be persecuted? If anyone says he does not want me to rule him, then it is up to him to stay or go. Those who have just stood up are not necessarily the best just because they agree with my uncle.

'My relatives who refuse were asked to stand before you. Now let my relatives who agree with me stand up for you to see.'

Thirteen men rose. 'I want it known that I also have uncles on my side. I now ask those who say I must not come to this land to stand, by which I mean Bamangwato tribesmen, not my relatives.' At different points in the crowd, forty men stood up. 'Now I ask those who say let the woman come to stand up.'

Almost as one, 4,000 men rose. As they did so, they began to chant 'Pula, pula' the Setswana for rain and a word used to signify great approval. As they chanted, so they stamped, and the dry dust of the Kgotla ground began to swirl in clouds around them. Men from every section of the tribe shouted their support. Radipophu Sekgoma, whose instincts had been with Tshekedi at the beginning, applauded his new chief. Goaletsa Tshukudu, who had turned the course of the Kgotla on the second day with his suspicions of Tshekedi's real motives, cheered till he was hoarse. But there were also lesser men shouting and stamping their feet. George Keikameng, a young man of 24 who worked as a shop assistant in Mafeking and had begged his boss to allow him to hitch a ride to Serowe for the great Kgotla, roared his support, as did Kefhalotse Mathware, a man in his early 30s trying to build a small business of his own, supplying the outlying farmers. And, of course, there were Seretse's constant supporters, Goareng Mosinyi, Phetu Sekgoma, young Simon Lekhutile and the others.

As the red dust swirled around them they could see Seretse on the platform, laughing, leaning back in his chair and slapping his thigh.

When, finally, the roar subsided, Tshekedi adjourned the meeting. As the men returned to their huts, they found the women filling the streets. The chanting and the roars had been heard throughout Serowe and everybody realised that some momentous decision had been reached. Naledi Khama, Seretse's younger sister still in her teens, had come rushing from the house where she was staying with Seretse to try to discover the cause. As Seretse climbed up the hill towards her, surrounded by his jubilant supporters, his victory was obvious. A wave of relief washed over the village that finally, after so many months, the matter was settled. The cooking fires did not burn so late that night. The Bamangwato went early to their beds.

The next day the mood of the tribe was positively truculent as Tshekedi opened proceedings by asking his friend, Chief Bathoen, to address the Kgotla. 'Let us take care,' the Chief of the Bangwaketse began, 'before it is too late. Once you said that Seretse was wrong, now you say he is not. Yet you are the same people. I was afraid yesterday that we were forgetting our laws by letting a child give instructions to the tribe before he is placed upon the throne.'

Hisses and grumbles of dissent filled the air and Tshekedi had to call the tribe to order.

Turning to Seretse, Bathoen continued: 'Son of the Chief, whether you stay and rule us, or whether you go, while you live so the tribe will be divided. The chieftainship of the Bamangwato was a thing of honour, now it is defiled. Yesterday you called upon your supporters to stand. It is the first time I have seen such a thing – two chiefs, one properly installed, one not yet installed, but both giving orders in the Kgotla.'

Sensing the growing hostility all around him, Bathoen sat down. It was time for Tshekedi, still defiant, to speak to the tribe for the last time. 'You think you have humiliated me, but in fact you have honoured me because you have done all you could to slander me before our visitors and yet they know the slander is not true. Had you waited, you would have heard what I had to say. I refused to take a vote but Seretse called for one. It is not our custom to take such votes. You obviously did not trust me to decide according to the will of the Kgotla. You were wrong. If you had done so, it would have been possible for the woman to come here and, although we might have been sorry for it, we should not have been divided as we are now. I shall move away from here now. It will take a few weeks to hand over the papers in my office and to gather my possessions together but I will not stay here.' Before Tshekedi closed the Kgotla for the last time and gave the tribe permission to return home to their huts, Ellenberger, the Government Secretary, spoke to the crowd.

'I have heard your decision and I shall report it to the Resident Commissioner who will pass it on to the High Commissioner and to the Secretary of State in London. Until the government signifies its approval of a change, the administration will continue as it has until now. I am satisfied with the way the meeting has been conducted and shall inform the Resident Commissioner accordingly. To Seretse I would offer my good wishes, to Tshekedi I would express my esteem and regard. There is one matter I must allude to: it was suggested at the meeting that Tshekedi had as his motive the wish to keep Seretse from the chieftainship. I wish to say to you that the government entertains no such suggestion or belief. On the contrary, Tshekedi's record of public service to the tribe has always been of the highest order.'

As the Bamangwato went back to their homes and Tshekedi began his preparations to leave, Seretse telegrammed his news to Ruth and Ellenberger composed his official cable to the Resident Commissioner in Mafeking. Most that day thought the matter was at an end. None could have known it was just the beginning.

9

The Perfect Chief

Seretse's victory now burst upon the British public. The stringers and local correspondents had sent back graphic accounts of the tribe's decision. Any reader who had ignored the story so far, could avoid it no longer. Although the press's estimates of the number of those present were high and they still insisted on calling Ruth a 'secretary' – she never did learn to type – the facts were basically correct. Fleet Street grabbed the story with both hands. Domestic news that summer was depressing and dull. It was dominated by the worsening economic situation and the fragility of the pound. The American and Canadian post-war loans were running out and the nation was preparing for a massive and humiliating devaluation of sterling. Now here, if they played it right, the papers had a story to rival a Rider Haggard fantasy, tales of Imperial Africa, and a white English girl as queen of 100,000 tribesmen. That should quicken the pulses on the top of the Clapham omnibus.

On Friday 24 June, the front pages were full of just one story: 'Seretse's Tribe Accepts Ruth as Queen' shouted the *Daily Graphic*; 'Tribesmen Hail Ruth as Next Queen, 6,000 Cheer at Rally', proclaimed the *Daily Mirror* reporting: 'Former London typist Ruth Williams will be the next queen of the 100,000-strong Bamangwato tribe in Bechuanaland. By 6,000 votes to 40, the tribesmen agreed to accept Seretse Khama as the future chief – with his white wife.' The Sunday papers followed up with full length features splashing file photographs of a laughing Ruth and Seretse. The *Sunday Express* emphasised what it saw as the split in the tribe. Beneath a two-year-old picture of Tshekedi looking stern they ran the caption: 'I am hurt deeply. I go.'

By Monday, 27 June, the events in Serowe were provoking solemn leading articles in the quality papers as well. The *Manchester Guardian* pointed out that approval by the British government of Seretse as chief would 'scandalise' a great many white South Africans. On the other hand, 'rejection might irretrievably offend' blacks throughout Africa. 'In the history of Bechuanaland this is, on its lesser scale, a crisis comparable with the abdication of Edward VIII and its possible implications are almost unlimited.'

The *Daily Mirror*, in its main comment column, was in no doubt about what was at stake.

> What lies before the British Government is a democratic decision of the tribe and it would be liable to give rise to harmful misunderstanding not to accept it. Whatever happens, the British Government must not appear to take the least notice of impertinent intervention from South Africa or do anything to weaken the trust of Bechuanaland that Britain will shield her from South African racial policy. The Protectorate's greatest fear is engulfment by the Union. Better informed Africans throughout British Africa will watch this decision closely.

The British, in the closing days of June 1949, had no intention of not following established policy. In Serowe, District Commissioner Lawrenson, flanked by his newly arrived successor Richard Sullivan, told reporters: 'The tribe's decision to accept Seretse as chief is regarded by the British Authorities in the Bechuanaland Protectorate as final.' Vivian Ellenberger, the Government Secretary, was meanwhile reporting to his boss, Anthony Sillery, the Resident Commissioner in Mafeking. As he had earlier told the tribe, Ellenberger said that the Kgotla had been properly constituted and appeared to reflect the overwhelming feeling of the tribe. By the morning of 26 June, the day after the Kgotla, Sillery had cabled a full account to Baring, the High Commissioner in Pretoria. Baring, along with the rest of South Africa's diplomatic community, had now left Cape Town as they did every year at the close of the South African parliamentary session. At the time of the Act of Union in 1910 it had been decided that South Africa would, in effect, have two capital cities – a legislative one in Cape Town where Parliament sat, and an administrative one in Pretoria from where the bulk of the civil service would operate. The decision had recognised the continuing existence of the two factions within the Afrikaner nation: the 'Trekkers', those who had struck out alone to be free of the British and who looked to the northern city of Pretoria as their capital, and those other Afrikaners who had stayed behind in the country's mother city. Wise though this may have been, it meant that twice a year, at great expense and with considerable disruption, the country's politicians and diplomats had to upsticks and travel the 900 miles separating the two capitals.

At least, as far as Bechuanaland was concerned, Baring was now much closer to the protectorate than when he was in Cape Town and he cabled Sillery asking him to invite Seretse to come to Pretoria for talks as soon as possible. The High Commissioner, though intrigued at the fact of Seretse's marriage to a white girl, felt no sense of alarm at what had happened. The previous year he had recommended to London that they should do all they could to stop the wedding but that had been because of Tshekedi's warnings of disruption and riot. Britain had no money to spare for Bechuanaland's development let alone getting involved in some expensive peace-keeping role there. If the regent told him that there would be violence if the marriage went ahead, then he would be failing in his duty not to try to prevent it. As it had turned out, Tshekedi had been wrong. He was leaving Serowe and an as yet uncertain number of senior tribesmen were going with him, but nothing like a serious split had occurred. A vote of 4,000 to 40 seemed pretty decisive and there were now reports that even old Phetu Mphoeng, the man who had installed both Sekgoma and Tshekedi on the throne and who had supported the regent throughout the crisis, had now defected to Seretse's supporters. The conclusion was obvious: the way to avoid trouble now was to accept the overwhelming decision of the tribe and recognise Seretse as the chief of the Bamangwato.

According to the protectorate's statutes, in particular Proclamation Number 32 of 1943, 'Chiefs are chosen by the Tribe in Kgotla. Names must be submitted for the High Commissioner's recognition and the Secretary of State's confirmation. The High Commissioner may direct a Judicial Inquiry to be held where it is alleged that the Chief is unacceptable, unworthy or not a fit and proper person.'

It didn't seem to Baring as if Seretse fell into any of those categories. He was the recognised heir to the throne, he was probably one of the best educated blacks in the whole of southern Africa and he undoubtedly commanded the overwhelming support of his tribe. Baring prepared to recommend to London Seretse's immediate confirmation.

In the end, forty-three people would leave Serowe to follow Tshekedi. They included some of the tribe's most senior members and experienced administrators. Gorewang Sekgoma and Badirwang Sekgoma, the two surviving brothers of the great Khama left as did seven other members of the royal family. With them went thirty-four other village headmen and tribal tax collectors. The administration would take time to recover but the British didn't doubt that it would. As they prepared to leave, Tshekedi and his supporters issued a signed declaration 'on the crisis that has arisen from the marriage of Seretse Khama and Ruth Williams.' They maintained that the recognised laws and customs of the Bamangwato had been violated and the known procedure disregarded. 'Under our custom, Ruth could never be Queen of the Tribe or mother of the chief-to-be. We challenge the present decision and call for a public inquiry.'

As he packed his possessions, Tshekedi was a bitter man. He was bitter about the way the tribe had repaid him after more than twenty years of devoted service and bitter about the way in which he felt the British had deserted him when he needed their help. He had faced adversity in the past, of course, and now he was doggedly determined to force the British to rule on Ruth's status and shake them out of their traditional pose of inactivity. This could only be done, he was convinced, by a judicial inquiry and on 7 July, he went with Douglas Buchanan to see Baring in Pretoria. Baring made himself unavailable to see the deposed regent but his officials told Tshekedi that the High Commissioner had no intention of holding a judicial inquiry and gave him the strong impression that within weeks London would confirm Seretse as chief and Ruth as queen.

Before the week was up, Seretse arrived in Pretoria to see Baring who welcomed him enthusiastically. The High Commissioner said he would welcome some indication of Seretse's plans and policy, advising him against any persecution of those who had supported Tshekedi. Baring estimated that confirmation from London would take about three weeks to come through and asked Seretse to avoid bringing Ruth to the protectorate until after he had been installed as chief. Seretse therefore left Pretoria with the clear impression that his acceptance by the British was a mere formality. Baring was later to insist that all his advice to Seretse had been conditional, that is, *if* Seretse were to be confirmed as chief. Whatever the truth, there seemed to be no obstacle in Seretse's way and soon after his return to Serowe,

Sillery, the Resident Commissioner, was urging Baring that the installation should take place as quickly as possible.

At that moment, Sir Evelyn would have found it impossible to believe that within less than a week he would be conniving to frustrate the democratic wish of the Bamangwato and doing all in his power to make sure that the installation never took place. The reason lay not in Bechuanaland but in South Africa and once again in the old Afrikaner divisions between those who trekked and those who didn't.

10
God's People

During the Boer War of 1899–1902, the British High Commissioner to South Africa, Baron Milner of St James and Cape Town, had declared that Britain's intention was 'to knock the bottom out of the great Afrikaner nation for ever and ever Amen'. Since at least 20,000 of the 26,000 women and children who died in Kitchener's concentration camps were under the age of 16, it did look as if the British had tried to sink almost an entire generation.

After the war, Lord Milner set about absorbing the Boers into the British Empire. To do this successfully, he decided, all the symptoms of what they regarded as their special identity should be eradicated. His main target was Afrikaans, the language of the Boers and now so different from Dutch as to be a separate tongue. The speaking of it was outlawed in the schools and those caught talking it were punished and humiliated. He also tried to encourage British immigration to South Africa so that English speakers might outnumber the Boers. This he would never achieve and Afrikaners continued to dominate white politics.

Realising this, many of them accepted the British proposals in 1910 to make them a self-governing dominion within the Empire even though that entailed a pledge of loyalty to the British Crown. Thus, within a decade of the Boer War ending, the people of South Africa found themselves ruled by Afrikaners again, though this time by men like Louis Botha and Jan Smuts who were openly dedicated to reconciling the English and Afrikaans traditions. But other powerful Boers resisted them. General Barry Hertzog, who like Smuts and Botha had been a Boer War commander, felt that in reconciliation lay the seeds of the destruction of the Afrikaner nation. He became a rallying point for all those activists who had resisted Milner's attempts to obliterate Afrikaner culture and who felt that the sacrifice of the war would be wasted until the Boer nation was free of the

British Empire. In 1914, with the outbreak of war against Germany, London asked South Africa to attack the German colony of Southwest Africa. For Hertzog and his supporters the prospect of fighting *for* Britain was too much. What was more, Germany had supported the Boers in their war with the British and had donated generously to the welfare of destitute Afrikaners when the war had ended. Smuts and Botha had felt bound by their pledge of loyalty given at the Act of Union and also believed that Southwest Africa was properly part of South Africa anyway and here was a chance to make it so. While many Afrikaners accepted this, the number against the war was so great that Hertzog decided to found his own political party, the National Party, dedicated to Afrikanerdom and the preservation of all that was unique to it. Until it came to power, its supporters believed, the Afrikaner nation would never be free, no matter how much British rule was dressed up in the clothes of a self-governing dominion.

Jan Smuts, meanwhile, was attacking Southwest Africa. With Botha he forced a German surrender, and was then asked by the British to do the same in German East Africa. Now with the rank of a Lieutenant-General in the British Army, Smuts again led his troops to victory before being invited to London to join the Imperial War Cabinet. In less than seventeen years, Smuts had gone from being one of the most wanted men in the Empire to part of the élite at the centre of its affairs. After the war, he became Prime Minister of South Africa. He also helped set up the League of Nations establishing himself as a major player on the world stage.

But as Smuts' international acclaim grew, so, in almost equal measure, it fell among his own people, the Afrikaners. Many activists accused him of selling out to the enemy and turning his back on his nation's destiny. In a general election in 1924 he was swept from power by a coalition, the largest member of which was Hertzog's National Party. Circumstances were now to ensure that more and more Afrikaners would turn to the National Party for their salvation.

As hard times in the 1920s forced the largely rural Afrikaner people into the cities, they fell prey once again to the hated British. While the political leaders might be Afrikaans, the mines, the factories, and the shops were run by English speakers who exploited the unskilled Boers. Often literally barefoot and destitute, they felt disinherited in their own land

and flocked to Hertzog's banner. For more than 120 years the British had been at their backs and now they were as much in thrall as ever. Only complete political power would deliver their country back to them and they now set out purposefully to achieve it.

Alongside the National Party, two other institutions were to help them win their victory. The first had been formed in 1918. The Afrikaner Brotherhood or 'Broederbond' was established as a secret society, exclusively Afrikaans and designed to promote Afrikaner interests against the rest of the world. As its power grew, every initiate was forced to swear an oath: 'He who betrays the Bond will be destroyed by the Bond. The Bond never forgets. Its vengeance is swift and sure. Never yet has a traitor escaped his just punishment.' The Broederbond aimed to make prominent Afrikaners in every city, town and village members of their secret society, dedicated to helping other Afrikaners attain power, influence and wealth. With the help of a young Cape Town newspaper editor called Daniel Malan, the northern-based organisation began to spread throughout the country. Although the main impetus still came mainly from the northerners, who had suffered the most in the Boer War and who still looked to the 'trekkers' as their ancestors, the Broederbond and the National Party, with the help of Malan and others, became genuinely nationwide movements.

The third note in the triad was the Afrikaners' place of worship, the Dutch Reformed Church. Since those early days, alone on the Cape plains with only their Bibles and guns, the Afrikaners had looked to their faith to sustain them. As refugees from religious persecution in Europe came to join them, their fervour had increased and, like the tribe of which they read in their Old Testament, they came to see themselves as a chosen people, sustained and protected by their God for a purpose. That purpose, they had little doubt, was to carry the bright, pure light of true Christianity into the dark continent. Now with the Afrikaner nation's identity threatened, the political, social and religious aims of the Boers came together. Daniel Malan, for instance, was a political activist in the National Party, a secret organiser in the Broederbond and also a minister in the Dutch Reformed Church. On those three fronts, Afrikanerdom advanced.

As the 1920s became the 1930s, the Afrikaners began to develop the political philosophy that would ensure their survival. When the British had been overcome, there would still be the blacks. The tribes of South Africa outnumbered all the whites by four to one and the Afrikaners by more than six to one. Blacks competed with unskilled Boers at the gates of the English-speakers' factories; poor whites and blacks sought houses in the same areas; more than a million mixed-race or 'Coloured' people, almost all with Afrikaans names and speaking Afrikaans, were living testimony to the danger of contact and equality.

Out of this evolved the philosophy of staying apart or 'apartheid'. The white man, not least the British white man, had already enforced an unofficial apartheid throughout the world wherever white had met black. Usually it had the force of custom rather than law. None the less pernicious for that, it did allow the perpetrator the luxury of either denying its existence or excusing it as a temporary measure. For the Afrikaner, insecure and threatened, 'apartheid' would need to be part of the political fabric of the state before he would feel secure. At the same time, to avoid the moral embarrassment of the obvious injustice such a policy would entail, the Dutch Reformed Church was on hand to imbue it with the blessing of God. As in the eighteenth century when they had found in the Old Testament an excuse for practising slavery, once again the clergy turned to the Scriptures. There they read that God had created many different races and it was clearly against His will to allow them to mix and eventually become one. Apartheid was essential to God's purpose and without it there was darkness and chaos.

As the Afrikaner intellectuals in the Broederbond evolved the policies, so the Dutch Reformed Church bestowed their blessing upon them and the National Party prepared to make them flesh. So intense had this nationalism become that it left General Hertzog, champion of the Afrikaner and founder of the National Party, behind. The old Boer General felt that the culture of his people was now secure after his coalition government had introduced reforms in education and national language. Now he believed that the future of South Africa lay in Afrikaans and English speakers working together, reconciling their differences and, each secure in his own identity, striving together for a more prosperous South Africa. In the early 1930s he led his party into a merger with Smuts. Once again 'reconciliation' seemed to threaten the Afrikaner's extinction and Daniel Malan in the Cape and the Transvaal activist Johannes Strydom declared the formation of a new, 'purified' National Party, untainted by any belief in cooperation. When the British Empire declared war on Nazi Germany, Smuts, as Prime Minister, Minister of Defence, and Chief of Staff, led the whites into the fight against Hitler. English and Afrikaans speaking South African alike died on the battle fields of the Second World War but at home the 'purified' Nationalists cheered every German victory, sabotaged rail and telegraph communications and were interned for the duration. By the war's end, Smuts' international reputation was at its zenith. A close friend of Churchill's and a powerful voice in the conduct of the war, he was promoted to the rank of Field Marshal. But as he became a statesman with a world vision, he lost sight almost completely of the fears and aspirations of his own people. While his eyes were fixed on distant political peaks such as the establishment of the United Nations and the evolution of the British Empire into a Commonwealth of equal nations, Smuts overlooked the realities beneath his feet.

Post-war South Africa found Malan's National Party armed with the cohesive policy of apartheid, guaranteeing superiority over the blacks, and promising social and economic reforms that would return control of South Africa's wealth to Afrikaner hands. Smuts and his party could offer no alternative to apartheid that was acceptable to the majority of white voters. To many they seemed 'soft' on blacks with no clear programme to prevent eventual black domination. Strydom in particular mocked the government for its indecision and lack of purpose. 'It is so clear and logical. If you say that you do not want to dominate the Native, it simply means that you stand for a policy of equality.' In a situation where blacks outnumbered whites four to one, equality meant domination. In the election of 1948, Malan's National Party scraped into power. 'Today,' said Malan when victory was his, 'South Africa belongs to us once more. For the first time since Union, South Africa is our own. May God grant that it will always be so.'

Within weeks the corner stones of apartheid were being laid. Fundamental laws began their passage through Parliament designed to enforce the separation of the races. By 1949, the Mixed Marriages Act made marriage between the races illegal even though there were less than a hundred such unions a year in the entire country. It was followed by the Immorality Amendment Act making sexual intercourse between different races a serious offence. The Group Areas Act, confining blacks to certain residential areas, reservation of thousands of different jobs for whites only and the whole legislative panoply of apartheid followed. At the same time, the civil service was being 'purged'. English speakers and 'Anglicised' Afrikaners were replaced wholesale by true supporters of the government drawn from the ranks of the Broederbond. At last the Afrikaner had come into his own. Now, after all this achievement, just as they were savouring the taste of controlling their own destiny, Afrikaners were being asked to stomach the installation of a black man and his white wife as chief and queen of the main tribe of a neighbouring territory. While the blacks in South Africa were being forced to accept the inevitability of apartheid, the British were about to give official blessing to the exact opposite. While the National Party and the Dutch Reformed Church preached there was no alternative to the policy of separation, their hated former masters seemed about to sanction the reverse. The British must not be allowed to let Ruth and Seretse Khama threaten the foundations of what was only just being built. They must and would be brought to heel.

11
For the Greater Good

Events in South Africa moved quickly once the Bamangwato had accepted their chief. If a spur to action were needed, then the press statements from the British apparently accepting the tribe's decision provided it.

Within hours of the Serowe decision hitting the South African press, Prime Minister Malan received a delegation from the Dutch Reformed Church. They said they deplored the possibility that the British might confirm the tribe's decision and called upon Malan to do everything he could to prevent it. A general conference of the church was already scheduled for the beginning of July and the mixed marriage would now be moved to the top of the agenda. The delegation hoped the conference would mobilise white opinion in the country and help force the British to think again.

But when Malan called his Cabinet together he found them deeply split over the crisis that the Bamangwato had provoked. Once again the Afrikaners were dividing between those from the Cape and those from the north. Paradoxically, it was largely because Malan was from the Cape that he had become leader of the 'purified' National Party when it split from old General Hertzog in the 1930s. So sharp were the divisions that the new party needed a Cape leader in order to become the countrywide force that could win a general election. Malan, of course, was also acceptable because of the power of his intellect and the depth of his commitment to Afrikaner nationalism, but the new government could never quite shake off the feeling that he ruled on the sufferance of the Transvaalers.

Johannes Strydom, leader of the National Party in the Transvaal, regarded himself as the guardian of the Afrikaner flame. He and his Transvaal Cabinet colleagues acted as the 'motor' for the new policy of apartheid, driving the government further and further down their ideological road. While some Afrikaner intellectuals balked at the emerging contradictions of apartheid – a policy that demanded the close involvement of cheap black labour in the industrial life of South Africa and yet, at the same time, insisted on the almost total social separation of the races – Strydom and his followers brushed all objections aside. At the same time, they championed every policy which they saw as lessening British influence. They had enthusiastically promoted one of the first acts of the new government which had been to overturn Smuts' plans to encourage more British immigration. New legislation made it more difficult for those already in South Africa to gain citizenship and thus the right to vote.

Now Malan found his Cabinet degenerating into factions over Ruth and Seretse Khama. The Prime Minister and his supporters advocated telling the British immediately that the installation of Seretse as chief of the Bamangwato was unacceptable to South Africa. The presence of such a prominent mixed marriage on their borders was provocative enough but for the British to sanction it officially was intolerable.

Strydom and his faction took the exactly opposite point of view. Nothing should be done, they argued, to prevent the British from installing Seretse and his wife in Serowe. The outrage in South Africa would not then be confined to Afrikaners but also to English speakers, many of whom found mixed marriages equally destabilising and offensive. As it was, the British colony of Southern Rhodesia was already grumbling loudly about the Bamangwato's decision. Rallying all white opinion in the country to this single issue, the government could then call a referendum to decide whether South Africa should annexe Bechuanaland and, more importantly, leave the British Commonwealth. At last, Strydom argued, the British were on the point of giving them the very weapon that would make South Africa free of them forever. With all white opinion mobilised, the government could declare a republic, free and independent like the old Boer republics before the British smashed them.

Malan adjourned the meeting before any decision could be reached. He was deeply distressed at the prospect of South Africa leaving the Commonwealth. Though he had as little affection for the British as any in the Cabinet, he could not possibly see how South Africa could survive alone in an increasingly hostile world. The country was industrially under-developed. Though it had massive mineral riches and agricultural resources, many of the whites – mostly his people, the Afrikaners – were unskilled and poorly educated. South African manufacturing was in its infancy and largely indebted to British investment. Apartheid was going to prove extremely expensive and South Africa would need all the economic help she could get. Internationally, criticism of South Africa was building up. The fledgling United Nations, the newly independent republic of India and the Soviet Union were all calling for the abandonment of apartheid. With the world dividing dangerously between East and West, with the superpowers developing nuclear weapons, with unrest and turmoil boiling up everywhere in the old European empires, did South Africa really want to be alone?

But how could Malan prevent himself from being politically outflanked by Strydom? If London did install Seretse as chief there would be a mighty outcry from South Africa's whites. The new government was trying to establish its authority and push through some of the most controversial legislation in the world. How could it possibly allow the British to defy it in its own backyard? Government supporters would demand action – even perhaps the military annexation of the protectorate. In the midst of all that, how could Malan resist Strydom's calls for a referendum on membership of the Commonwealth? His only hope seemed to lie in the British being persuaded to disqualify Seretse as chief.

Malan summoned Douglas Forsyth, his Secretary for External Affairs.

Forsyth was something of an anomaly in the new government. As soon as the new government had come to power, all the old Anglophiles at the top of the civil service had been purged and replaced by loyal Broederbonders. Few civil servants were more identified with the previous administration than Forsyth. At 53, he was a man of great authority. He had fought with the young Smuts against the Germans in South-West Africa nearly thirty-five years earlier. At the end of the First World War, he had joined the civil service. By 1941 he had not only become Secretary for External Affairs (the senior civil servant in the department) but also private secretary to Smuts himself. In this position, he had travelled to many countries building up personal relationships with bureaucrats and politicians around the world. Far from sacking him, the new Prime Minister insisted that he stay on. Malan, absorbed for all his political life with domestic matters, felt naked and vulnerable in foreign affairs. He needed Forsyth.

Forsyth noticed that the Prime Minister appeared very agitated, even distressed about the whole affair. He didn't yet know of the Cabinet split or that the Prime Minister felt he was fighting for his political life. A telegram was dictated to South Africa's High Commissioner in London, Leif Egeland, instructing him to arrange an immediate appointment with the Secretary of State for Commonwealth Relations, Philip Noel-Baker. Not knowing how the British would react and frightened of provoking an official policy statement to which he would have to reply, Malan insisted that Egeland's approach to Noel-Baker be on a semi-official or private basis.

The next morning, 30 June, Leif Egeland left South Africa House, the imposing stone High Commission that dominates the eastern side of Trafalgar Square, and travelled the quarter of a mile down Whitehall to the Commonwealth Relations Office between Downing Street and Parliament Square. He had been appointed to the London job the previous year by Smuts and was one of the Union's most polished diplomats. Gaining his first university degree in South Africa in 1921, he had come to England to study for his BA in jurisprudence at Trinity College, Oxford. In 1927, he had joined London's Middle Temple and returned to South Africa to become a distinguished barrister.

After the war he had joined the diplomatic service, being posted to Scandinavia before arriving in London.

The man he was meeting that morning, Philip Noel-Baker, the Secretary of State for Commonwealth Affairs, was some ten years his senior. Though not one of the most prominent members of Clement Attlee's Labour Cabinet, Noel-Baker was one of the most respected ministers in the government. Ernest Bevin, the Foreign Secretary and fiery anti-Communist, Aneurin Bevan at the Ministry of Health, Hugh Dalton and Herbert Morrison, even young Harold Wilson at the Board of Trade, all grabbed more headlines than he did. Yet Noel-Baker's academic brilliance and principled advocacy of peace had won him special respect. He had read History and Economics at King's College, Cambridge becoming President of the Union in 1912. Just two years later he had been appointed vice-principal of Ruskin College, Oxford. During the war, he had served with ambulance units, frequently under heavy fire, in both France and Italy. The Italians had decorated him for his outstanding courage. In 1929, he became Labour MP for Coventry and later Derby, being appointed immediately on his election to be the Parliamentary Private Secretary to the Foreign Secretary. Throughout the 1930s he had worked constantly for disarmament in an effort to avoid repeating the horrors he had known at first hand in 1914–18. He had worked hard establishing both the League of Nations and its successor, the United Nations, in the hope of guaranteeing world peace. Now, at the age of 60, he was about to be drawn into one of the most personally distressing episodes of his political life.

Egeland began by saying he had been instructed by his Prime Minister to 'represent urgently the grave concern' which his government felt about the possible installation of Seretse Khama as chief of the Bamangwato. As the British government knew, he went on, the repercussions of recognising such a man, married as he was to a white English woman, would be extremely serious. People of all races in southern Africa would regard official recognition of the man and his wife as a grave infringement of a basic principle. It was, of course, also possible that recognition of Seretse would split the tribe and the resulting turmoil would be in nobody's interest.

Relaxing into his theme, the High Commissioner explained that, knowing Africa as he did, it would be extremely difficult for Ruth to settle down in Bechuanaland. She would not just be lonely but isolated in every way. No one of either race would visit her or give her any social life of any kind. Egeland said she would certainly not be able to stand the strain of such an existence. He personally was prepared to wager a lot of money that she wouldn't last six months. Then, in accordance with Malan's wishes, Egeland concluded by saying that while he wanted to make it plain that his government felt extremely strongly about these matters, particularly since their interest was deeply involved, he was nevertheless making only semi-official or private representations. Thanking the Secretary of State for having seen him at such short notice, Egeland left.

Noel-Baker recorded the interview in his own hand, including the final observation. As the crisis deepened, ministers of the Crown would rely on the final paragraph of Noel-Baker's account to allow them to lie to both the House of Commons and the British people. They would maintain that no such meeting had ever taken place.

For the moment, the Secretary of State felt the South African reaction had been pretty much as he would have expected. He would take advice, of course, from his staff but there seemed no overriding reason to ignore the wishes of the tribe.

The following week in South Africa, the Dutch Reformed Church held its General Assembly. A resolution was put before the conference calling the Pretoria government's attention to the 'serious repercussions which the marriage of Seretse Khama with a white woman may have on race relations in South Africa'. One delegate said: 'The whites are a spearhead of Christendom and civilisation in a land containing eight million natives, of whom at least half are semi-civilised, unconverted or living in barbarism. Anything calculated to reduce the prestige and influence of the white man as the standard bearer of civilisation will harm the best interests of all people living in South Africa today.' As one South African newspaper, the *Natal Witness*, put it: 'Mixed marriage strikes at the very root of white supremacy.' Meanwhile, at the High Commissioner's residence in Pretoria, Sir Evelyn Baring had been welcoming Seretse and giving him the strongest impression that confirmation was a formality. Baring was quite clear about what his advice to London should be. The policy of indirect rule demanded that the tribe's decision should be respected. Although only 46, Baring had spent more than half his life in the service of the Empire and his advice carried great weight in Whitehall. His pedigree was impeccable. The son of Lord Cromer, the former Governor General of Egypt, Baring had progressed through Winchester, Oxford and the Indian Civil Service before becoming Southern Rhodesia's youngest ever Governor in 1942. There he had irritated the white settlers by his liberal and progressive attitudes to the 'natives'. He had upset them even more by his espousal of the increasingly dominant theme of 'trusteeship' in British colonial policy, an idea which had been developed to counteract the more extreme demands of the white colonial settlers.

From Malaya to Kenya and the Rhodesias, the settlers were demanding more rights, more land and more control over the 'native population', who were rapidly becoming disinherited in their own countries. Clearly, in the self-governing dominions, any commitment to the original inhabitants was long extinct. The aboriginal tribesmen of Australia and the Indians and Eskimos of Canada had already been overwhelmed. The millions of blacks in South Africa were increasingly in thrall and there was nothing directly London could do about it. In the colonies, however, the

British government decided its obligations were still alive. The new policy stated that colonial land was held 'in trust' by the Crown until such time as the native inhabitants were strong and competent enough to handle their own affairs. It was Britain's policy to ensure that everything was done to encourage the 'natives' to attain that happy state and to make sure that rapacious entrepreneurs and land-hungry white farmers didn't steal their birthright in the meantime. Though a policy more honoured in the breach than the observance, it did serve to set limits to white ambition and offer some prospect to blacks of eventual independence.

In 1945 Baring became High Commissioner to both South Africa and the protectorates. The South African appointment was the most senior diplomatic post in Africa but Baring was even more excited about his new responsibilities to Bechuanaland, Swaziland and Basutoland. Here, if anywhere in the Empire, the policy of trusteeship could be worked out in its purest form. As protectorates, rather than colonies, the three territories had never absorbed large numbers of settlers. Baring believed that Britain's overriding duty was to prevent South Africa gobbling up the three countries until such time as their populations were in a position to stand on their own feet. South African agitation for the incorporation of the territories had been constant since the 1910 Act of Union which seemed to suggest their eventual absorption. As the black man's lot in South Africa deteriorated, Pretoria's demands for the protectorates had grown louder. In white South African eyes, the existence in southern Africa of a parallel system of administration which allowed the 'natives' pretty much to govern themselves and, at the same time, held out the prospect of eventual independence, made the subjugation of their own blacks very much more difficult. Unfortunately, as international criticism of South Africa's racial policies grew, so it was becoming more difficult for Britain to accede to Pretoria's demands.

Baring, indeed, had been shocked at the conditions under which many blacks lived when he arrived in South Africa. The poverty in the black urban slums of Johannesburg and Cape Town was appalling and he occasionally visited the worst areas with Father Trevor Huddleston as his guide. Huddleston, a British worker priest with a profound sense of the injustice under which South Africa's blacks were labouring, became a great personal and spiritual friend of Baring.

When the National Party won the 1948 election Baring was

sure the Africans' lot would further deteriorate and, at the same time, felt that pressure on Britain to give up the protectorates might prove irresistible. Thus, he was about to advise London, a prompt recognition of Seretse as chief of the Bamangwato would send a clear signal to Malan that the British intended to pursue their policy in the protectorates and that they were not susceptible to pressure.

It was at that moment that Baring had a conversation that turned his intended advice on its head. Since coming to South Africa, Baring had struck up a friendship with Douglas Forsyth, the Secretary for External Affairs. Indeed after the 1948 election, Forsyth's remained one of the few friendly faces in a sea of increasingly hostile ones.

Now, secretly, on 7 July, Forsyth came to see him. Malan had told the civil servant of the split within the Cabinet between the Prime Minister and the Strydom faction. Forsyth, of course, shared all Malan's misgivings about leaving the Commonwealth. He believed that continued association with Britain was one of the best hopes of moderating the more extreme policies of the new government and warding off the international isolation he was sure those policies would create. He even looked forward, at the next election, to the return of Smuts. He saw as clearly as Malan the dilemma in which the Prime Minister found himself and he felt the only way to head off catastrophe was to tell the British what was going on at the centre of the South African government.

Baring listened to Forsyth with a sinking heart. To advise London as he had intended was to play right into the hands of Strydom and the most extreme wing of the National Party. With a referendum vote behind him, it was entirely possible that Strydom would invade the protectorates, taking by force what the British refused to hand over voluntarily. Had Britain the will and the wherewithal to win back territories more than 8,000 miles from home once they were lost? Baring doubted it and, if not, where did that leave the policy of trusteeship? Handing the Bamangwato and the rest over to the National Party would damn their future as surely as that of South Africa's own blacks looked already damned. Baring had not come to South Africa to preside over such a disgraceful episode in British colonial history. Far from selling out the protectorates, the maintenance of their independence was at the centre of his purpose.

As for the threat to leave the Commonwealth, the implications of that went to the very heart of vital British interests which he knew would be immediately apparent in Britain. It was not for him to spell those out since their significance went far beyond his authority. His priority must remain the protectorates. And yet, if he advised against recognition, what reason could be given? As it was, the press in England were waiting to see if London would 'give in' to the South Africans. And what of the Bamangwato and the trust they had put in the British through the years? If they were not to have Seretse, then who were they to have? On a more human level, what effect would refusal have on the marriage of Ruth and Seretse? The two had been through an extremely difficult year already. Might not Seretse's disqualification from the chieftainship prove too heavy a blow and break up their marriage? Was it right for any man to have that on his conscience? Baring turned to his spiritual adviser, Trevor Huddleston, for help. The priest agreed it was the most difficult of dilemmas. Giving in to Malan and his obnoxious government was anathema to both men. Maintaining British policy in southern Africa, which was seeming increasingly liberal and progressive in comparison with apartheid, provided a slim source of hope for many of the Union's blacks. As long as the British handled 'native affairs' differently, it proved that there was an alternative to apartheid. For the British now to bow to Pretoria would greatly enhance the new government's growing aura of invincibility.

And yet, what was the alternative? Putting aside the implications of leaving the Commonwealth, was it right to endanger the independence of the protectorates when there seemed good reason to believe that the British were unable to defend them? Was it right to subject hundreds of thousands of Africans to the evil policies of apartheid when it might be avoided? Huddleston's reluctant advice, and he has regretted it ever since, was that Baring should advise against recognition.

For a day or two more, Baring wrestled with his dilemma. Finally, he cabled Whitehall that Seretse should not be recognised as chief and then sat down to write a full account of his reasons. Heading his dispatch 'Top Secret and Personal' Baring addressed it to Sir Percivale Liesching, newly appointed Permanent Secretary at the Commonwealth Office in succession to Sir Eric Machtig. Baring wrote as follows:

My first reaction to the news of the tribe's decision was to recommend the recognition of Seretse. I thought that we should face as soon as possible the inevitable storm of criticism in Southern Africa. I have always felt and I still feel that where there is a straight and an unavoidable choice in our Territories between fostering the interests and preserving the confidence of Africans on the one hand and the maintenance of good relations with the Union on the other hand, it is our relations with the Union which must be sacrificed. This is the advice I would offer if consulted on a request by any South African Government for transfer of the High Commission Territories against the will of their inhabitants . . . I have, however, with great reluctance and after much thought come to the conclusion that in this case I should not advise on these lines. The result of the collision would, as I will endeavour to show, be disastrous.

News from Bechuanaland, said Baring, had shown that the number of people who were leaving the tribe with Tshekedi would deal a severe blow to the 'native' administration and that on its own should give pause for thought.

As regards the Union the situation is the gravest which has faced us since I first came to this country. When I was first informed of the result of the Serowe meeting I knew that there would be official protests and a loud public outcry. I then thought that South Africans would be less troubled by Seretse's position as chief than by the fact of a European woman and an African man living together as man and wife on the Union's borders. I believed that a result of the recognition of Seretse while he is married to his present wife would be a great impetus to the demand for the transfer of the High Commission Territories.

On the 7th July, however, I obtained my first opportunity of seeking Forsyth's help. In Cape Town he had discussed the whole matter with Dr Malan. Dr Malan had discussed the question with Ministers and was greatly worried and distressed. He spoke freely to Forsyth.

Two points emerge. First, official recognition of Seretse as chief so long as it implies the residence in Serowe of his English wife and the performance by her of the duties of the first wife of a chief is what really matters to the members of the Government and probably to most South Africans. The mere residence of Seretse and his wife in Serowe without official recognition is objectionable to them, but in Forsyth's view of subsidiary importance. He hopes that it might be avoided but it is the recognition of Seretse as chief which will be the match to set off the gunpowder. Huggins (the Prime Minister of Southern Rhodesia) has also written to me taking exactly the same point of view.

Secondly, the political consequences in the Union of recognition would be far more serious than I had realised. Recognition would naturally assist the fight for transfer, but this will not be the sole or the most important result. On the contrary, the Nationalists will be strengthened against the United Party (Smuts' party) and, worse still, inside the National Party, Mr Strydom will be strengthened against Dr Malan – and Strydom already controls a majority in the party caucus. He and his followers are eagerly awaiting recognition of Seretse. Nationalist feeling has already been inflamed as a result of the disputes over the Citizenship Bill (restricting British immigrants' rights to South African citizenship and thus the vote). The more extreme Nationalists will use the Seretse incident to add fuel to those flames. They will argue that our action demonstrates the folly of allowing the existence side by side in Southern Africa of two systems of Native administration diametrically opposed to one another. They will go on to say that South Africans should not and cannot be associated with a country which recognises officially an African chief married to a white woman and they will make Seretse's recognition the occasion of an appeal to the country for the establishment of a republic, and not only of a republic but a republic outside the Commonwealth. Dr Malan is desperately worried and feels that he could not successfully oppose an extremist offensive on these lines.

Forsyth himself says the extremist Afrikaners, encouraged by the move to independence in India, exploiting sentiments aroused by the Citizenship Bill and the emotions about to be inflamed by the unveiling of the Voortrekker Monument next December (to commemorate the Great Trek) would obtain a mandate from the electors for the severance of the Commonwealth tie.

Baring reminded Liesching that the Nationalists had always been more successful with an anti-Black call rather than an anti-British one. The large number of English-speaking whites would always object to that and this the extremist Nationalists had realised.

They believe that Seretse's recognition would enable them to exploit colour feeling in order to sever the tie with Great Britain without exasperating English speaking South Africans. They would appeal to the whole country on a common (white) South African dislike of the application in the High Commission Territories of British principles of native administration and on a common South African abhorrence of race mixture. They would thus fight the battle for a secessionist republic with the ideal war cry and at the ideal time; and Forsyth, following the hints dropped by Dr Malan during their conversation, believes that they would succeed . . .

These are Forsyth's views and I have never known him speak with such feeling. To argue that this incident on the edge of the Kalahari might lead to the complete secession of South Africa from the Commonwealth may seem far-fetched. Yet I am afraid that what Forsyth says has the ring of truth and I believe him . . . In all these circumstances I feel that we must play for time. I am well aware that if we do so we shall be accused of weakness . . . yet the political results of recognition would be so serious, and the effect on the tribe of a quick decision, if wrong, would be so bad that I have no alternative.

Baring said that by playing for time – say by establishing some small committee of inquiry to investigate Seretse's suitability as chief – a confrontation with South Africa would be postponed. As time went by, the tribe might reverse its decision or Seretse might even tire of Ruth. 'I recognise the disadvantages of the proposals I have made,' he wrote, 'but the consequences of recognising Seretse would be so serious that we should, I believe, do everything we can to avoid a collision on this issue with the Union.'

In support of his policy of prevarication, Baring concluded by turning to a literary authority: 'I remember reading in Edward Grey's autobiography a remark that war is never inevitable. Its consequences are so bad that if possible the issue should be postponed and no attention should be paid to the argument that "war must come some time – it had better come this year" . . . To my mind the same applies in this case.'

The High Commissioner then ordered the dispatch to be encoded and sent to London.

12

In the Interests of the Nation

Sir Percivale Liesching, Permanent Secretary at the Department of Commonwealth Relations, was a man of firm opinions. Neat, almost fastidious in his appearance, he had a reputation as a stern administrator who got things done. Indeed, he had been appointed to the post of senior civil servant at the Commonwealth Office to do just that. In 1947, with the coming of independence for India, the India and the Dominions Offices had been merged into the Commonwealth Office. But, with civil servants always eager to preserve their empires, the two ministries had only merged at the top. Beneath the Secretary of State and the Permanent Secretary two parallel bureaucracies floated like twin icebergs joined at the tip, duplicating jobs, supplies, paperwork and expense. Liesching had been brought in to put an end to such extravagance and he was going about it with his usual determination.

Educated at Bedford and Brasenose College, Oxford, Liesching had graduated just before the outbreak of the First World War. He had had, as they say, 'a good war' being mentioned in dispatches for his bravery. He had fought with the East African Expeditionary Force serving under the newly promoted Smuts and had developed a taste for Africa that would stay with him throughout his career. In 1920, he joined the Colonial Office, transferring five years later to the Dominions Office. In 1933, he had been posted to the High Commissioner's Office in South Africa as Political Secretary. There he had followed the fortunes of emerging Afrikaner political nationalism as well as the deposition and reinstatement of Chief-Regent Tshekedi over the McKintosh flogging melodrama.

Now at 54, athletic for his years and determined in his purpose, he read Baring's telegram with, he felt, a special insight. Before forwarding the dispatch to his Secretary of State, therefore, Liesching felt it would be useful for Noel-Baker's greater understanding if he added a few notes of his own. He began by describing a conversation he had had at lunch only the day before with Lieutenant-General Len Beyers, one of South Africa's Defence Chiefs.

> His particular angle was that to allow Seretse to be chief with his white wife would not be simply a matter between the United Kingdom Government, Bechuanaland and the Union but would light a fire throughout the British Colonial Territories in Africa which would not soon be quenched. He said that the very existence of white settlement in these territories depended, in view of the numerical inferiority and defencelessness of the white population, upon the principle that the native mind regarded the white woman as inviolable. Once the United Kingdom Government, in all its majesty, countenanced officially a marriage such as Seretse had contracted, the whole principle would be undermined. Repercussions, in his opinion, would be long and loud and also disastrous.

Without feeling the need to question the proposition that recognising Seretse would lead to wholesale rape throughout the Empire, Sir Percivale was then moved to add a few words of a more personal nature:

> I do not wish here to discuss at length the question of our attitude towards the Colour Bar on which, I dare say, I am as doctrinally correct as yourself, the Colonial Secretary and all those in this country who most strongly disapprove of discrimination based on racial colour. I have never, however, been able to reconcile myself to the ultimate logical consequences of this principle of non-discrimination when it takes practical forms affecting oneself or one's family in terms of miscegnation. Nor do I believe that many who hold their antipathy to the Colour Bar would, if confronted with the matter in personal terms, view with equanimity, or indeed without revulsion, the prospect of their son or daughter marrying a member of the negro race.
>
> I mention this controversial topic in order to argue that if it is true here, it must be all the more true in British Colonial Territories in Africa. South Africa might whip up feeling in

Southern Rhodesia, in Kenya and in Tanganyika. I have little doubt that Southern Rhodesia will react violently and there has always been an unholy alliance between the South Africans and the Kenyan settlers over native policy and the Colour Bar. Tanganyika can be just as easily infected. In short, there may be a very bitter harvest here and account should be taken of the possibility.

South Africans frequently found Sir Percivale receptive to their remarks and opinions. The previous week, he had reported to Noel-Baker that at the end of a regular High Commissioners' meeting, Mr A. A. M. Hamilton, the Second Secretary at the South African High Commission, had told him that Ruth was pregnant and a room in a Johannesburg nursing home had been reserved in her name. The news had already been telegrammed to Baring in Pretoria before it was found to be false.

Noel-Baker, meanwhile, was understandably confused. Within the space of less than two weeks, the advice from his officials had gone into reverse. Only three days before, Noel-Baker had authorised an off-the-record press briefing welcoming Tshekedi's decision to leave Serowe. 'The regent is in disfavour but Seretse and his white bride are promised support from 90 per cent of the tribesmen,' one of his officials had told the *Daily Graphic*. Now what had seemed a perfectly straightforward decision at the beginning of the month, with both the Resident Commissioner in Bechuanaland and the High Commissioner in South Africa apparently advocating confirmation, had turned into a dilemma with apparently lethal consequences. Baring's analysis of the political implications was frightening. As the Cabinet minister responsible for Bechuanaland, he knew how vulnerable the territory was and the financial and logistical impossibility of defending it from a determined South African attack.

However, as Baring had known, it was the threat that South Africa would pull out of the Commonwealth that weighed most heavily with Noel-Baker. The implications of South African withdrawal went to the heart of some of Britain's most vital British interests, both public and secret. The most obvious public one was the newly born concept of a Commonwealth of Nations to replace the old idea of Empire. The shattering of the British economy in the Second World War and the emergence of America and the Soviet Union as the two giants on the world stage had prompted a fundamental reassessment of Britain's imperial legacy. Unable and unwilling to resist the growing demands for independence in India, Pakistan, Burma and Ceylon, and fully aware that many more would soon follow in their steps, Britain had been searching for a new formula to accommodate both its present and former possessions. The idea of a club of nations, some still governed by Britain, others independent like the old dominions of Canada, Australia, New Zealand and South Africa and the newly free Asian countries bound loosely together for mutual benefit had been widely canvassed by Attlee's Labour government and largely accepted. Burma apart, India, Pakistan and Ceylon had welcomed the idea and in April 1949, two months before the Bamangwato crisis, the Commonwealth Prime Ministers Conference met in London to seal the new relationship. Within a week the Labour government's intense preparation over the previous three years had borne fruit. The nations declared that 'they remain united as free and equal members of the Commonwealth of Nations, freely cooperating in the pursuit of peace, liberty, and progress'.

As the first among equals, Britain set great store by the Commonwealth. Mutually beneficial trade deals on raw and manufactured goods were important to Britain's recovery and the club lent Britain the aura of still being a world power, almost, if not quite, still up there with the big boys.

If South Africa, one of the Commonwealth's most important members, were to desert the new clubhouse before the paint was even dry, the organisation would be dealt a damaging, if not fatal, blow. The much lauded prospect of a group of equal sovereign states being able to work out mutual problems against the backdrop of a special relationship would be seen, at its first test, to be a mirage. What had appeared to be one of the most successful diplomatic coups in living memory could turn into a disaster.

But South Africa's membership of the Commonwealth had an even deeper significance and one which was even more closely bound to British ambitions. Prime Minister Attlee and Bevin, the Foreign Secretary, were convinced that possession of the atomic bomb was essential if Britain was to remain a world power and the weapon's development had become a top priority.

The British nuclear programme had been severely delayed since the end of the war when the Americans suddenly refused technical cooperation. During the war, the British had made great contributions to the Manhattan Project, the top secret

Anglo-American programme that finally produced the bombs that defeated Japan. During the war, Churchill and the American President, Roosevelt, had reached at least two documented agreements that America would help Britain to develop her own nuclear bomb when the war was over. But so secret had the whole affair been that when, on Roosevelt's death, he was succeeded by Harry Truman, the new President was told nothing of the agreements. At the same time, Congress, jealous of America's unique nuclear possession, began passing legislation banning the dissemination of nuclear technology. The British programme was stalled. One of the very few people outside the immediate circle of those involved in the Manhattan Project who had known of its existence was Jan Smuts, the Prime Minister of South Africa. Churchill, because of his close personal relationship with the Field Marshal, had told him of the bomb's development.

Soon after Attlee had come to power, large uranium deposits had been discovered in South Africa and the British thought they saw a way of breaking the blockade in the flow of American technical assistance. The one chink in America's armour was the world shortage of suitable uranium. Mining techniques were uncertain and deposits still largely undiscovered. The shortage of uranium was the one factor preventing the Americans building a massive stockpile of atomic bombs. If the British could guarantee what looked like one of the biggest uranium deposits in the world, then they would have the leverage to force the Americans to cooperate with them on their own atom bomb. In November 1945, the British and Americans had agreed to pool all the supplies of uranium in the world that they could get their hands on but, considering the American reluctance to honour all their agreements, this did not bother the British unduly.

The month after the Anglo-American agreement on sharing uranium, Attlee sent a cable marked 'Top Secret and Personal' to Field Marshal Smuts. 'I should be most grateful . . . for your favourable consideration of the proposal that, subject to South African needs, an option should be granted to His Majesty's Government in the United Kingdom for the purchase of all disposable surplus over a term of years . . . It would be of considerable advantage . . . if agreement could now be reached.' Smuts replied six days later saying it was too early to make any commitment as no one knew how much uranium was in South Africa nor how much the price should be. 'You can of course count on us to be continually alive to the need of control to ensure that supplies of this new source of frightfulness and power will not find their way into hands that might abuse it,' Smuts wrote back. That was all very well, the British thought, but it was hardly the point. As an internal memorandum to the Dominions Office explained: 'The telegram [Smuts' reply] has caused us great consternation and embarrassment here since it is clear that without some definite assurance of supplies from South Africa in the future, our whole programme for the development of atomic energy and also our bargaining position with the Americans would be greatly prejudiced.'

The next month, January 1946, the Dominions Office cabled the newly arrived High Commissioner to South Africa, Sir Evelyn Baring. They sent him a full account of the background, suggesting to Baring that Smuts should be put in the picture. 'We should hope that . . . he would appreciate the vital need . . . for the UK Government to be assured of raw materials and to be put in the strongest possible bargaining position *vis-à-vis* the Americans on whom we are still dependent for much in this matter.'

Negotiations continued slowly as the extent of the South African deposits was assessed, but by October 1947 Baring was able to tell his Secretary of State that Smuts would probably agree that South Africa should sell all its uranium to Great Britain and nothing to the Americans. Negotiations continued and a final contract was due to be signed at the end of 1948. But in June of that year the fiercely anti-British Malan government had come to power and all further progress was stalled. By 1949, the Americans had joined negotiations for South African uranium but still deferred to the British because of their 'special relationship' with Pretoria.

The discussions remained top secret in both London and Pretoria. Indeed, at least ten British Cabinet Ministers knew nothing about the atomic weapons programme at all and probably no more than five, including the Prime Minister, knew anything of the negotiations with South Africa. Noel-Baker and Liesching at the Commonwealth Office, of course, were centrally involved as was Baring in Pretoria. Leif Egeland, the South African High Commissioner in London, was briefed and all contact between the two countries on this matter went through Douglas Forsyth as Secretary for External Affairs.

By the spring of 1949, the reality of South Africa's economic plight was giving Pretoria second thoughts about refusing to negotiate the sale of this precious new ore. The cost of the programme of rapid industrialisation had already forced Malan's government to call in a massive 9 million ounces of gold loan that the pro-British Smuts administration had agreed with London in 1947. The terms of the deal had been very favourable to the British – the South Africans were to receive half a per cent a year in interest – but now the gold was needed to pay the bills at home.

Malan now said he was ready to talk about selling uranium. On 7 June, Mr E. H. Louw, the Minister of Mines, announced in the House of Assembly in Cape Town that British and American government representatives would shortly visit South Africa to discuss the production and purchase of uranium. On 8 July, as the British were waiting to be given a definite date for the meeting, British diplomats in America picked up a rumour originating from the South African embassy in Washington. The talks, the diplomats had heard, were now likely to be postponed. The reason given would be that one of the South African scientists concerned with the negotiations would be away at an international conference for the next month or so, but 'it was also hinted that there are other reasons, apart from the scientist's conference, for the delay'. As Noel-Baker was replying to Baring's bombshell telegram of 11 July spelling out the implications of recognising Seretse as chief, he received, on 13 July, by hand, a note from High Commissioner Leif Egeland. 'My dear Philip,' the South African envoy wrote, 'I am writing in connection with the proposed visit to South Africa of representatives of the USA and UK Governments for the purpose of discussing matters associated with the production of uranium in the Union. I have now been advised that it is doubtful whether the Union Government will be ready to hold the tripartite discussions on South African uranium production before November.'

Of course, there could have been many reasons for such a delay. The emerging technology of uranium mining presented many difficulties and there was no generally accepted world price. But there was no doubting that the timing of the postponement was unfortunate with the Seretse affair at the top of the two countries' diplomatic agenda. Just as Pretoria had agreed to restart negotiations on uranium after a year of delay, so the Seretse affair had soured relations between Britain and

South Africa and had deeply split the Malan Cabinet. There was no indication that the two events were directly related but the South Africans were soon to put similar pressure on the British. Pretoria was eager to be given 'special status' in return for allowing Britain and America to buy her uranium, whereby she would be helped to develop her own nuclear energy programme. On 4 November, Baring telegrammed London to say that the South Africans had told him that if Britain helped South Africa achieve special status it would offset the bitterness in Pretoria being caused by Britain's refusal to transfer the protectorates. Anyway, whatever the real reasons for the postponement, it was an unwelcome complication for Noel-Baker. 'My dear Leif,' he wrote, in reply to the South African High Commissioner, 'Many thanks for your letter . . . We shall now make our plans on the assumption that (our discussions) will take place in November. May I take it that you will be confirming this nearer the time? We are anxious as you know that the discussions should be held as soon as they profitably can be.'

Eagerness for the talks to begin was increased only six weeks later when, to the complete surprise of every Western intelligence agency, the Russians exploded their first atomic bomb.

Meanwhile, Noel-Baker was wrestling with the immediate and practical problems before him. Clearly, he would have to refuse Seretse's recognition and he would have to convince the Cabinet.

Baring's advice was sound but the High Commissioner had given him no suggestion as to how such a decision could be explained in public. When he had turned to Creech-Jones, the Secretary of State at the Colonial Office, he had received no help there either. Creech-Jones had agreed entirely with the decision to refuse Seretse's recognition but 'we must not do it too quickly. To do it now will look racial and we must get it over to administrative grounds. To refuse recognition at this moment will look like too substantial a concession to South African opinion.' Although Noel-Baker could not see how the decision could be explained, he was certain of one thing: the British government could never admit to giving in to South African pressure. That, at all costs, must be kept secret and denied at every opportunity.

In South Africa, Forsyth had told Baring of Egeland's 'semi-official' meeting with Noel-Baker and, when replying to the Secretary of State's further inquiries, Baring, in passing, had written: 'You have already received representation from the Union Government.' Noel-Baker, with his pencil, underlined the sentence and wrote, in the margin, an instruction to his secretary: 'Omit in printing.' Two lines further on, Baring had written: 'The Prime Minister of Southern Rhodesia has stated in the Legislative Assembly that his Government too is addressing to me an official protest.' The Noel-Baker pencil underlined the giveaway 'too' and again wrote against it in the margin, 'Omit'. The Secretary of State's sensitivities were high indeed if he found it necessary to censor secret departmental papers. Whatever the reason, one thing was clear: the cover-up had started.

Noel-Baker and his staff then began work on a memorandum to be put before the Cabinet on 21 July. In it he deployed all Baring's and Liesching's arguments against recognition of Seretse, concluding: 'We cannot exclude the possibility of an armed incursion into the Bechuanaland Protectorate from the Union if Seretse were to be recognised forthwith, while feeling on the subject is inflamed.'

Noel-Baker then went on to rule out any decision to recognise Seretse immediately and presented the Cabinet with two options: first, that the government declare there and then that Seretse should not be recognised; and, secondly, that they play for time by setting up a judicial inquiry to look into the whole affair. The first course, Noel-Baker admitted, carried with it the disadvantage that it was almost impossible to justify on any grounds that could be made public. The second course, while it couldn't 'be assumed that the enquiry would result in a report unfavourable to the recognition of Seretse', seemed preferable since 'the eventual decision [to recognise or not] would still remain with the High Commissioner'. Noel-Baker called upon his colleagues to decide quickly between these two courses of action. 'Seretse's wife is likely to leave for South Africa within a short time and, if she joins him there before we have made any announcement, the position will have become much more difficult, since the press would sensationally represent this as the arrival of a white "Chieftainess". It would be very difficult to overtake the implications of this and any subsequent announcement would look like a harassed rear-guard action.' By the time the memorandum was completed, on 19 July, there was never again any serious discussion in the British government about whether or not to recognise Seretse Khama as chief of the

Bamangwato. The decision had already been taken and was never challenged internally. From now on, the debate would be about the best ways of not recognising him and of explaining that non-recognition to a disbelieving public.

Sir Percivale Liesching, at any rate, was immensely pleased with the course of events. In a 'private and personal' letter written in longhand, he thanked Baring for his

extraordinarily valuable reports over this terribly difficult Seretse problem. I cannot go into detail as time is too short, but I should like you to know that among ministers here there has now developed a complete unanimity against recognition of Seretse with Ruth as his wife. It was very difficult to estimate how ministerial opinion would go on this and Creech-Jones (Colonies) has come out entirely on the right side. My Secretary of State has been very sensible from the first. Your reputation here is exceedingly high, as well it might be, and your judgement is trusted to an extent which has never been exceeded in the case of any High Commissioner I have known.

13

No Alternative

Seretse's telegram announcing his victory had arrived at 34 Adolphus Road, Finsbury Park at about the same time as the press. Ruth was now under siege in her ground-floor flat, unable to leave her front door without being followed. Seretse and Ruth had agreed that neither would speak to the press until after his installation. Their quotes in the past had been distorted and there seemed no reason to antagonise the British authorities further as things seemed to be going their way.

But Ruth's silence only whetted Fleet Street's appetite. Reporters and photographers camped outside the house and neighbours were showered with gifts to persuade them to keep the pressmen alerted.

One morning in early July, Ruth, in desperation, jumped over her back garden fence in an effort to elude the pack. Neighbours spotted her and the reporters gave chase. Ducking into someone else's garden, Ruth watched her hunters race by. After a few minutes, she walked quietly to the nearest bus stop. As she stepped on to the bus, a voice said quietly behind her: 'Good morning, Mrs Khama.' The reporter joined her on the top deck, she enduring his persistent questions, he her icy silence. The next day, Ruth asked the girl in the upstairs flat – all those in the house had taken Ruth's side – to put on dark glasses, a head scarf and long coat and walk around the block for her. The girl did, pursued by the press, and Ruth made her escape.

Ruth was now beginning to feel the pressure. Anxious to join her husband, alone and under siege, she was sleeping badly and in a high state of tension whenever she tried to leave the house. Some of Seretse's friends from the students' hostel and the Inner Temple law schools came to stay with her during the day to bring her comfort. This immediately increased press speculation. On 2 July, the *Daily Express* reported:

Ruth Williams airmailed a letter to her husband from London

yesterday. Dressed in a red and white striped summer frock, her blonde hair tinged with red, she left her flat to post it. She rarely leaves her flat and yesterday she was escorted by a Negro in sports coat and flannel trousers. He said she did not want to make a statement. When asked if he was a guard appointed by her husband, Seretse Khama, he did not reply. Ruth then said: 'I have no statement to make, not because I am prevented from talking but because it is not my wish to talk.'

Ruth, to her great joy, was now fully reconciled with both her parents. They suggested that she move back home to Lewisham but still keep up the pretence of living in the flat. She therefore made sure that she appeared in Finsbury Park at least once a day bringing back with her small amounts of clothes that would not arouse suspicion. In the flat, she packed the rest of her belongings into large trunks and her allies in the flat above agreed to send them off after her final departure.

Although Ruth was anxious to travel to Bechuanaland as soon as possible, Seretse had cabled that Baring had asked her to delay travelling until after his installation.

On 2 July, the South African press, quoting government sources, had reported that Ruth should not try to land in the Union on her way to Bechuanaland as she would not be a welcome guest. This meant that she would have to fly the five-day route on the BOAC Flying Boat from Southampton to Victoria Falls on the border between Northern and Southern Rhodesia. Unknown to Ruth, the Commonwealth Relations Office checked with BOAC all the reservations for the next three weeks to make sure that she had not booked a seat without telling them. The airline was very helpful but warned that she might still apply for a cancellation under an assumed name.

Sir Percivale Liesching was anxious to find out her intentions and John Keith, the Chief Welfare Officer at the Colonial Office, was asked to contact her. Liesching also wanted the rumour that she was pregnant checked out. On 13 July, Keith met Ruth for lunch. He found her eager to cooperate with the government and reported that she had no intention of travelling to Serowe without telling the authorities. She told him that the press was a great nuisance and the *Daily Express* and the *Mirror* were troubling her badly. The *Mirror*, she said, had offered her £100 for her story but she had turned them down.

Meanwhile, in Serowe itself, one of Fleet Street's most colourful reporters had arrived to make the story his own. Noel Monks was the *Daily Mail*'s Africa Correspondent. A big, burly, silver-haired, 45-year-old Australian, with a full, fleshy face and a pugnacious jaw, Monks had deservedly earned his reputation as one of Fleet Street's finest by courageous reporting in the Second World War. Both in the Tunisian campaign and at the D-Day landings in Normandy, Monks' direct style and fresh eye for detail had produced some of the finest reports. Now, on behalf of the *Daily Mail*, he roamed Africa documenting the emerging independence movements and the gradual decline of the old colonial empires. His racy style engaged the casual middle-brow reader.

In Serowe, he was initially stalled by Seretse's refusal to speak to him or any reporters. Inquiries among the white trading families in the village – perhaps eighty people in all – led Monks to report that the majority of them were against Ruth coming to Serowe. Many of them disliked the idea of mixed marriages; the idea seemed unsettling, unworkable and, to some, distasteful. At the same time, the white traders owed their livelihood in Serowe to the goodwill of the chief. Whereas Tshekedi was against the marriage, the tribe were now for it. Seretse, as chief, would have the power to throw the traders out if they offended him so few people were prepared to speak publicly.

Monks, however, found Tshekedi a willing interviewee and only too willing to be quoted. Standing by the tombs of the chiefs cut into the rock overlooking the Kgotla ground, Tshekedi told Monks: 'All my work in the past twenty-two years, the plans I have for the tribe's future welfare, all now go overboard – because of a white woman 6,000 miles away who has never seen Africa in her life.' Tshekedi then went on to describe how a chief of the Bamangwato must be prepared to house and feed up to 250 people at any one time. Men who had travelled from distant villages seeking redress for some wrong would be the guests of the chief until the matter was resolved. At the same time, important people from other tribes, often with their families, would come on lengthy visits and there were also sometimes refugees needing temporary hospitality. The welfare of all these people was traditionally the responsibility of the chief's wife. 'A chieftainess who could not even speak the language would be completely stumped,' Tshekedi told Monks.

Those London papers as yet unwilling to send their own men to Serowe found South African pressmen happy to earn extra money reporting for them. A 'special correspondent' wrote a full page article in the *Sunday Express* describing the outrage and scandal the marriage was causing in South Africa and Rhodesia. Turning to the Bamangwato capital, the correspondent wrote: 'To a European, Serowe is just a dump. Three hundred miles from Mafeking, its mud huts house 30,000 natives with a few isolated tin houses where the white traders live. Even the hut of the chief is little different from those of the people.' Describing local taxation, the article described how if Seretse decided to 'acquire concubines, as he is entitled to do under tribal law, he must pay twenty-five shillings tax for each, but no more than three pounds, fifteen shillings whatever the number'.

Meanwhile, Baring had been analysing the Afrikaans press coverage of the affair and it seemed to bear out Forsyth's story of the Cabinet split. There were two main Afrikaans newspaper publishing companies in South Africa, one in the Cape and one in the Transvaal. Both, since their inception, had faithfully followed the political lines laid down by the National Party in their own area. Baring had found that *Die Burger*, the mouthpiece of the Cape National Party, had mentioned the Serowe crisis almost every day, warning the British that the South African government would not be able to stand back if Seretse were confirmed as chief of the Bamangwato. *Die Transvaler*, however, organ of the Transvaal National Party, had mentioned the matter only once, warning ominously that it presented 'a challenge to the statesmen who still hold the fate of Christian Western Civilisation in their hands'. Apart from that the newspaper had not mentioned the affair, bearing out Forsyth's view that the Transvaal extremists wanted to do nothing to dissuade the British from installing Seretse as chief.

At 10 a.m., on Thursday 21 July, Noel-Baker brought the marriage of Ruth and Seretse before the British Cabinet for the first time. Referring the Prime Minister and the assembled ministers to his memorandum, he repeated the view that there could be no question of immediate recognition of Seretse. The Cabinet quickly agreed that a judicial inquiry 'would afford time for reflection by all the parties concerned'. The issue, they stressed, was not one of the merits or demerits of mixed marriages and the government should vigorously rebut any suggestion that their attitude 'was in any way determined by purely racial considerations. The principal objective of policy must be to safeguard the future well-being of the Bamangwato themselves and there could be no doubt that the recognition of a Chieftain with a white wife might have consequences gravely prejudicial to good government and to the stability of the local native administration.'

The Cabinet meeting closed by agreeing that the inquiry should be set up as soon as possible.

The Commonwealth Office now moved swiftly. Aware that Ruth was preparing to leave for Bechuanaland, Baring was told to go to Mafeking and tell both Seretse and Tshekedi of the Cabinet's decision. This he did on 26 July. Tshekedi was delighted, feeling at last that the British had taken the advice he had been giving for months. Seretse wanted to know what precisely the inquiry would be inquiring into. The tribe had overwhelmingly acclaimed him as chief, everything he had been told since, including by Baring himself, had indicated that the tribe's decision would be confirmed. What then had suddenly arisen to create doubt and require a judicial investigation? Could this possibly be fear of South Africa? The High Commissioner replied that the terms of reference of the inquiry would be announced in due course but the purpose of the tribunal would be to discover whether or not Seretse was a suitable person to be chief. He asked both men to keep quiet about the inquiry until the official announcement was made the following Saturday, 30 July. On Friday the 29th, Noel-Baker's office wrote to Leif Egeland's private secretary at South Africa House. 'You will recollect that your High Commissioner came to see Mr Noel-Baker on June 30th to discuss the Seretse affair. Mr Egeland will, I think, be interested in the enclosed text of an announcement which is to be made tomorrow on this subject.'

The next day, Baring announced the inquiry in Cape Town and Anthony Sillery made the long dusty drive to Serowe to break the same news to the tribe.

Baring was delighted by the Cabinet's decision. On 31 July, he wrote to his wife who was on leave in England: 'I received a telegram from the Cabinet. It was more satisfactory than my wildest hopes. Not only did they accept the proposal for a judicial inquiry but it is clear partly from the telegram, and partly from a letter Liesching wrote to me, that they accept the main point, i.e. the impossibility of recognising Seretse as long as he is bound to Ruth.'

Not knowing that his fate was already decided, Seretse cabled Ruth to come and join him.

14

'Mrs Jones' Flies Out

On the evening of Monday, 15 August, Ruth's parents drove her to London's Victoria station. She had put in her usual appearance at the flat in Finsbury Park and the press had, she hoped, no idea that she was leaving for Serowe.

The British authorities had been told of her plans and had raised no objection. All felt it best that she should travel under a different name so a 'Mrs Jones' had bought a ticket for the BOAC Flying Boat to Victoria Falls.

Ruth was now very excited at the prospect of joining Seretse and seeing his country and its people for the first time. Her anxiety about the press, however, was now approaching paranoia. Her parents wished her a warm and tearful goodbye as she boarded the train for Southampton and the Flying Boat. After a night in the airline's Southampton hotel, Ruth and the other passengers arrived at the quayside departure buildings early the next morning.

Suddenly Ruth's pulse began racing wildly and she slunk to the back of the hall pulling her hat low over her eyes. There were reporters and photographers everywhere. A passenger waiting next to her asked her if she knew what was going on. Who was on their flight who was so famous? Ruth, frightened and lonely, didn't reply. Then the star of the show arrived. A young South African ballet star who had just completed her highly acclaimed London debut was flying home. Most of Fleet Street had arrived for farewell interviews and photographs. Gratefully 'Mrs Jones' checked her bags and boarded the aircraft.

At 9 a.m. the huge airplane lifted off from Southampton Water and headed south. After nights in Sicily, Luxor in Egypt and Entebbe in Uganda, the four-engined airliner began its final approach up the Zambesi Gorge towards Africa's mightiest waterfall.

By this time, reporters and neighbours in Finsbury Park had realised that Ruth had eluded them and Fleet Street had a dozen reporters waiting at the landing stage upstream from the falls. The Flying Boat, strangely silent as the roar of the falls drowned out the noise of its engines, glided through the plumes of spray thrown up by the falling torrents to touch down on the Zambesi River. Slowly, a great cumbersome boat now, the airliner manoeuvred towards the landing stage as the waiting reporters pressed forward. This time, the ballet star was ignored and all eyes and lenses were on 'Mrs Jones'. The *Daily Mail* reported: 'As she stood at the 400-foot Falls the tall, slim girl with red-gold hair said "This is wonderful!" When tourists asked if she was Mrs Khama, she smiled and hurried into the tearoom at the airport station. She was besieged by amateur photographers with cine and miniature cameras. Hundreds of holidaymakers turned their backs on the wonder of the waterfall to gaze at the "White Queen".'

That night a local British official joined her for dinner at the hotel and told her a small private charter plane had been booked for the following morning to fly her the 125 miles over bush and scrub to Francistown, a cattle and trading centre in Bechuanaland. The pilot had been told to fly a slightly longer route along the edge of the Kalahari so as not to offend the Southern Rhodesians by flying over their territory. They, like South Africa, had announced that Ruth Khama would be a most unwelcome visitor. The official said that Seretse had been told of her arrival time and would be at Francistown's grass airstrip to drive her the final ninety miles to Serowe. He added that he felt the plane should take off very early the next morning to avoid the press.

At 6.30 a.m. the next morning, the small plane, piloted by a Mr R. Hart of Zambesi Airways, took off and headed south for the forty-five minute flight to Francistown. Waiting at the airstrip in Francistown was not Seretse but a Mr George Jacobs who lived in Bulawayo, Southern Rhodesia's second city. He had been in Francistown on business and was waiting for his aircraft to take him home. He took only an idle interest in the small plane landing from the north until it taxied close to him and stopped. Nobody got down from the plane. Walking towards the aircraft he saw a young woman in the passenger seat shielding her face from him. Could this be the famous Ruth Khama herself? He had heard on the radio that morning that she had landed at Victoria Falls the night before. Taking out his camera, Jacobs circled the small plane trying to take Ruth's

Clement Attlee.

Patrick Gordon-Walker.

The Right Revd William Wand, Bishop of London.

Sir Evelyn Baring.

Philip Noel-Baker.

Ruth's sister Muriel and their Mother and Father.

Tshekedi Khama.

Ruth and Seretse in London – the first picture to be taken after news of their marriage was released, October 1948.

M. Cert.
S.R.

CERTIFIED COPY of an ENTRY OF MARRIAGE.

Pursuant to the Marriage Acts, 1811 to 1939.

[Printed by Authority of the Registrar-General]

Insert in this Margin any Notes which appear in the original entry.

Registration District KENSINGTON

1948. Marriage Solemnized at the Register Office in the

District of KENSINGTON. ROYAL BOROUGH OF KENSINGTON. (METROPOLITAN BOROUGH) in the

No.	When Married.	Name and Surname.	Age.	Condition.	Rank or Profession.	Residence at the time of Marriage.	Father's Name and Surname.	Rank or Profession of Father.
201	Twenty ninth September 1948	Seretse Khama	27 years	Bachelor	Law student	10, Hampden Hill Gardens W.8	Sekgoma Khama (deceased) Khama	Native Chief
		Ruth Williams	24 years	Spinster	—	3 Belmont Hall Court 6.8.13	George Williams	Commercial Traveller

Married in the Register Office

by licence before me,

This Marriage was solemnized between us { Seretse Khama Ruth Williams }

in the Presence of us { J Zimmerman Muriel Williams Kathleen Ainley }

J. H. Mooney Registrar

C. E. Weston Superintendent Registrar

I, CECIL E. WESTON, Superintendent Registrar for the District of KENSINGTON in the ROYAL BOROUGH OF KENSINGTON do hereby certify that this is a true copy of the Entry No. 201 in the Register Book of Marriages No. 279 for the sous district of KENSINGTON in the Superintendent Registrar

now legally in my custody. WITNESS MY HAND this 5 day of July 1949. C. Weston

CAUTION.—Any person who (1) falsifies any of the particulars on this Certificate, or (2) uses as true, knowing it to be falsified, is liable to Prosecution.

The marriage certificate.

Seretse pleading his case at the Kgotla, November 1948.

Ruth waves at the plane at Mahalapye airstrip as Seretse is flown on to Gaberone, March 1950.

Ruth meeting Seretse as he arrives for a weekend visit, 16 April 1950.

Ian Khama installed as Paramount Chief in 1979.

Seretse and Ruth with baby Jacqueline and Naledi arriving in exile in England, to be met by Ruth's mother, August 1950.

The twins Tshekedi *(left)*and Tony *(right)*Khama with their elder sister
Jacqueline, 1989.

Lady Ruth Khama at home in Botswana, 1989.

picture. Each time he approached, she turned away from him hiding her face with her hat.

Within a few minutes – to Ruth it seemed hours – a big, turquoise Chevrolet appeared, bouncing across the rough grass of the airstrip. In it was a laughing Seretse and at his side, his cousin and close friend Goareng Mosinyi. Jacobs, his camera still in his hand, watched as the American sedan drove right up to the aeroplane, parking beneath its wing. As Seretse opened the car door and Ruth opened the plane's, they formed an effective screen hiding their embrace from the frustrated Jacobs. Safely in the front seat, snuggled close to Seretse, Ruth managed to give the amateur photographer a final wave as the car roared away.

It took two hours for Seretse to guide the Chevrolet along the dusty dirt roads from Francistown to Palapye. August is still winter in Bechuanaland, dry and crisp in the mornings and pleasantly warm by mid-morning. Warm too was Ruth's welcome. Though her arrival was unannounced, Seretse's car was well known throughout the Bamangwato Reserve. As they drove past workers in the fields, groups of bystanders on streets and herdsmen chivvying cattle along the roads, shouts of welcome went up the moment Ruth was spotted. Once or twice Seretse had to stop the car as people demanded the right to shake Ruth's hand. Between times, Ruth and Seretse chatted, Goareng joining in and quickly forming a firm friendship with Ruth. Seretse told Ruth how, since the Kgotla meeting, he had become the head of the tribe in everything but the official confirmation which the British were withholding. Why had the British suddenly made this about turn? Pressure from Pretoria could be the only reason. But if London was going to give in to what could only be racist demands, how could they explain that to the world? It might prove so embarrassing for them that the British might still decide that recognising Seretse was the lesser of two evils. Whatever else, the British would have to come up with some acceptable reason why Seretse wasn't suitable to lead the tribe. What that could be, Seretse couldn't imagine. He was the rightful heir, accepted by the overwhelming majority of the tribe, extremely well educated and well travelled. What reason would they find?

By 10 a.m. they were driving into the small railway hamlet of Palapye passing bystanders whose faces suddenly lit up in recognition. Through streets of people cheering Ruth's arrival, they arrived at the house of Mrs 'Ma' Shaw, who ran the town's largest trading store. A friend of Seretse's since he had been a little boy, she had offered the couple a bed in her house until they found somewhere in Serowe. Ma Shaw's house was a large, single-storey house with plastered mud-brick walls. At each corner was a lofty, semi-circular room topped with a conical, corrugated iron roof. Ruth and Seretse were installed in one of these. Next door to Ma Shaw lived her only son Tommy and his new wife, Barbara, herself newly arrived from England.

But Fleet Street was not to be denied. Outwitted by the early departure from Victoria Falls, the pack had chartered planes of their own and flown to Francistown. There they had hired cars and set off in search of Africa's most newsworthy couple. As is usual, most of them stuck together. Nothing haunts a reporter more than the fear of being scooped on a major story. The deadly telegram from the London editor reciting the opposition's front page exclusive has damned many a promising career. The way to avoid that was to hunt as a pack, corner the quarry together and share the meat. The procession of rented cars moved off down the dirt road toward Palapye and Serowe. Only the *News of the World* decided to go it alone. Outdistancing the others, the *NoW*'s man drove straight to Serowe to find that Ruth and Seretse had not arrived. Never lost for a story, the reporter cabled London: 'White Queen and Husband Disappear'. The story read: 'The journey from Francistown to Serowe should not have taken more than four or five hours. Yet, nearly 12 hours after their departure they had still not arrived.'

By mid-afternoon, however, the rest of the press had found them. Stopping in Palapye, they had soon discovered Seretse's Chevrolet parked outside Ma Shaw's. The low garden fence was about thirty yards from the house and Tommy Shaw had to marshal them behind it, threatening them with the police if they trespassed on his mother's property. Tommy then decided he'd better move into his mother's house as long as Seretse and Ruth were staying there. Fleet Street's finest looked a pretty untrustworthy lot to him. Seretse felt well able to deal with the reporters. He and Ruth decided they still wouldn't talk to the press, knowing that the British would be looking for any excuse to use against them at the judicial inquiry. An impromptu or distorted remark in the newspapers could provide the British with just the ammunition they needed. Ruth had long since begun to resent the newspapers. The tensions and anxieties that had developed when she had been under siege in London now returned. The pressure of being a national figure, watched wherever she went, was starting to take its toll. She felt she might escape it once in Africa but now the newspapers were back in greater numbers than ever.

That night, at about 2 a.m., Tommy Shaw was woken up by a rustling sound and a beam of light shining through his window. Some of the press, frustrated by being kept on the road, had decided to try for a photograph of Ruth and Seretse in bed together. Unfortunately for them, the first bedroom window they tried had been Tommy's. Ma Shaw's son, his gun in his hand, persuaded the journalists that future such adventures could prove unacceptably dangerous.

The following morning, Sunday, Seretse decided to take Ruth to Serowe for the day. Ruth in a pink floral frock, hatless and hanging on to her husband's hand, ran with him in a mad mid-morning dash through the press ranks for the turquoise Chevrolet. As they roared off down the arrow-straight dirt road to Serowe, Fleet Street, crammed into three hire cars, gave chase. At speeds touching sixty and seventy miles per hour, the powerful American car was soon outdistancing the pursuers. At one point, cresting a rise, they saw another car of reporters coming back from Serowe in the middle of the road. Seretse swerved into the scrub, the heavy sedan bouncing over rocks and bushes before regaining the road in a cloud of dust.

Soon they heard another noise, this time from above. Noel Monks, doyen of correspondents and now the resident journalistic master of Serowe, had taken to the air. Taking off from a flat field outside the Bamangwato capital, Monks and his photographer had been attracted by the clouds of dust thrown up by Seretse and his high speed pursuers. Monks ordered the pilot to investigate, and the plane swooped low over the speeding Chevrolet, the *Daily Mail* photographer snapping away.

Seretse now felt things were getting a little out of hand and that a tour of Serowe really wasn't on. Instead, he decided to show Ruth the house he had in mind for them both. It was in the southern approaches to the village and they therefore would not have to go into Serowe bringing their travelling circus of press with them. Sheltering in a friend's house opposite, Seretse showed Ruth the bungalow he had in mind. It was being built for a white official called Brian Murcott but the District Commissioner, Richard Sullivan, had said he would raise no objection to Seretse moving in instead. On slightly raised ground with land sloping down to the road, the large bungalow had a huge bow window and a shady and spacious verandah. As soon as the water supply was arranged, they would move in.

Once back on the road to Palapye, the race continued. Audrey Blackbeard, daughter of Serowe's schoolteacher and Joe Burgess's assistant in the Post Office was, that Sunday afternoon, in Palapye representing her village in a local tennis competition. Suddenly, roaring engines, blaring horns and clouds of dust stopped all play as she and everyone else watched Seretse's Chevrolet, pursued by the press, race around three sides of the court, skid to a halt outside Ma Shaw's, and Ruth and Seretse, hand in hand, charge through the garden gate and into the house. Moments later, the reporters in their cars arrived and took up their positions on guard outside the garden fence.

Seretse could not afford to be away from Serowe and the high speed chases were becoming ridiculous. He therefore took up an invitation from the Revd Alan Seager, the LMS's resident missionary, and his wife, to spend some time in their house in Serowe until their own was ready.

On Tuesday morning, at a more sedate pace, the press in eager attendance, they drove back to Serowe and the Seagers' house. The previous Saturday, on the morning when Ruth touched down in Bechuanaland for the first time, Tshekedi had packed three red lorries high with his possessions and had left the Bamangwato Reserve. True to his promise never to share Serowe with Ruth, he had accepted an offer from Chief Kgari of the Bakwena and moved into voluntary exile.

Once in Serowe, Ruth was greeted wherever she went. Spontaneous demonstrations happened wherever she appeared, women chanting and ululating, men clapping and cheering. When, on the following Monday, 29 August, the couple moved into the Murcott bungalow, a daily stream of visitors arrived to greet the chief's wife formally. Every member of the royal family who had remained in the Bamangwato Reserve, headmen from surrounding villages and other tribesmen waited patiently outside the house for their chance to welcome Ruth. Many brought simple gifts and all brought a smile. Outside the bungalow, church and school choirs sang songs of greeting and a huge banner welcoming Ruth was stretched across the main village road. The *News Chronicle*'s reporter witnessed one typical incident: 'When Ruth Khama stepped out of a Serowe store here today a group of women set up a welcoming chant. Soon thousands of natives were milling around the London-born wife of the chief-designate.'

That same day, 29 August, South African Prime Minister Daniel Malan had told a National Party meeting in the Transvaal: 'Will you be surprised if Seretse's subjects or any black man here in South Africa says "If Seretse Khama can have a white woman, why can't I?" ' The Khama's marriage was the most powerful argument in favour of apartheid, Malan said. A week later, the Prime Minister announced to another meeting that all South Africans would soon be required to carry identity cards showing the holder's race. This would enforce segregation and 'protect the European race'. In this context, he said, the 'marriage of Ruth Williams to Seretse Khama is nauseating'.

It is difficult to say how many of Serowe's whites shared the opinion of the South African Prime Minister. Those who did were faced with the dilemma that showing their distaste risked giving offence to the chief designate. That in turn carried the danger of being ordered out of Serowe. Most whites simply made sure they didn't meet Ruth, thus protecting their sensibilities without causing offence. One white trader explained her fears to young Maria Stoneham. Maria and her husband John had come from South Africa to start a garage business in Serowe. Her greatest fear, the white woman explained to Maria, was that the Khamas would want to send their 'Coloured' children to the white, traders' school in Serowe. 'That would put us in a right pickle as Coloured children are the last thing we want at the school, isn't that right, Maria?' Maria Stoneham made no answer. She and her husband were 'Coloureds' themselves as everyone in the village knew. Indeed her own children had been refused entry to the same school. The woman, apparently completely unaware of what she had said, walked off.

But there were many honourable exceptions to the rule of prejudice. The Shaws, of course, and the Blackbeards were friends from the start. Audrey's older brother Colin had been close to Seretse since they had both played together as boys. Other trading families like the Woodfords and the Watsons welcomed his Ruth with an open heart. Phineas McKintosh, too, who had demonstrated his colour blindness back in the 1930s and caused the great flogging crisis, was also warm and hospitable. An English couple who lived in Palapye, Alan Bradshaw and his wife, struck up a warm relationship with Ruth

119

and Seretse, a friendship which would, before long, cost Alan Bradshaw dear.

All these remained, however, in the minority. Even the Revd Seager and his wife, both close friends of Tshekedi, found it difficult to be friendly to the new arrival. After the six nights that Ruth and Seretse spent under their roof, Seager wrote to Ronald Orchard at LMS headquarters in London.

> We found them pleasant enough company except for the fact that they were late for every meal they had with us. But we did not really see a lot of them and there was disappointingly little opportunity for establishing friendly relations. There has been no formal welcome of her. There were demonstrations of welcome in the town but they were of an undesirable character although there was no real disorder.
>
> My own impression is one of disappointment. I had tried to convince myself that perhaps I was prejudiced against it and that it might look better when I saw them together. On the contrary it looked worse, not merely from the point of view of colour but from their attitudes to each other and to the tribe. They seem very much in love but completely unconcerned as to the effect of their actions on the tribe.

Far from being unconcerned, Seretse was at the centre of tribal affairs. In the Kgotla, at meetings in the surrounding villages, out at the cattle-posts, and in discussions in his new bungalow, Seretse was chief of the Bamangwato in every way apart from British recognition. Still refusing to speak to the press, he and Ruth were pestered at almost every turn. Ruth had endured more than a year of their persistence. Now, finally, secure in her husband's love and surrounded by the warmth of the tribe, she gave up her battle to suppress the deep anxieties that had grown up during the previous year. One day, at lunch, with Seretse and half a dozen others round the table, she suddenly felt the room swimming. She struggled to her feet only to fall to the floor. Serowe's doctor diagnosed nervous collapse. For the next few days she slept soundly, aware of nothing. In all she stayed in bed for six weeks. During that time she swore that she would never let worry endanger her health again. It was an important oath to take. Her troubles were far from over.

15

Loaded Dice

The Commonwealth Relations Office, meanwhile, was trying to rig the judicial inquiry. Having persuaded the Cabinet to set up the machinery to disqualify Seretse from the chieftainship, they now had to ensure that it did. The problem, of course, was that the sole objection to Seretse – his marriage to a white woman – was the one reason they could not give for objecting to him. Indeed, the Cabinet, aware of the political gelignite with which they were dealing, had specifically ordered that 'general issues of racial relationship' should be 'excluded from the scope of the enquiry'.

The Commonwealth Office could not even turn to Tshekedi for help because his objection to Seretse was also centred on the marriage which he maintained was against tribal law and custom.

The safest course was to try to get the whole thing over to what Creech-Jones called 'administrative grounds'. If they could make sure that the inquiry found that proper procedures had not been followed at the Kgotla, then it followed that Seretse had not been correctly elected by the tribe. But such an 'administrative' route was obviously not enough on its own. As an internal Commonwealth Office memo of 3 August said: 'We must guard against terms which might make it likely that the report would be so limited to procedural flaws that the only reasonable action would be to hold a fresh Kgotla; for, if the latter (as is not unlikely) came to the same decision as its predecessor, we should be worse off than ever.'

If, on the other hand, the terms of reference were widened to include more general issues on which to find Seretse unsuitable, it was highly likely that the question of his marriage would then crop up which is what everybody was trying to avoid.

Throughout the month of August, the department's senior civil servants wrestled with the problem. Noel-Baker had charged the two senior ministers below him to supervise the search for the right terms of reference. These were old Lord Addison, the last Dominions Secretary and spokesman for Commonwealth Affairs in the House of Lords, and the Commonwealth Office's very energetic Parliamentary Under Secretary, Patrick Gordon-Walker.

The latter now took a very close interest in the marriage crisis. As his officials passed various suggestions for the inquiry's terms of reference across his desk, Gordon-Walker rejected them all. He had taken the extreme view that the tribunal should be given no chance at all to make any recommendations. He was not prepared to take any chance that Seretse should be recognised for confirmation 'which would really put us in the soup'. It would be much better, he reasoned, if the inquiry were limited to reporting on 'the considerations that should determine whether Seretse Khama should be recognised as chief'. That way, he said, the Commonwealth Office retained all the options in its own hands and eliminated the risk of the inquiry coming out with exactly the wrong finding.

Gordon-Walker's suggestion was telegrammed to Sir Evelyn Baring in Pretoria. The High Commissioner immediately pointed out that the inquiry had been called under a specific law, Bechuanaland Protectorate Proclamation Number 32 of 1943. This said: 'The High Commissioner may direct a judicial inquiry to be held where it is alleged the Chief is incapable, unworthy or not a fit and proper person.' In other words, Baring said, the tribunal was obliged to recommend whether Seretse should be chief or not.

Gordon-Walker's immediate reaction to Baring's telegram was to suggest that a new Proclamation be passed to allow the tribunal to report just on 'the considerations' that should decide whether or not Seretse should be chief. Baring's reaction, supported by many in the Commonwealth Office in London, was that to change the law at this stage would immediately increase public suspicion of the whole exercise when the government was trying to pass it off as routine and administrative.

Baring felt that the tribunal would have to be allowed to rule on Seretse's suitability to the chieftainship and in this he was supported by Sir Walter Harragin, the High Commissioner's legal adviser and the most senior judge responsible for Bechuanaland. While agreeing with Gordon-Walker that the tribunal must, as far as possible, be prevented from recommending that Seretse should be chief, Baring pointed out that the obvious answer was to make Harragin the chairman of the inquiry. As chairman he would be able to reduce substantially the risk of it coming to any embarrassing conclusions.

'I feel that we have, therefore, to balance the risk of receiving a specific recommendation as a result of the Judicial Enquiry against either the disadvantages of special legislation or the rejection of the view of the Chairman of the Enquiry.'

Baring thus suggested that the terms of reference should be 'to report on whether Seretse Khama is a fit and proper person' to be chief of the Bamangwato. Baring continued: 'Harragin, who has seen all the correspondence, is satisfied that the above term of reference is adequate for our purpose.'

Whitehall agreed. It was also decided to charge the inquiry with investigating whether the Kgotla meeting was legitimate or not. If it was found to be so, then it would give the inquiry a more even-handed appearance while a new Kgotla could not be called since the inquiry would also have found that Seretse was not 'a fit and proper person' to be chief anyway.

All that now remained was to find two people to sit alongside Harragin at the inquiry. The obvious choice was Anthony Sillery, the Resident Commissioner in Mafeking, but he was thought to be too sympathetic to the Bamangwato and had, ever since the June Kgotla, been urging Baring to install Seretse as chief. Instead, his deputy, Nettleton, was appointed. The third member of the tribunal was to be R. S. Hudson, head of the African Studies Branch of the Colonial Office in London. All available information about him pointed to a sober person well aware of the implications of all the issues involved.

Thus armed with what appeared to be a fairly unbeatable hand, Noel-Baker went to Attlee at the beginning of September for his agreement. On 6 September, the British Prime Minister replied that he was satisfied and on 15 September Baring announced the inquiry's terms of reference. They were:

(1) To report whether the Kgotla held at Serowe between the 20th and 25th June, 1949, at which Seretse Khama was designated as Chief of the Bamangwato tribe, was properly convened and assembled, and its proceedings conducted in accordance with native custom.

(2) To report on the question whether, having particular regard to the interests and well-being of the tribe, Seretse

Khama is a fit and proper person to discharge the functions of
Chief.

When Tshekedi read the terms of reference he immediately
wanted to know from the British why there was no mention of
the marriage and whether or not it contravened tribal law and
custom. After being assured that those matters would be
covered by the investigation, he was then astounded to be told
'for the sake of convenience and clarity you will be treated as
plaintiff and Seretse Khama as defendant at the inquiry and you
will have the usual rights of a plaintiff in a civil action'. The final
subtlety that the British had dreamed up was to make it appear
as if Tshekedi was the whole reason for the inquiry. At one
stroke they had created the impression that, if it weren't for him,
Seretse might already be chief. Suspicion that the British were
being bullied by the South Africans was thus skilfully diverted
and laid at the feet of the deposed and angry regent.

Tshekedi was in no doubt that the tribe would see the inquiry
as an attempt by him to wrest the chieftainship from Seretse
and, far from trying to calm tensions in Serowe, the British had
succeeded in inflaming them. He immediately wrote to Baring
formally renouncing all his rights to the chieftainship in an effort
to undo the harm the British had deliberately done. He received
no acknowledgement.

The British were in no mood to be deflected from their
purpose. Throughout September, Malan kept up the pressure,
denouncing the marriage and insisting that, because of it, he
would soon be requesting formally the transfer of all the High
Commission Territories to South Africa. That was the only way
to eliminate further provocation, he said. Then on 31 October,
the day before the inquiry opened in Serowe, South Africa
announced that Ruth and Seretse Khama had been declared
Prohibited Immigrants. Neither could now set foot on South
African soil. The implications for Seretse were severe. The
British administration of Bechuanaland was headquartered in
Mafeking, across the territory's border in South Africa. That was
where the Resident Commissioner and his senior staff sat and to
where the chiefs of all the tribes had to come on regular
protectorate business. For Seretse to be unable to visit Mafeking
would make it almost impossible for him to carry out his duties
as chief.

The next day the judicial inquiry opened in Serowe inside a

large marquee erected in the middle of the village. More than 3,000 tribesmen had assembled for the hearing and they all sat in a vast semi-circle around the entrance to the huge brown tent, unable to hear what was going on but determined to show their support for Seretse.

In case the point had somehow been missed, Sir Walter Harragin began by saying that it was because of Tshekedi that the inquiry was being held. The inquiry's job, Harragin said, was to examine the doubts that had arisen in the minds of the High Commissioner and the Secretary of State about Seretse's suitability to be chief of the Bamangwato. 'As to why they should have any doubts, it is necessary to refer to a public declaration that was made by the Regent, Tshekedi Khama, requesting that a judicial inquiry should be held.'

This, of course, as the British well knew, was a smear. Tshekedi had called for an inquiry to rule on the legitimacy under tribal law of Seretse's marriage and thus the rights to the chieftainship of any children that Ruth might have by Seretse. Tshekedi had not suggested that Seretse was not fit and proper to be chief, rather that Ruth should be disqualified from being his wife. What was more, when he had proposed the idea of an inquiry to the British, they had said there was nothing further from their minds and that they could see no reason why Seretse should not be installed as chief.

However, the feeling already engendered towards Tshekedi was enough to make him frightened to come to Serowe. After Harragin's opening address, Buchanan, acting for the former regent, asked that the tribunal be moved to Lobatsi, a town 250 miles away and well outside the Bamangwato Reserve so that Tshekedi could give his evidence without any fear of reprisal. Harragin reluctantly agreed and suggested that all the proceedings should be moved to Lobatsi. After conferring with the tribe in the Kgotla, Seretse announced that as the tribunal was concerned with the Bamangwato, then Serowe was the only proper place for the tribunal to sit. What was more, he said, the tribe had decided that he should boycott the Lobatsi proceedings as a protest. Harragin said the inquiry would reconvene in Serowe after Tshekedi's evidence had been heard in Lobatsi.

On Friday 4 November, Tshekedi Khama stood before Harragin and the others to give his evidence. He began by protesting that he had never called for an inquiry into whether or not Seretse was suitable to be chief but only whether his marriage was legitimate under tribal law. He also resented, he said, being regarded by the British as the 'plaintiff' in the affair and Seretse designated the 'defendant'. 'With all respect, I do submit that this places me in a position which is not of my making. I had and have no desire to be party to any litigation.'

However, never a man to pass up an opportunity, Tshekedi then proceeded to mount the most effective case he could to prove that Seretse's marriage would be harmful to the tribe and that therefore the inquiry should disqualify Ruth as the tribe's 'queen'.

He began by asserting that the marriage flouted tribal custom because neither he nor the tribe had been consulted beforehand as they had the right to be in the case of the chief's bride. Next he said that the June Kgotla had been illegal since tribal meetings are not allowed to vote.

In passing he pointed out a 'weakness in the present system' of British administration of the protectorate. In the old days, before the British, a chief could stamp out rebellion by force when he first saw it. Since the British arrived, the power of the chief to take up arms had been taken away and Tshekedi had been forced to watch the rebellion fester and grow. 'I was therefore helpless and a state of chaos and anarchy has resulted.'

The ex-regent then, unwittingly, moved closer to the very heart of the matter.

> The duty of Seretse, if he wished to be Chief, was to have regard to the interests and well-being of his people. Had he considered their interests he must have realised that in the circumstances existing in South Africa his marriage was not in the interests of the Tribe and that it could only embitter the relations of the Tribe with neighbouring states. That it has already done so is evidenced by the attitudes of the Rhodesian and Union Governments. The acceptance of Seretse and his wife as respectively Chief and Queen of the Tribe will more seriously embitter such relations.

The next plank in Tshekedi's platform was that the British themselves would be the cause of ridiculous confusion if Ruth were confirmed as the chief's wife. The statutes and proclamations passed by the British concerning Bechuanaland distinguished between 'native' and British law and the different rights enjoyed by 'natives' and those of European descent. 'The impossible position arises therefore,' Tshekedi said, 'that the Queen of the Tribe is someone to whom native law does not apply.' Thus, for example, the native courts would have no jurisdiction over Ruth as the Phineas McKintosh incident of fifteen years before had demonstrated. Then an attempt to enforce 'native' law on a white had caused an armed intervention by the British and the deposition of the chief.

Finally, at the express wishes of the tribe, the British had banned the sale of liquor to 'natives'. Ruth, as a European, was perfectly free to buy alcohol. The result, Tshekedi said, was that 'the principle of prohibition is in fact being disregarded by the purchase of liquor by Seretse's wife and its supply by her to her husband and other natives at her house. Such a supply is indeed a contravention of the laws of the Territory – the Proclamation of April 4th, 1892, Section 11!'

Satisfied that he had deployed every argument available to him, Tshekedi thanked the Commission and concluded his evidence. The three commissioners, the stenographers, the secretaries and the lawyers, then packed everything up and began the long, hot journey back to Serowe.

On 14 November, packed once more inside the big brown tent, the 3,000 tribesmen again sitting patiently in the hot sun outside, the judicial inquiry reopened. Seretse, dressed in a dark suit, took the stand. From the first, he established a completely different atmosphere. Whereas Tshekedi had been suspicious, defensive and tense, reading, whenever possible, from lengthy submissions prepared beforehand, Seretse appeared relaxed and quiet spoken. He answered all questions put to him fluently and with courtesy and spoke without notes. He admitted from the beginning that he had married without the tribe's consent and that that had been against tribal custom. He understood why the tribe should be angry about it but he had asked them for their forgiveness and they had given it. This was far from unprecedented, as the tribe knew, Seretse said. The last three leaders of the tribe, including Tshekedi, had all married without consent. In each case, once they had obtained the forgiveness of the tribe, nothing further was heard about the matter. The question of the chief's wife, Seretse said, was entirely something for the tribe to consider and had nothing to do with the British. If the Bamangwato had accepted Ruth and forgiven Seretse, why should the British insist on punishing him? He had married his wife for love, he told the Commission, and the tribe knew he would never give her up.

When asked about Ruth's practice of buying alcohol, he admitted that he drank liquor but he suggested that he was as able as any European to decide whether or not to drink and how much. There had never been any suggestion from anybody that he drank to excess.

Looking directly at the commissioners he said: 'I claim the Chieftainship because it is due to me, and the tribe wants me. My morals are as good as any chief or regent in the Bechuanaland Protectorate. My educational qualifications are probably better.'

The commissioners then put to Seretse that it was impossible for him to carry out his duties as chief because the South Africans had banned him from entering their country and the headquarters of the British administration was in Mafeking. On average, they pointed out, the chiefs had to visit Mafeking once every six weeks. Seretse replied that it was a strange situation for the tribe and him to be punished and penalised because the affairs of their country were administered from another country which was hostile to them. As a compromise he suggested that meetings involving him could perhaps be held on the border itself, some fifteen miles from Mafeking, if the British could not be persuaded to move their headquarters into the country they were administering. After hearing evidence from experts on tribal law and history, the economic dependence of Bechuanaland on South Africa and other issues, the inquiry closed.

There had been no doubting the positive impression that Seretse had made. Quiet and imposing, often witty, he had answered all questions easily and openly. During adjournments, Ruth, recently recovered from her nervous collapse, had brought tea and sandwiches for him and the couple would sit quietly together in the shade until it was time to resume. Not one piece of evidence against Seretse's character had been produced. His legitimate succession to the throne had never been challenged and it was obvious that the overwhelming majority of the tribe wanted him to be chief. Even the London Missionary Society was no longer in any doubt about that. A. J. Haile, the LMS's Africa director, had been invited down from Bulawayo to give evidence at the inquiry. When he returned home he wrote to Ronald Orchard in London: 'I met and spoke to many Africans that I knew and there is no doubt about it – Seretse has a very big following and the feeling against Tshekedi is deep and bitter; his stock is at its very lowest.' Haile reported that families had been asked to give £1 per household towards Seretse's legal expenses 'and the money is pouring in'.

Sir Walter Harragin began to wonder if the judicial inquiry had been such a good idea after all.

16

Cover-up

The commissioners completed their report on 1 December and it landed on Noel-Baker's desk three days later. The report, as he turned the pages, filled him with gloom. Point after point made by Tshekedi had been examined by the inquiry and found to be wanting. On the regent's central claim that, according to tribal law, Ruth could never become the queen of the tribe nor her children heirs to the throne, the inquiry sided completely with Seretse. Acceptance by the majority of the tribe had legitimised the marriage and any subsequent offspring and, as the inquiry reported, 'we agree with Seretse that it is for the tribe, and not for the Government, to decide who is to be Queen of the Tribe'.

Similarly, Tshekedi's objections that Seretse had shown himself irresponsible by persisting in the marriage were dismissed as were all his complaints at the way the June Kgotla had been conducted. On Tshekedi's charge that Ruth supplied alcohol to Seretse and others at her house, the report found 'there is no suggestion that [Seretse] drinks to excess . . . and we are not prepared to find that Seretse is thereby unfit for the chieftainship'.

The commissioners included an attempt at a character analysis of the young would-be chief:

> It would be incorrect to think of him as an African well satisfied with a mud and wattle hut, and with crude sanitary conveniences. Though a typical African in build and features, he has assimilated, to a great extent, the manners and thoughts of an Oxford undergraduate. He speaks English well and is obviously quick to appreciate, even if he may not agree with, the European point of view. Thus he was an easy witness to examine, he immediately understood the questions and answered them without hesitation, clearly and fairly, and we have no hesitation in finding that, but for his unfortunate marriage, his prospects of success as Chief are as bright as

130

those of any Native in Africa with whom we have come in contact.

It was beginning to look to the Secretary of State that the judicial inquiry was digging a hole so deep that the government would never be able to climb out of it.

The commissioners then turned to Tshekedi's assertion that the marriage had ruined Bechuanaland's relations with South Africa. 'We are aware of the attitude that has been taken up by the Union of South Africa and Southern Rhodesia, for we have read the utterances of the Prime Minister of the Union and the debates in the Southern Rhodesian Parliament, and we are also aware of how dependent the Bechuanaland Protectorate is upon the good offices of the Union and Southern Rhodesia.' The report then referred to a recent parliamentary statement by Patrick Gordon-Walker. An MP, Mr Platts-Mills, had asked the Under Secretary for Commonwealth Relations: 'Could you give a solemn assurance that the attitude of the Government will be in no way prejudiced by the fact that Seretse Khama married a white woman? Will you convey that attitude to the Government of South Africa, which has looked with greedy and race-ridden eyes on this problem?' Gordon-Walker had replied: 'I do not think there is any need to give such an assurance. The Government of South Africa does not come into this matter at all.'

Gordon-Walker was hoping, of course, that the judicial inquiry would provide the clothes to hide the nakedness of such a lie. But it was not to be. In the absence of everything else, the inquiry was left with no alternative but to find South Africa as the sole reason for rejecting Seretse. 'The attitude of the vast majority of the European population and many of the Africans in the Union and Southern Rhodesia to this marriage cannot be ignored, and, in spite of the Under Secretary's reply, we have no hesitation in saying that in practice an unfriendly policy in the Union or Southern Rhodesia would have devastating effects on the Bechuanaland Protectorate.'

Similarly, the announcement from Pretoria that Seretse and his wife were Prohibited Immigrants made it impossible for Seretse 'to carry out his duties as Chief' since he was barred from setting foot in South Africa. He was therefore unable to visit the administration headquarters in Mafeking or attend any of its regular meetings. The cost of moving the headquarters to a town within the protectorate was estimated by the inquiry as £1 million and would take a very long time to achieve.

Our conclusions on the questions referred to us in the terms of reference can therefore be recorded as follows:

(1)   We are of the opinion that the Kgotla held at Serowe between the 20th and 25th June, 1949, at which Seretse Khama was designated as Chief of the Bamangwato Tribe, was properly convened and assembled, and its proceedings conducted in accordance with native custom.

(2)   That having regard to the interests and well-being of the Tribe, Seretse Khama is not a fit and proper person to discharge the functions of Chief.

The Commissioners then gave the reasons for their findings:

(1)   Being a prohibited immigrant in the Union of South Africa, he will be unable to efficiently carry out his duties as Chief.

(2)   A friendly and co-operative Union of South Africa and Southern Rhodesia is essential to the well-being of the Tribe and indeed the whole of the Bechuanaland Protectorate.

Almost as an afterthought, the report then added: 'His recognition will undoubtedly cause disruption in the Bamangwato Tribe.' The report totalled some 150 paragraphs yet it devoted only three to Tshekedi's allegation that recognition of Seretse would disrupt the tribe. In those three paragraphs, the commission conceded that any potential disruption had been considerably lessened by Tshekedi's decision to leave the Reserve. '[Tshekedi] has outstayed his welcome and . . . is at present the most unpopular man in the tribe,' the report found. Similarly, although Tshekedi would be taking experienced advisers with him, 'the actual number leaving the Reserve is small and in due course may be expected to drift back'. Nevertheless, though largely unjustified in the body of the report, the danger of disruption became the third of the report's reasons for rejection. Perhaps Sir Walter Harragin had hoped it would provide some small crumb of comfort for the Commonwealth Secretary.

The report concluded:

In finding Seretse unfit and improper, we wish to emphasise the fact that, should conditions change, as they well might in a variety of ways, Seretse Khama should be allowed to assume his duties as Chief. He is admittedly the lawful and legitimate heir and, save for his irresponsibility in contracting this unfortunate marriage, would be, in our opinion, a fit and proper person to assume the chieftainship.

What a mess! Noel-Baker was in despair. Harragin had obviously done his best and managed to arrive at the right conclusion but the reasons given had made the whole exercise a complete waste of time. It was useless for the commissioners to cite South African hostility to the marriage as the main reason for recommending non-recognition of Seretse. The point of the inquiry had been to come up with some other reason. Worse than that, by setting up the inquiry, the government would now find it very embarrassing not to be bound by its findings. The press and the British public were waiting to hear what it had discovered and what the government's decision would be in the light of those findings.

Apart from having gained precious time, the commission had landed them all in a worse mess than ever.

Noel-Baker wrote to his Prime Minister, Clement Attlee:

TOP SECRET
Dear Prime Minister,
I have now received the report of the Judicial Inquiry into the question whether Seretse Khama should be recognised as Chief of the Bamangwato . . . While it comes down against recognition . . . the report will not be an easy document to defend.

The report is an inflammable document and, I am afraid that if any hint of its contents got out before we are ready to publish it and announce our considered decision, a position which is already difficult enough will be made even more difficult. There is, therefore, something to be said for limiting the circulation of my [accompanying] memorandum to a very small number of people at this stage. You may think it sufficient that you, the Colonial Secretary and I should have it for the present. If on the other hand you wish it to be more widely circulated, I suggest that it might be well to recall copies after Ministers have read it.

Noel-Baker accompanied this letter with a summary of the judicial inquiry's report, giving its two findings and its reasons for them. 'I have no reason,' the Commonwealth Secretary wrote, 'to question the rightness of the second finding but I am considerably embarrassed by the reasons on which it is based. Publication of this report will, I think, be unavoidable and I confess that I should find it very difficult to defend in Parliament a decision to refuse recognition of Seretse which rested solely or primarily on the grounds mentioned.'

Attlee, also aware that the matter now had all the potential of a major political scandal, agreed that Noel-Baker's memorandum should be restricted to himself and Creech–Jones, the Colonial Secretary. The Commonwealth Secretary was now left with the problem of coming up with an alternative strategy before the end of January.

Far from the snow and freezing fog of London, Seretse and Ruth waited to hear their fate in the midsummer heat of Serowe. As the weeks had passed since the end of the judicial inquiry and there had been no announcement from London, their suspicions had increased. Though both felt that the hearings had gone well for Seretse and the commission had heard nothing that could disqualify him, both were becoming convinced that the British were wilting under pressure from South Africa and were searching for some reason that would allow them to do Pretoria's bidding. At the same time, they were also celebrating a secret. Ruth was pregnant and the baby was due in May or June – Ruth was in a muddle over her dates. The birth would clearly be an event of great political significance and would increase pressure on the British to allow them to stay. Whatever happened, both agreed that it was vital for the baby to be born in Serowe.

The British were also extremely interested to know whether or not Ruth was pregnant. Barbara Shaw, Tommy's English wife, was about the same age as Ruth and was also a blonde. She had been having regular medical check-ups recently and, early in January, had taken the train from Palapye to see her specialist in Bulawayo, Southern Rhodesia's second city. All went well and she returned home. Some weeks later, she returned to Bulawayo to be told by her doctor that minutes after she had left the surgery on the previous visit, a man identifying himself as a member of the British Secret Service had arrived. He had asked the doctor whether or not Ruth Khama was pregnant and, if so, when the baby was due. When told that the woman he had followed from the railway station to the surgery was Barbara Shaw and not Ruth Khama he appeared flustered and left. Clearly, someone had seen Barbara getting on the train at Palapye and had telephoned the British authorities in Bulawayo who had followed the only young, blonde Englishwoman to arrive.

As it was, news of the pregnancy reached the British soon afterwards. Although they could not find out exactly when the baby was due it increased the general sense of urgency in Whitehall to come up with a new strategy as soon as possible. Noel-Baker agreed with Attlee that the Cabinet meeeting of 31 January must be their deadline.

The inquiry's report had landed the government in such a mess that the growing feeling within the Commonwealth Office was that it should never be published. The only answer now seemed to be to try to talk Seretse into relinquishing the chieftainship voluntarily. If he could be persuaded to do the 'proper thing' for the 'sake of the tribe and all the people in Bechuanaland' then the situation could still be saved. He would, of course, have to agree to a self-imposed exile. It would be impossible to allow him and his wife to carry on living in Serowe even if he wasn't chief. If Seretse refused to cooperate, the British would have to announce that he was not going to be recognised, he would have to be removed from the Bamangwato Reserve by force if necessary and everybody would have to live with the consequences. The advice from both Sillery in Mafeking and Baring in Pretoria was that Ruth and her husband should not be in Serowe when the announcement that Seretse was disqualified was made. The tribe would be angry anyway at London's decision but the local authorities would have a better chance of keeping the lid on things if the couple at the centre of the storm were elsewhere. Sillery also recommended that the announcement should be made during the next few weeks. It was the time of the brief rainy season and many of the people were out in the fields tending their cattle and crops. Serowe was half deserted at that time of year and that too would reduce the risk of large-scale violence. Noel-Baker therefore decided that Seretse and Ruth should be invited to London 'for talks'. There he would appeal to Seretse's 'better nature'. To sweeten the pill, he would offer him money on a regular basis – as a sort of generous allowance – and government help to find accommodation in London and a good job. Clearly, if such a strategy succeeded, all the government's problems would be at an end. It wasn't much of a plan but nobody could think of anything better.

On 26 January, Noel-Baker put the final touches to a memorandum to be put before the following week's Cabinet meeting. He began by stressing that the judicial inquiry had recommended that Seretse was not a fit and proper person to be chief. He said that he agreed with that finding and then proceeded to list all the reasons that he had hoped the inquiry was going to produce but hadn't. He maintained that the June Kgotla had not really voted in favour of Seretse but had rather voted against Tshekedi. Furthermore, recognition of Seretse as chief would deeply split the tribe and encourage opposition to the Bamangwato from other tribes. Seretse was also too irresponsible to prove a wise chief. He had wilfully opposed tribal custom in persisting with his marriage and there was evidence that he had been drinking liquor.

Lastly, turning the inquiry's major reason into an afterthought, Noel-Baker said there was the danger that recognition would unite and inflame public opinion in South Africa.

As regards the judicial inquiry's other finding, that the June Kgotla had been properly convened, Noel-Baker said he wasn't sure that this was necessarily the case. There was strong evidence that it had not been a fair representation of tribal feeling and he said that the chiefs of several of the other tribes in Bechuanaland opposed Seretse becoming chief.

Noel-Baker, of course, was unable to call on the inquiry's report to support any of these views. In fact, on nearly all of them the report offered flat contradictions. Nevertheless, the Secretary of State pressed on, explaining that he now proposed to invite the couple to London for talks. 'I am advised,' he wrote, 'that Seretse has indicated in recent conversations that an adverse decision would not surprise him, but that he would in such an event be fairly hard up. The local authorities [in Bechuanaland] consider that he may agree fairly readily to go to London for discussion and accept the offer of a generous allowance.'

Finally, Noel-Baker asked his Cabinet colleagues to agree to what he proposed as quickly as possible.

It is of the utmost importance that the decision should be announced without delay since:

(1) Dr Malan has announced his intention to present a demand by the Union Government for the transfer of the High Commission Territories. It would be deplorable if the announcement of our decision not to recognise Seretse should follow this demand and should thus appear to be taken, not on its merits, but under Dr Malan's pressure. On the other hand, an early announcement might result in a demand for transfer not being presented at all.

(2) Seretse's wife is due to give birth to a child in May or thereabouts. Seretse is unlikely to leave Serowe willingly without her. I am most reluctant to leave them both in Serowe for much longer. An offer of the best medical attention in London in her confinement may prove a strong inducement. If action is not taken in the next two or three weeks it will, for this reason, have to be postponed until the late summer . . . The danger of minor disturbances and possibly of a major outbreak of violence increases as time goes on. For all these reasons it is imperative that a decision should be reached immediately.

On Tuesday morning, 31 January 1950, Noel-Baker presented his case to the Cabinet. There is no record of anyone challenging the absurdity of the Secretary of State's position. The last time the affair had come before the Cabinet, Noel-Baker had explained that Seretse must be banned from the chieftainship because, if he weren't, extremely dangerous consequences from South Africa would follow. A judicial inquiry had then been set up to disguise the real reason for disqualifying him but hadn't managed to come up with a single one other than South African hostility. Noel-Baker, nevertheless, was now listing a lot of reasons of his own, few of which appeared to be supported in fact, and was advising that the inquiry report be suppressed and that Seretse be invited to London and offered money to give up the chieftainship of his own accord. So important was the issue that Sir Evelyn Baring had been brought all the way back from South Africa to attend the Cabinet meeting. In spite of the facts – or perhaps because of them – Noel-Baker, supported by the High Commissioner, carried the day and the Cabinet agreed to invite Seretse and Ruth to London 'for talks'. The official Cabinet minutes recorded that in these talks, an offer of an allowance and other appropriate forms of help should be made to Seretse on condition that he should not return to the Bechuanaland Protectorate. Ministers hoped that it might then be possible to avoid publication of the report of the Judicial Inquiry. Ministers considered it was unnecessary to decide at the present stage what action should be taken if it should prove impossible to persuade Seretse to relinquish the Chieftainship.

Discussion closed with the Cabinet Secretary being instructed to recall all copies of Noel-Baker's memorandum referring to the inquiry's findings.

By Thursday 2 February, Noel-Baker, Gordon-Walker, Liesching and Baring had agreed a telegram to be sent to Sir Walter Harragin who was standing in for Baring while the latter was in London. The telegram contained instructions for Sillery, the Resident Commissioner in Mafeking, on how to go about inviting Ruth and Seretse to London.

Marked 'TOP SECRET AND PERSONAL' Sillery was to tell Seretse that Noel-Baker wanted 'to see him and his wife to discuss his future'. Seretse was to be assured that the British government would provide the finest medical care for Ruth while she was in London. 'If Seretse raises any questions about their passage back or the cost of the passage, Sillery should say that he will not be out of pocket over the journey. We hope that Seretse will agree to bring Ruth. Sillery should do his best to persuade him to do so.' Finally, the telegram said the couple should arrive in London not later than 16 February as Attlee had called a general election for the end of the month.

The next day, Sillery sent a telegram to Seretse asking him to meet him the next day in Lobatsi for urgent talks about 'the future'. The marriage crisis was now entering its most dangerous phase.

17

The Invitation

During the Christmas and New Year period Ruth and Seretse had broken their pledge not to see any of the press. The exception to their rule had been perhaps the most celebrated feature photographer in the world. Margaret Bourke-White, the American star photographer for *Time* magazine and *Life* magazine, specialised in touring the world to capture dramatic pictures of world figures. She had photographed Mahatma Gandhi shortly before his assassination in 1948 and had been most recently in the Soviet Union with Joseph Stalin.

Now she was in Serowe. Both Ruth and Seretse admired her work and since they were not obliged to give interviews which could be distorted and make a sensitive situation worse, they agreed to be photographed. The most striking picture which she took shows them close together, he some four inches taller than she, both looking to the right of the camera. Facing one light source, they stand in starkly contrasting brightness and shadow, their different skin tones forming part of the whole. Seretse's face is calm and assured, the eyes level and steady, a man sure of himself and his destiny. At his side, Ruth stands with her chin lifted aggressively, defiantly, challenging the world – or at any rate the British government – to part her from her love.

The day after receiving the telegram from Sillery, Seretse and Ruth set out to see him in Lobatsi. Sillery told them that, following the judicial inquiry, everything was now up for review. The Secretary of State was therefore inviting Seretse and his wife to London to discuss the future. Of course, travel and accommodation expenses would be paid by London and the best medical assistance available would be on hand for Mrs Khama during her confinement. In response to his questions, Seretse was assured that neither of them would be prevented from returning to Serowe if they so wished and Sillery, on behalf of the local administration, agreed that no British official would address the Kgotla while he was away. There was no need for him to give a written guarantee of Seretse's right to return and anyway he was not empowered to draw one up, and time was very short if the talks were to be completed before the British general election.

Sillery told them he had already booked two seats on the Flying Boat leaving Victoria Falls on 10 February. Seretse said he would agree to go on that day. Ruth said nothing. Sillery cabled Baring after they had left: 'They were neither very communicative and I could form no very clear estimate of their attitude.'

In fact, their reactions to the invitation were quite different. Seretse felt that if the British were prepared to give their word that they would both be able to return, that was enough for him. He could see no reason why they should not both accept the British proposal. Ruth, however, was deeply suspicious. She had never been involved in any talks before so why was her presence so important now? The British had never courted her opinions in the past and yet now her participation appeared vital. What were the British up to? Why had they not released the finding of the judicial inquiry? Why was a written guarantee of their freedom to return so difficult to provide? Exhausted after travelling more than 500 miles in one day, they both arrived back in Serowe late on 5 February.

The next day, Seretse called the elders together in the Kgotla and told them of the British invitation. He said he felt both he and Ruth should accept but he also told them of his wife's suspicions. The mood of the Kgotla was with Ruth. What possible proposals could the British have in mind that could not be put to Seretse alone? Ruth was a British citizen and, therefore, the British might be able to stop her leaving Britain once she went back there. Then Seretse would be forced to choose between her and the Bamangwato. The advice to their chief was that he should go alone. As a Bamangwato tribesman, at least he could not be stopped from returning. Ruth was safer in Serowe.

Sillery had now arrived in Serowe and was staying with Sullivan, the District Commissioner. As the Kgotla entered its second day, he cabled Baring about its course. In response to insistent demands for information from Liesching in London, Baring reported that the tribe were suspicious that Ruth would be kept in London and that the Commonwealth Office should prepare itself for Seretse arriving alone.

Then, the following day, 8 February, Sillery had brighter

news. He had invited them both to lunch and was able to report to Baring:

> Ruth was gay and excited apparently at the prospective journey and showed particular interest at talk of shopping. Seretse, engrossed in his own thoughts, had a poor appetite and showed curiosity about his return journey. We parried his questions. Ruth is the dominant personality. They are both hard up and sensitive about this. This suggests the possibility of His Majesty's Government obtaining their co-operation by emphasising security resulting from generous allowance consequent on voluntary abdication.

Sillery's cable lifted spirits in London. Perhaps they would both come after all and perhaps they would see the sense of accepting the government's money. Noel-Baker, meanwhile, was trying to ensure that the affair did not damage the government in the general election campaign that was just getting under way. Contacting senior MPs in the Conservative and Liberal parties, Noel-Baker told them of the great sensitivity of the matter and that the government hoped everything would soon be settled. 'I shall try to do nothing,' he wrote, 'that will help the press to inflame the matter and I remain as anxious as ever that candidates of different parties should not try to use it in the Election.'

Then, at five past four on the afternoon of 9 February a top priority telegram arrived at the Commonwealth Office.

SECRET. FLASH, FLASH.
SERETSE ONLY, NOT RUTH, LEFT FRANCISTOWN BY AIR THIS MORNING.

A few minutes later, a fuller explanation arrived. Sillery, via Baring's office in Pretoria, cabled: 'Ruth has jibbed at last minute. Seretse's supporters demanded written guarantee that she will be allowed to return to the Protectorate. Since I was unable to furnish this they have brought pressure to bear on her and I am sure against her personal inclination she has decided to stay.'

Sillery was undoubtedly trying to excuse his earlier misreading of the situation. Ruth, from the moment she first heard of the invitation, had no intention of going. Seretse, though reluctant to go on his own, had finally agreed to her staying and they had quietly said goodbye to one another that morning, hoping their separation would be short.

Baring was now becoming concerned that Noel-Baker's indecision was jeopardising the entire government policy on the marriage crisis. With Liesching's support, he had forced the Secretary of State to change his mind the previous July when, on almost the eve of the crucial Cabinet meeting, Noel-Baker had suddenly wanted to talk to Seretse to see if he could persuade him to relinquish the throne voluntarily. They had pointed out to him then that if Seretse refused to step aside the government would have put itself into a worse situation, having shown its hand and then having to impose by force what it had failed to achieve by consent. While Noel-Baker was angry that the whole strategy of the judicial inquiry had failed, Baring set little store by Noel-Baker's renewed plan to try to talk Seretse into quitting. Now that Ruth had refused to go with him, the chances looked even slimmer. As far as Baring was concerned, there was no alternative but to tell Seretse he would not be made chief of the Bamangwato and then to ban him and his wife from the protectorate. The political consequences would be extremely difficult but they would be as nothing to the implications of allowing the matter to stagger on. Trying to talk Seretse out of the chieftainship was a waste of time and, as would have been the case in the previous July, would leave the government in an even more embarrassing position when he turned them down.

Now, with Ruth staying behind in Serowe he felt Noel-Baker's chances were even smaller. With Seretse on the second day of his Flying Boat journey home – from Uganda's Lake Victoria to Luxor on the Nile – Baring telegrammed London with suggestions on how to encourage Ruth to change her mind and join her husband. 'I suggest that it would be wise to make this [allowance] generous and to increase it if Ruth joins him. On the assumption that they would both enjoy Government hospitality, I suggest a rate of £40 a month for Seretse and £60 if Ruth joins him.' He advised London that Seretse should be told that no discussions would be held until he sent for his wife. The alternative, Baring pointed out, was that he would relay everything to her, she would relay it to the tribe and would try to 'provoke demonstrations by his supporters'.

The Commonwealth Office, however, rejected Baring's advice. As an internal memo on the High Commissioner's cable stated:

'If Seretse refuses to send for Ruth and we refuse to talk to him until he does, he'll then go back to Serowe and we can't stop him. If he went back, could we possibly repeat the process and summon him (and Ruth) again? We should have got into a position at once dangerous and ridiculous.'

Ruth and Seretse's senior advisers, including Phetu Sekgoma and Goareng Mosinyi, were determined that the government should know that the Bamangwato were ready for any false moves. With the help of Percy Fraenkel, Seretse's South African-based lawyer, they wrote to Noel-Baker saying that they were pleased that 'our Chief' had been invited back to London for talks.

> But we regret that our Queen has been unable to come to you also as you wished. We were prepared to give our consent as the Bamangwato people that our Chief, accompanied by his wife, should come there to you, in compliance with your request, provided that the Bechuanaland Protectorate Administration gave us the undertaking in writing promising the safe return of our Queen back to the Bamangwato country after the proposed consultation had concluded. But the officers of the Administration refused to make this promise and assurance. It is for this reason that we have not found the way clear to permit her to undertake the journey to you.
>
> Our apprehension arises from the inimical talk from two neighbouring countries, namely the Union of South Africa and Southern Rhodesia, in the strong objections they have expressed against the marriage of our Chief and also from the traditional fear we have long had of both these countries. We as a free people deny that they have any right to try even to influence the eventual decision which rests solely with ourselves and your Government. Assuring you of our genuine loyalty to His Majesty and His Government, we are, Sir,
> The Bamangwato.

As Seretse began the last leg of his journey – from Sicily to Southampton – Noel-Baker's civil servants finished their final briefing papers for the Secretary of State's crucial meeting. There had been discussion for almost a week about who should actually attend. On 7 February, the Prime Minister had asked the Lord Chancellor, Viscount Jowitt, to sit in with Noel-Baker on the first meeting with Seretse. Sir Percivale Liesching,

143

however, had tactfully explained to Attlee that Seretse would complain that the government was trying to overawe him with too many Cabinet bigwigs and that the Lord Chancellor would be better left in reserve for any subsequent meetings. Attlee agreed.

On the afternoon of 15 February, Seretse's Flying Boat touched down on Southampton Water. Liesching had asked John Keith from the Colonial Office – one of the few Government officials in London who had actually met the young chief – to meet Seretse at Southampton and to drive him up to London in a government car. Liesching hoped that Keith would be able to assess Seretse's state of mind and thus give Noel-Baker some warning of the attitude he would adopt at the following morning's meeting. Also there to meet Seretse was a Sergeant Ewing from Scotland Yard who had been detailed by the Commonwealth Office to be his bodyguard. While Seretse found Sergeant Ewing very useful at Southampton in keeping the press away from him, he was not at all keen to have him as a constant companion. It was soon agreed that the policeman would return to Scotland Yard but that he would be on call if Seretse should need him.

Seretse chatted openly with Keith on the two-hour drive from Southampton to London. He told him that he and the tribe felt the British government were not considering the interests of the Bamangwato so much as the reactions of the South African government, 'and it's not my job to pull the Government's chestnuts out of the fire'. Ruth hadn't come with him because nobody trusted the government, he said.

At ten past six in the evening, the government Humber swept across Westminster Bridge, passed the House of Commons, turned right into Whitehall and stopped outside the Commonwealth Office. There to meet Seretse was Sir Percivale Liesching. After courteous inquiries about Seretse's journey, the Permanent Secretary began a little probing of his own. 'The Secretary of State invited Mrs Khama as well as yourself to take part in the discussions of these difficult matters because he believed that it was in the interests of both of you, as well as of the Bamangwato Tribe, that various aspects of the matter which affect you so nearly should be discussed with you jointly.' Liesching paused to allow Seretse to reply. The young man, relaxed in the office armchair, looked at him but said nothing. Liesching was puzzled. It wasn't as if they hadn't put him at his ease, offering tea and solicitous inquiries about his journey. Nor, indeed, did Seretse look dour or obstinate, quite the opposite in fact. Liesching decided not to pursue the matter but said: 'Well, I won't press you further to say anything on that point if you prefer not to discuss it, but I would urge you very earnestly to reflect upon it in the interval between now and your meeting with the Secretary of State tomorrow morning.' With that, Seretse was shown back to the government Humber. He was driven up Whitehall, skirting Trafalgar Square and South Africa House, and into Charles II Street just off the Haymarket. There, in Airways Mansions, the government had rented him a small apartment.

Back at the Commonwealth Office Liesching was debriefing Keith on his conversations with Seretse on the journey from Southampton. Next Liesching briefed Noel-Baker. The meeting was scheduled for 11.30 the following morning. Noel-Baker was not looking forward to it.

18

Money on the Table

The next morning Seretse was shown into Noel-Baker's rooms at the Commonwealth Office. The Secretary of State strode across the carpet to greet him, shaking him by the hand and leading him to a large conference table. Seretse was accompanied by Lord Rathcreedan, the senior partner in a London firm of solicitors. Percy Fraenkel, Seretse's lawyer, had contacted them and asked them to send a representative to the meeting on his behalf. Seretse sat at the table with Rathcreedan at his side and Noel-Baker sitting directly opposite him. The Secretary of State was flanked by Viscount Addison, the old Dominions Secretary now promoted to the position of Lord Privy Seal, on one side, and Sir Percivale Liesching on the other. Next to Sir Percivale sat Sir Sidney Abrahams, one of the Commonwealth Office's legal advisers. After the introductions, Noel-Baker said he hoped Seretse had had a nice flight and thanked him for not talking to the press both in Serowe and on his arrival in Britain. The Commonwealth Secretary then asked him why he had not brought his wife. 'It really is in both your interests that she be here. Is there any chance that you might send for her?'

Seretse replied by asking why Noel-Baker had sent for her. She had never been consulted before and 'to speak frankly, the Tribe believes that this is a trick on the part of the British Government and that they would have difficulty in getting her back'. Speaking quietly and reasonably, without a trace of anger, Seretse continued: 'We asked for a guarantee about her return but this was refused. This confirmed the Tribe's suspicions and, I must confess, I have come to share them myself.'

'Don't you think her presence would be helpful now?' Noel-Baker asked.

'That depends on the outcome of this conversation. Can't a guarantee be given now?' Seretse looked along the line of men facing him. Nobody replied.

Eventually Noel-Baker spoke: 'Don't you think it would be in

146

the interests of the tribe if you gave up the chieftainship voluntarily? If you did, we would advance you £1,100 a year as an allowance and we would help you find some suitable employment. We would exclude Tshekedi from the Bamangwato Reserve and we would do everything possible to obtain the best medical attention and accommodation for Mrs Khama during her approaching confinement.

'If you were to agree to all this,' the Secretary of State continued, 'all we would ask was that you keep quiet about it until after the General Election. We regard this as a friendly proposal on behalf of the British Government to diffuse a potentially explosive situation which threatens the best interests of the Bamangwato. While you are away from the Reserve, we would institute a period of direct rule and would promise to keep the whole affair under constant review.'

Noel-Baker sat back in his chair. Seretse, his voice still low and without emotion, leaned forward. 'The Tribe and I believe that the Government is refusing to confirm me as Chief of the Bamangwato because you are frightened of annoying Dr Malan and the rest of the South African Government. You are also frightened of offending the whites in Southern Rhodesia who, like the South Africans, believe in persecuting African people. It has been very difficult for me to believe that the Government would act like this particularly towards the people of one of its own Protectorates. Nevertheless, it looks like you would rather hurt the Tribe than annoy Dr Malan.'

Noel-Baker responded immediately. 'It is no part of our policy to placate the South African Government at your expense or that of the Tribe. I say that categorically and I want you clearly to understand it. I will tell you in strict confidence – and on the understanding that you will not quote me on it – that we differ greatly on many areas of policy from the governments of both South Africa and Southern Rhodesia. Anybody who follows our Colonial policy at all closely would realise that it has always been the intention of the British Government to do what they thought was right regardless of the views of either South Africa or Southern Rhodesia.'

Noel-Baker looked directly at Seretse throughout his speech. Those either side of him, emboldened by the Commonwealth Secretary's bravado, stared too at the young Chief. In the face of such unanimity, Seretse felt there was little else to say. 'I am in no position to take any decisions myself as the Tribe must decide everything in Kgotla. It might help us all to reach a decision if we could see a report of the Judicial Inquiry into my suitability. May I see a copy?'

Noel-Baker's eyes dropped to the note pad in front of him. 'I fear I cannot,' he said.

Sir Percivale Liesching suggested that perhaps the meeting should adjourn for a week or so to allow Seretse to reflect on what had been said. If necessary, there would be time for consultation by telegraph with Serowe. It was agreed that the men would meet again on Saturday 25 February.

Before walking back up Whitehall to his flat, Seretse said goodbye to Lord Rathcreedan. He had been very disappointed in him. Throughout the meeting he had said nothing. He had offered no comments on the offers made or the conditions attached. Perhaps he didn't understand anything about the case. In fact, Rathcreedan had been given hardly any notice of Seretse's arrival and had been unable to prepare himself for the meeting. Anyway, in the face of such big guns, Seretse felt he needed more support. He would have to send for Fraenkel and he wanted him next to him in time for the meeting on the 25th. There was a fixity about Noel-Baker's position, an unwillingness to find some middle way, a take-it-or-else attitude about him which depressed Seretse and made him fear the worst.

After telegramming South Africa to ask Fraenkel to join him, Seretse sent a brief cable to Ruth and the tribe saying that nothing would be decided for at least another ten days.

Liesching had asked John Keith to stay in touch with Seretse and provide him with a constant assessment of the young man's moods and plans. The following morning Keith met Seretse and by mid-afternoon a full account of their conversation was in Liesching's hands. The Permanent Secretary then immediately sent an account of it to Noel-Baker.

Liesching listed the points that Seretse had made to Keith:

(1) He could not make any decision on his own. He would lay himself open to the charge of having sold his birthright for 'a mess of pottage'. If the tribe wanted him to resign, then he would be prepared to do so.
(2) If the British Government did not want him to return to Serowe then they should say so publicly.
(3) He was going to send for his own lawyer as the people deputed to help him had been useless.

Liesching then continued: 'Mr Keith told me he was much impressed with Seretse's exposition of what had occurred yesterday. He felt that Seretse was a gentleman and had a lot of moral courage and was behaving very well here, especially in his attitude to the press.'

Noel-Baker picked up his pencil and underlined the words 'Seretse was a gentleman'. In the margin he wrote: 'I agree. And this is our best hope. But it is very hard to deal with him properly without a frank discussion of race relations in the Union [of South Africa]. Can we risk this?'

In truth the Commonwealth Secretary was becoming sickened by the whole business. A gentleman of high ideals he had wanted to resolve the crisis from the beginning by honest persuasion rather than subterfuge, intimidation and bribery. His distaste at what he was required to do had increased considerably when he had actually met Seretse for the first time. While one part of his mind saw that government policy to placate South Africa was unavoidable, another part was repelled by the lies necessary to carry it through. He began to doubt whether he had the stomach for it. Luckily for him, his release was not far away.

Sir Percivale Liesching was untroubled by such doubts. His political masters had formulated a policy which required execution. That policy had largely been formed on the basis of advice given by him and other public servants and was obviously in the government's best interests. What was needed now was a decisive plan of action to carry that policy through with rigorous determination. Sir Percivale now drew up a list of recommendations for the Secretary of State which he also telegrammed to Baring.

The obvious point to emerge so far, he wrote, was that Seretse won't make a decision for himself but insists on referring everything to the Kgotla.

To let Seretse return to the Reserve, even for a brief period, will be dangerous. He and the Tribe would confirm each other in resistance and any chance of eventually getting him and Mrs Khama out of the Reserve peacefully would be seriously prejudiced. It seems probable that if His Majesty's Government decide that he cannot be recognised (and maintain the offer to him of a conditional allowance and other help) he will abide by the decision and accept the offer. He will probably

149

ask to return briefly to settle his affairs but this must be refused.

Liesching wrote that the other complication was clearly Ruth's pregnancy. The government's information was that the baby was due in May but press reports were now indicating July. If a decision not to recognise Seretse was to be imposed, 'it remains to be discovered: whether Mrs Khama can safely be moved to England; if not, whether she can go to some place in the Protectorate outside the Reserve; or whether, until she can travel to England, Seretse should be allowed to reside with her at such a place'.

Noel-Baker did not reply to Sir Percivale's recommendations. The urgency of making a decision had receded a little with a request from Seretse to postpone the 25 February meeting to 3 March. Fraenkel had cabled him from South Africa that that was the earliest date he could arrive in London. Noel-Baker had no objection to that as, like every other politician in the country, he was now caught up in the general election. When it was all over, he would find that the Seretse crisis was no longer his responsibility.

On Thursday 23 February, the nation went to the polls. Attlee and his Labour government were defending a record which included the most radical period of social reform the country had ever known. The establishment of the welfare state with the provision of free health care for everybody and the support and maintenance of the unemployed, the sick and the elderly had dominated domestic politics since the end of the war. At the same time, the government had embarked on a course of nationalising major industries and services. Abroad, relations with the Soviet bloc had degenerated into the Cold War, India and Pakistan had gained their independence and Britain was trying desperately to disengage herself from expensive overseas commitments. By 1950, the British people had put up with shortage and rationing for nearly a decade. Far from German and Japanese surrender ushering in a new era of peace and prosperity, the end of the war had exposed Britain's economic exhaustion which was verging on collapse. The five years of Labour rule had been characterised by one financial crisis after another with American and Canadian loans just helping the country to avoid bankruptcy. It was, then, with very mixed feelings that the electorate cast its votes on 23 February. While the social reforms still commanded a majority of public support, poverty at home and the diminution of prestige abroad made many wonder whether the time had not come for the return of Winston Churchill.

In the event, the government scraped home with a majority of just seventeen seats over the Conservatives and the other parties. There had been a 3 per cent swing away from Labour to the Conservatives. Two days after the election, on Saturday 25 February, Attlee called a special Cabinet meeting to take stock of the new situation. Attlee told his colleagues that although all the results were not yet in, it was clear that the Labour Party would have an overall majority. The proper course, the Prime Minister said, was for the Labour administration to remain in office. It must, however, be recognised that, with so small a majority, life would become very difficult in the House of Commons. There would be no question of attempting to carry through any of the major controversial legislation which had been promised in the party's election manifesto. The government would have all its work cut out managing to get a majority on any vote. Attlee closed by saying that he would shortly be announcing his new Cabinet which would meet for the first time on the following Thursday, 2 March.

When the new Cabinet was revealed, Noel-Baker had been demoted from Commonwealth Secretary to Minister of Power. He had not been in the best of health and the Seretse affair had taken its toll. He hadn't fought Attlee's decision to move him. His place was taken by his energetic junior minister, Patrick Gordon-Walker. A much more decisive man with a less squeamish approach to the more ambivalent side of politics, Gordon-Walker had been closely involved with the Seretse affair for eight months. It was just as well, since not only had the Bamangwato moved to the top of his ministry's list of priorities but it was about to top the government's too.

During the political turmoil of the election, Sir Percivale Liesching had been busy. He had asked Keith to see Seretse again and the former had reported that the young chief was now depressed, determined not to bring his wife to London and determined – 'no matter what happens' – to go home immediately after the next meeting.

Sir Percivale Liesching prepared a memo for his new Secretary of State. He advised that 'we ought not to let him go back to the Reserve'. Liesching pointed out that although the British could not stop Seretse leaving England 'we can exclude him from the Protectorate. As Seretse is banned from South Africa and Southern Rhodesia, he may realise that it is better for him to stay in London.'

Sir Percivale found Gordon-Walker refreshingly decisive after his predecessor. The new Commonwealth Secretary accepted his advice immediately and both agreed that Seretse would have to be banned from the Bamangwato Reserve for at least five years. They both felt that by imposing this decision on Seretse the young man would be excused the charge of letting the tribe down. They would be doing him a favour by letting him off the hook, so to speak. This was an important point, they felt, and should be pointed out to the Cabinet.

Liesching cabled Baring with the new decision and then, with Gordon-Walker, they discussed it with Attlee. The Prime Minister agreed and it was proposed that when Gordon-Walker met Seretse on 3 March, provided that he hadn't had a dramatic change of mind, he should be asked to wait for a very few days more while the government prepared its announcement.

On 2 March, the new Cabinet met for the first time and discussion was restricted to the contents of the King's speech to be read out at the opening of the new Parliament. The very next day, Friday 3 March, at 10.30 a.m., the Cabinet met again. The first subject on its agenda was 'Bechuanaland Protectorate: Chieftainship of the Bamangwato Tribe'.

Gordon-Walker began by saying that he was scheduled to meet Seretse that very afternoon. Although his predecessor had failed to persuade Seretse voluntarily to relinquish the chieftainship, he said he would certainly try again. Gordon-Walker told his colleagues that although Seretse might agree to what the government asked, he was frightened of being seen by his supporters to have 'given in'. Seretse was likely to insist, Gordon-Walker said, that any decision to disqualify him should be imposed on him rather than that he should be asked to agree to it. The Secretary of State was therefore asking the Cabinet for authority to impose its decision on Seretse and to tell him that he was banned from returning to the Protectorate for five years. To soften the blow, he proposed that the government should say that they were not disqualifying him from the chieftainship but postponing making a decision for at least five years to see how things turned out.

In the discussion that followed, the majority of ministers felt there was probably no need to specify the number of years but rather to say that postponement should last for a 'substantial period of years'. Apart from that, the Cabinet agreed to Gordon-Walker's proposals without a murmur.

Thus armed, the Commonwealth Secretary prepared for the afternoon's meeting.

Meanwhile, Percy Fraenkel, Seretse's lawyer, had arrived in London and had asked the Commonwealth Office for a record of the 16 February meeting so that he could know what had already been discussed. Liesching told his officials to make an account of the meeting available but that it should be censored first. He told his officials to cut out Noel-Baker's remark that 'the United Kingdom differed greatly on certain things from the Government of South Africa' and his assertion that 'it was the intention of the United Kingdom Government to do what they thought was right regardless of South Africa's views'. These omissions should not be mentioned to Fraenkel, Liesching instructed. In fact, Liesching said, he should be assured that it was a full account of the conversation. Liesching also pointed out the changes to Lord Addison. 'The Lord Privy Seal will, of course, appreciate that only this version [the censored one] should be produced for reference at the meeting.'

At three o'clock on the afternoon of 3 March Gordon-Walker sat down opposite Seretse for the first time. He was flanked, as Noel-Baker before him, by Lord Addison and Liesching and with Sir Sidney Abrahams, the legal adviser, also present. This time, Seretse had the support not of Lord Rathcreedan but of Percy Fraenkel.

Gordon-Walker began by apologising to Seretse for the delay caused by the general election and then he asked him if he had made a decision.

'As I said at the meeting with Mr Noel-Baker, I must consult the Tribe before any such decision could be taken.'

Fraenkel then spoke up. He said that the government had given his client no reason why he should not be installed as chief. Instead of that, they were asking him to give up his birthright on the vague grounds that to do so would be 'in the best interests of the tribe'. Seretse was eminently suited to be the Chief of the Bamangwato and the tribe had given him their wholehearted support. 'There is no danger at all of internal troubles if Seretse is installed,' the lawyer said. 'I cannot say what repercussions there might be if he is not.'

Gordon-Walker replied: 'It is our information that there is in fact serious danger of dissension. If Seretse agrees with our view that he should resign voluntarily, we think it proper that he should be given a suitable allowance and such assistance as he requires in obtaining suitable employment.'

Seretse said the government's objection was ridiculous. 'I know of no previous occasion when a Chief has been asked to give up his Chieftainship because of dissension within the tribe. In my case, it is obvious to everyone that I have done more to unify the tribe than to divide it.'

But Gordon-Walker was in no mood for prolonged conversation. 'Please give me your decision,' he said.

'It is not mine to give,' Seretse replied. 'I must consult with my tribe and obtain their consent.'

Gordon-Walker then got to his feet and said he would now put the matter to the Cabinet and would have a government decision for him shortly. He was sorry, he said, for the continued delay but the matter would finally be settled very soon.

After Seretse and Fraenkel had left, Liesching ordered a full record of the meeting to be typed up and that evening it was sent to Attlee at Number 10 Downing Street. The next day Gordon-Walker and Liesching walked the short distance to Number 10 to see the Prime Minister. Having read the record of the meeting, Attlee agreed with the two men. A decision to refuse to recognise Seretse would now be imposed and Seretse would also be banned from the protectorate for at least five years.

Gordon-Walker then drew up a Cabinet memorandum on Seretse's refusal to resign voluntarily. In it he asked for Cabinet authorisation to tell Seretse that the government would postpone a decision on whether or not he should be recognised as chief for a period of not less than five years. He pointed out that although the Cabinet wanted no fixed time mentioned, some indication would have to be given in order to persuade tribal elders to volunteer to be part of any interim administration and to give the British government some protection from what would otherwise be continuous pressure to end the period of non-recognition.

A message was taken to Seretse asking him and Fraenkel to attend a meeting with the Secretary of State at 6 p.m. on 6 March. At 2.30 p.m. that afternoon, Gordon-Walker presented his proposals to the full Cabinet. They were accepted without qualification. Gordon-Walker and Liesching then went back to the Commonwealth Office to prepare for the final meeting.

19
Tricked!

At six o'clock, Seretse and Fraenkel arrived at the Commonwealth Office. Fraenkel had asked Lord Rathcreedan to come along with them. He was now much better briefed and Seretse's lawyer wanted as many witnesses as possible to what was about to take place. As soon as everyone was seated, Gordon-Walker began. 'The Cabinet has carefully considered the position now that you have refused to resign voluntarily and has decided that we must withhold recognition from you.' He paused briefly but Seretse made no reply. 'We must do that for a period that is long enough for the tribe to settle down and to see whether the present difficulties will disappear. This period will not be less than five years.

'On behalf of the Government, I would like to offer you an allowance of £1,100 a year on condition that you don't return to the Protectorate without permission. It is very important that you say nothing to the press about this until Monday 13 March, as we wish to make the announcement simultaneously in the House of Commons and to the Tribe in Kgotla.

'I would be very happy to arrange for Mrs Khama to be flown back to London, receive proper attention and make all the necessary hospital arrangements for her. You will no doubt have to offer her some explanation before 13 March and I would be grateful if you would show me first what you propose to tell her. Of course, it is a further condition of the £1,100 allowance that your wife also remains outside the Protectorate.'

There was silence in the room, all eyes on Seretse. Slowly, quietly, he asked: 'Am I to understand I'm being kicked out of my own country? That seems to me a very improper thing to do.'

'We can't allow you to go back for at least five years,' replied Gordon-Walker. 'We have the power to exclude anyone we please from the territory. The decision has been taken with great care and it is thought, on the whole, to be the wisest and fairest solution.'

Percy Fraenkel interrupted. 'The High Commissioner gave an assurance that if both Mr and Mrs Khama came to England, they would both be allowed to return.'

Sir Percivale Liesching leaned forward. 'May I be allowed to answer that, Secretary of State? When the Resident Commissioner was asked for an assurance, he made it clear that he could not give such a guarantee.'

After another pause, Seretse spoke, this time his voice betraying his anger. 'I'm well aware that the Government has the power to exclude me from my own country but I feel strongly that I have been tricked into coming here and now I'm not allowed to return. Why did you invite me here? I am bitterly disappointed at the way I have been treated. It was too much, I suppose, for you to recognise me as chief since I had broken all the rules and married a white woman. The protectorate is very small and weak compared with Southern Rhodesia and South Africa, but I didn't expect a British government to sacrifice me and my people to them. We have trusted the British since the days of my grandfather. This will destroy not only their faith but the faith of all the Colonial peoples in the integrity of the British. Why didn't you make it clear at the very beginning that you had no intention of recognising me?'

'We wanted to give you the chance to resign voluntarily,' said Gordon-Walker.

Lord Addison tried to mollify the bitter young man sitting before him. 'We're not talking about permanent exclusion,' he said soothingly. 'This matter will be looked at again in five years.'

'I am being excluded from my country on the vague grounds that my recognition will not be in the interests of the tribe. I can't believe this is the true reason. You all know there wouldn't be any disturbances if I was recognised – the whole tribe supports me. I've felt that there was something else in the background ever since you decided it was necessary to hold a judicial inquiry. I don't think there's any chance of me going back in five years or ever. You'll always find some good reason for keeping me out of my country.'

Gordon-Walker decided it was time again to deny South African pressure. 'We've done our best to look at the problem from the point of view of the best interests of the tribe. I must emphasise that our decision was not reached through fear of any attitude that the Union of South Africa might take up. I understand that this decision must worry and upset you and I hope, later, you'll see the position more calmly. We'll look at it again most carefully in five years, you have our word on that.'

Lord Rathcreedan then spoke up for the first time. 'I'm not clear what the reasons for not recognising Seretse are? Is it the possibility of disturbances?'

'This is the major reason, yes,' said the Secretary of State. 'There's undoubtedly tension in the tribe. Tshekedi is still a powerful force although he will, of course, be kept out of the reserve.'

'Tshekedi will be living next door to the reserve and I'll be 6,000 miles away,' Seretse said. 'Is there no appeal over all this? Must I just accept this injustice?'

'The final decision must take place somewhere,' replied Gordon-Walker. 'This has now been done and there can be no further appeal.'

'What happens if I decide to defy you and go home anyway?'

'We can't, and we won't stop you from leaving England but the moment you arrive in the protectorate you will be removed.'

Rathcreedan then asked how the government could take such a decision without giving reasons. 'Don't you have to show good cause?'

'I'm answerable to the House of Commons and not to a court of law,' Gordon-Walker replied. Turning to Seretse, he continued: 'What are your views on the return to England of Mrs Khama?'

'I don't suppose we have much option, do we?'

'We have the power to remove her, of course, but we wouldn't want to press it at the moment. If you insist that she stay where she is until after the baby is born, His Majesty's Government will respect that wish.'

Seretse said he would let the Commonwealth Secretary know as soon as he had decided. 'Where are we supposed to live while we're in England?'

'Well, we'll do all we can to help you find suitable accommodation,' replied Gordon-Walker.

'I must point out,' Sir Percivale said hurriedly, 'that as soon as the proposed allowance starts to be paid to you, you will of course be responsible for meeting your own expenses for accommodation.'

Fraenkel then asked, as he had at the previous meeting, if they could be shown a copy of the judicial inquiry's report. 'If it was a public inquiry, then surely the conclusions should be published?' he said.

Gordon-Walker got to his feet. 'I'm afraid not,' he said. Then, thanking everyone for coming, he walked from the room.

With Fraenkel at his side, Seretse caught a taxi back to his flat in King Charles II Street. Although he had, in a sense, largely resigned himself to the British refusing him, he was angry and upset at the way they had done it. It was deceitful and underhand to go through this pantomime of asking him back 'for talks' when all they wanted to do was to get him into their hands before announcing he was banned. On the way to his flat he stopped to send a telegram to Ruth. 'TRIBE AND I TRICKED. BRITISH GOVERNMENT TO TAKE OVER TERRITORY. AM BARRED FROM WHOLE OF BECHUANALAND PROTEC-TORATE. LOVE SERETSE.'

He then telephoned the major newspapers to tell them he was holding a press conference in his flat.

Within the hour, his tiny apartment was bursting with reporters and photographers. In deference to what he had believed was the British government's good faith, he had hardly spoken to a reporter for more than two years. Now a bitterly disappointed man, Seretse was determined to expose the deceit. It was high time, he felt, that the British people knew what sort of government they had elected.

In a steady voice he explained what he had been told. 'I have been offered an annual allowance of £1,100 if I will live in England and relinquish my claim to the chieftainship. I have refused the offer. I have therefore been banned from my country for at least five years.

'I was told that it was a Cabinet decision that I should not be allowed to return. I was also told that my wife could be excluded immediately from the territory but for reasons of health they would not insist on my wife's return here for the time being. Mr Gordon-Walker would give no reason why I should be excluded except that it might cause disturbances if I were confirmed as Chief of the Bamangwato.

'My tribe has not rejected me. Without their consent, I cannot give up the chieftainship. I was invited to come to this country for talks with an assurance that I would be allowed to return home. Now I have been told that I will not be allowed to return. I consider that I have been tricked in a way that I would not have thought possible by a government of Britain.

'From the very beginning when I was asked to come to England my people suspected a trick. For that reason they insisted that my wife should remain with them while I was away. At my meetings I was told not to say anything to the press until next week because they wanted to announce the whole thing simultaneously in the House of Commons and in Africa. I am seeing you now because I feel I have been double-crossed.'

Seretse said he did not agree that there would be disturbances if he returned but there might be strife if he didn't 'because of the government's trickery'. He said he knew that police reinforcements were being moved into the Bamangwato Reserve which meant that 'the government was convinced that its attitude isn't popular with my people. All of us at home have believed for a long time that there is South African pressure behind all this. The fantastic thing is that the British government believes that my white wife and I will be a disturbing influence in the territory and that the people who have asked us to rule them will revolt as soon as we accede to their request.

'I maintain that it was because the British government wanted to appease Dr Malan and to keep the Union of South Africa in the Commonwealth that they have done what they have. We are just a small, backward race and it is quite easy to deal with us. If any government can do anything lower than this, then I would like to know what it could be.'

Back at their offices, the journalists prepared their front pages. The *News Chronicle* telephoned Gordon-Walker at his home. 'This is all rather startling,' the Commonwealth Secretary said when told of Seretse's press conference. 'I do not think there is anything I can say at the moment.'

Noel Monks in Serowe cabled back to the *Daily Mail* the first reaction from Ruth: 'Nothing will shift me from my husband's house.'

Ruth had also replied to Seretse's telegram. 'Everyone here extremely distressed,' she cabled. 'Please advise if coming back at all.'

The next morning, 7 March, Seretse's story was in every newspaper. Lengthy accounts of the press conference and photographs of the young chief dominated the front pages and several papers also carried background articles on Seretse's marriage to Ruth and the hostile reception it had received in South Africa.

Gordon-Walker was annoyed and wrong-footed. He sent a request to Seretse to attend another meeting on the following day. The young man was clearly set on a blaze of publicity and he must do all he could to dampen down the flames. Next he sent an explanatory note to his Prime Minister, Clement Attlee. It was obvious that he would have to make a statement to the House of Commons by the next day at the latest and all plans of delaying the announcement until 13 March must now be scrapped.

'Our greatest difficulty, I think,' the Commonwealth Secretary wrote, 'concerns the question of publication of the report. The report itself is a lamentable document. The inquiry was public; it is known the report has been received; Seretse has publicly declared that we have refused to show it to him. We are likely to be very strongly pressed to publish it.

'The report contains so much explosive material that it would be far better not to publish it at all if it can be avoided.'

Gordon-Walker continued by saying that he had contacted several senior Conservatives including Anthony Eden and had got their agreement not to object to a statement that the report would not be published. 'If, therefore, we can restrain or withstand potential critics within our own party, it ought to be possible to avoid publication altogether.'

Attlee replied: 'I agree it would be better not to publish.'

Early the next day, senior Conservatives called at Gordon-Walker's office to discuss his statement to the House that afternoon. Following instructions from the Tory leadership, it was agreed that the Seretse affair would be dealt with in a manner designed to ensure 'that this should not unduly embarrass the government'. It was agreed that the Conservatives would restrict their criticism of the government to their indecision and delay and they would allege that there had been too much 'shilly-shallying'. In reply it was agreed that the government would say that the length of time taken showed the care and deliberation with which the matter had been dealt.

Hoping that at least one problem was solved, Gordon-Walker prepared to meet Seretse again. At 11.30 the young African was shown in, his lawyers at his side. The atmosphere between them was cold and distant.

Gordon-Walker began: 'I have read with the greatest surprise the reports in the newspapers yesterday. I thought that there had been a clear understanding and agreement between us that we would make no statements to the press.' The Secretary of State paused, looking Seretse in the eye. His adversary stared back at him but made no reply.

'The result of all the publicity is that I can no longer talk as freely as I have until now as I can no longer trust that our confidence will be respected. I can't, therefore, tell you any details about what action we propose to take or the reasons for it since I can't rely on you not passing on all my remarks to the press.' He paused again. Still there was no reply.

'Have you decided whether Mrs Khama should join you here in London?'

'I don't want her moved,' Seretse said quietly.

'Well, as I said last time, if that is what you want then we shall respect your wishes.'

Lord Rathcreedan then pointed out that Seretse would have to go back to the protectorate anyway. Tshekedi and he were becoming locked in a legal dispute over the ownership of Seretse's father's cattle and he would have to be allowed to go back to prepare his case.

Gordon-Walker said he accepted that but 'no interference whatsoever in the affairs of the reserve or the protectorate will be tolerated. We are not prepared to allow interference from any quarter. I really don't want to say anymore at present since I can't be sure it won't be twisted and given to the press.' With that, the Secretary of State indicated that the meeting was closed and Seretse and his lawyers left.

Three hours later he stood up to address the House of Commons. First, he sketched in the background of the marriage and the various tribal Kgotlas ending in June 1949 when the 'assembly declared their acceptance of Seretse as chief, notwithstanding his marriage'. He then went on to explain that the government 'viewed with grave concern the danger which recognition would cause to the unity and well-being of the tribe and the administration of the protectorate'. Having failed to persuade Seretse to resign voluntarily, the government was now withholding recognition for at least five years during which time Seretse would not be allowed to visit the Bechuanaland Protectorate. The House had been growing increasingly restless as the Secretary of State spoke. Now, one of his own backbenchers, the Revd R. W. Sorensen, the MP for Leyton in London's East End, stood up to interrupt.

'Is the minister aware that this matter is already having very grave repercussions in many parts of the world, particularly the Commonwealth? Can he give an assurance that the statement, reported in the press, that Seretse had been tricked has no foundation? Further, may I ask whether in this matter the minister has had any communication from the Union of South Africa?'

As Gordon-Walker had feared, the most dangerous opposition was going to come, not from the Conservatives on the benches opposite, but from his fellow Labour MPs behind him. The Labour Party had become increasingly opposed to all forms of racial prejudice and South Africa's apartheid policy in particular. Black people's groups in Britain and around the Commonwealth had welcomed the election of a Labour government for this very reason. To many in Labour's ranks, the decision to ban Seretse looked like a sell-out to racism. But Gordon-Walker had no alternative but to keep up the pretence the government had been following for nearly eight months. If he must deny South African pressure, then he would do it utterly and unequivocally.

'We have had no communication from the government of the Union nor have we made any communication to them. There have been no representations and no consultation in this matter.' On the question of whether or not he had been tricked, Gordon-Walker replied that the exclusion order would have been served on Seretse whether he had come back to London or not. The question of trickery did not arise since he was in the same position as if he had not accepted the government's invitation.

On that point, Winston Churchill, the leader of the opposition, got to his feet. The Tories had agreed not to criticise the merits of the decision, not to recognise Seretse as chief and not to press the Commonwealth Secretary to publish the inquiry report. But the question of whether or not Seretse had been tricked into coming to England seemed, to the great man, to offer fair scope for debate.

'Have we not, as it were, enticed this man to come over here to have talks on the whole question? Now that he wishes to go back is it not a fact that if he puts one foot across the border of his native land he is to be stopped by force? . . . Will the minister give full consideration to the point of honour which is involved?'

Gordon-Walker assured Mr Churchill that the decision had

been a very difficult one to take. 'I have done my utmost throughout to preserve honour between man and man in this matter.'

The attacks on the Commonwealth Secretary continued. The Labour MP Fenner Brockway asked if he was aware of 'the very grave concern among all sections of our community at the fact that a colour bar has determined the decision of the government on this matter?' Another Labour MP, Tom Driberg, asked Gordon-Walker where Seretse should go in order to be with his wife.

The minister replied that as Seretse was to be allowed for a short time to return to Lobatsi, a town inside the protectorate but outside the Bamangwato Reserve, in order to prepare his legal case, it could be arranged for Ruth to be brought there shortly before her confinement.

At that, Churchill returned to the question of trickery. Whether or not Seretse was enticed to London, should he not be reunited with his wife before any further action was taken?

'I could not give an undertaking that Seretse Khama could go back to the Reserve to meet his wife,' Gordon-Walker said. 'There are obviously very grave difficulties about peace and order at this critical moment.'

Churchill got to his feet again. 'It is a very disreputable transaction,' he said. Turning to the inquiry's unpublished report, he said that while the government maintained that the question of mixed marriages and South African opinion had not influenced their decision in any way, 'can [the minister] give the assurance that none of that was mentioned in the report?'

Gordon-Walker said he would not like to say anything one way or the other about what was in the report. 'It is only one of the many factors we have had to take into consideration in coming to our decision. It would give a disjointed appearance if this one factor of those we have had to take into account were made public. I hope, therefore, that I shall not be pressed to make the report public.'

As the debate ended, it was clear that the government had done nothing to allay the suspicions of the House. In fact, the more members thought about it, the more difficult the government's position seemed. There was widespread suspicion that the government was giving in to South Africa. If that wasn't true, then surely the simplest course was to publish the information on which they had taken their decision.

Outside Parliament there was immediate protest at what the government had done. The National Council for Civil Liberties said: 'We are profoundly disturbed at the government's statement. We cannot see any reason for this action other than Seretse Khama's marriage to a white woman.' Two thousand women who were attending an International Women's Day celebration in central London that afternoon passed a spontaneous resolution condemning without reservation the government's ban on Seretse. The next morning, Joseph Mitchell, secretary of the League of Coloured Peoples representing more than 20,000 British blacks, held a protest meeting. There, Leary Constantine, the famous West Indian cricketer now in London studying law, announced the formation of the 'Seretse Khama Fighting Committee'. Damning editorials appeared in newspapers from India to the Caribbean. In South Africa itself, the South African Indian Congress sent a telegram to Prime Minister Attlee telling him that the ban on Seretse had 'reduced British prestige on this continent to its lowest levels'.

In Johannesburg, *Die Transvaler*, mouthpiece of the Transvaal National Party, could find no words of praise for the British either. It dismissed as 'pure diplomatic eyewash' the claim by Gordon-Walker that the Seretse ban was not influenced by South Africa. The decision had been based on only one reason: 'Seretse's marriage to the former London typist Ruth Williams'. If Strydom's grand strategy of using British recognition of Seretse as the reason to march out of the Commonwealth had failed, the least he could do was exploit London's embarrassment to the full.

The government could find no consolation anywhere. Even *The Times* was unequivocal in its condemnation.

If the Bamangwato do not object to a white consort and the prospect of a half-breed succession it would not seem to be for the Imperial Government, pledged before all nations to respect the equal rights of all races, to overrule them in their own domestic concerns. There, if principle were to prevail over expediency, should be an end to the argument . . . No good can come of compromise involving injustice to individuals if its aim is to blur the outline of the truth.

Most popular support in Britain for Seretse centred around his enforced separation from his pregnant wife. Gordon-Walker had recognised this and he telegrammed Baring in Pretoria for advice.

> The question of Ruth is difficult. The least desirable eventuality is that she should refuse to leave the reserve. If she does so and insists on her confinement taking place there, then I think we must be prepared to let Seretse join her there under suitable surveillance in order to be with her for a few days at the critical time. Obviously this is a situation to be avoided if possible and I hope you may be able to do something to avert it in your conversations with Ruth. In general there is at present no reason to suppose that Seretse will be cooperative in any respect and we must shape our course on the assumption that he will be as awkward as possible.

Baring, meanwhile, was preparing for the difficult task of announcing the government's decision officially to the tribe. So difficult had things become in London that Gordon-Walker insisted on keeping in direct contact with Baring throughout his trip to Serowe. It was therefore arranged that the High Commissioner's Assistant Chief Secretary and the cypher staff would be on 24-hour duty, maintaining constant contact by telegraph with the Bechuanaland administration in Mafeking. There, officials would maintain 4-hour-a-day radio contact with Serowe.

For his part, Baring was delighted with the way things had gone. He cabled a reply to Gordon-Walker:

> I am most grateful for the firm line taken by the United Kingdom government. A major disaster has been avoided and the effect on relations with the Union Government has been admirable.
>
> I agree with you that we should avoid forcing Ruth to move before the baby is born. I too hope that she will join Seretse at Lobatsi. I will try to suggest this to her but am told that she is so perverse that a direct suggestion might have the effect of confirming her in her idea of staying at Serowe.

Baring then turned to a brief analysis of the Afrikaans press. All had welcomed the British decision, all had called for South African support for it, all, that is, but one. 'The editor of *The Transvaler* is obviously angry and criticises the slowness of the

UK government in reaching a decision. No appeal for support is made and this lends colour to the view that Strydom's followers, as distinct from the more moderate Nationalists, hoped that we would recognise Seretse.'

Things at his end were going well at last. He set off for Serowe in high spirits.

20
Midsummer Madness

As support for Seretse built up in London and around the world, it flooded into Serowe. Telegrams offering Ruth encouragement bombarded the tiny Post Office, often from the most unlikely sources. One, signed simply 'Victorian Grandmother', read: 'God will not seek thy race; He will not ask thy birth; He will demand of thee: What hast thou done on earth? Carry on.'

Ruth's parents cabled her: 'Keep smiling. Love from all. Chin up.'

Closer to home, her new friends, black and white, rallied round. The tribe had long since accepted her as its own and she and the senior figures, Phetu Sekgoma, Goareng Mosinyi, Radipophu Sekgoma and the rest, spent long hours deliberating the best tactics to thwart the British. Ruth's new friends among the white population also brought her comfort. The Blackbeards, the Woodfords, the Shaws and the rest all stood by her. Alan Bradshaw and his wife, Doris, became particularly close. They lived in Palapye where he worked recruiting local black labour to work in South Africa's gold mines and Ruth would often drive the forty bumpy miles to stay with them for the weekend. They had become firm friends with Ruth almost from her first night in Bechuanaland. 'Ma' Shaw, with whom Ruth had spent her first night in Bechuanaland with Seretse, was a firm teetotaller and would not allow alcohol in her house. Alan Bradshaw had taken pity on the Khamas and had invited them to his house for a welcoming drink the night after Ruth's arrival. All four had been very close ever since. Being British himself – he was born at Sharpness, near Gloucester – he was incensed at Ruth's treatment and shared his feelings with anyone who would listen. The local British officials soon began to feel his presence was 'unhelpful'.

Ruth's other great ally was Dr Don Moikangoa, the senior black doctor at Serowe hospital. Because he was black, the British would not allow him to hold the top post of Senior

Government Medical Officer which was reserved for a Dr Gemell. Ruth, however, refused to see any doctor other than Don throughout her pregnancy and he became one of her staunchest allies. When, within days of the government's announcement, Ruth received telegrams both from Seretse and her mother urging her to stay put in Serowe no matter what the British did, he reinforced the advice.

Finally, Ruth found support in the most unlikely source of all. The reporters, who had plagued her for eighteen months and had been largely responsible for her nervous breakdown the previous year, arrived back in Serowe in force the moment Gordon-Walker's decision was announced. Led by the *Daily Mail*'s incorrigible Noel Monks, they suddenly found themselves with a story bigger than they had ever hoped. Ruth, forcibly separated from her husband, the white queen of the tribe, pregnant and defiant, was irresistible copy. On her side, she suddenly recognised a community of purpose. The way to attack the government now was through public opinion and the way to British hearts was through Noel Monks and his colleagues.

Noel was the first to be allowed into Ruth's home. He had a way of suggesting what he felt were improvements to what Ruth had to say and, as long as she agreed, that was what he filed. As a result, while the sentiments were hers, they tended to appear clothed in unusually racy language. On 8 March, the morning of the first parliamentary debate on the marriage crisis, the *Daily Mail* carried a Monks' piece from Serowe headlined: 'Ruth: They'll Have to Carry Me Out of Here – Feet First'. The story underneath purported to be Ruth's first reaction to what had happened:

> It's like a bad dream. And to think they nearly got me there too. It makes one ashamed of being British.
>
> No colour bar and British democracy – my eye! Queen Victoria would turn in her grave. It was my husband's grandfather who sought Queen Victoria's protection. A precious lot of protection the Bamangwato are being given now. Those little nitwits in the administration who have been hoping and praying that I would get fed up in a few weeks and scamper off back home to London are going to be disappointed. I'll stick here till they carry me out feet first.

Noel Monks knew a good story when he saw one. With support

at every hand, Ruth was feeling strong and determined when she and the tribe received a message from District Commissioner Sullivan that Baring wished to summon a Kgotla to explain the government's policy to the tribe. The High Commissioner would be arriving in Serowe in five days time on 13 March.

Early on the 12th Baring's party left for Serowe. It included Nicholas Monsarrat, the Director of the United Kingdom Information Office based in Johannesburg. Aged 40, Monsarrat had joined the Diplomatic Service after serving throughout the war in the Royal Naval Volunteer Reserve. By the war's end, he had started to write novels based on his wartime adventures at sea and had already published three books by 1950, one of which, *Three Corvettes*, had sold well. By the time he boarded the train for Bechuanaland, the manuscript of perhaps his most famous novel, *The Cruel Sea*, was already with the publisher. Many people were soon to wonder whether it was his fascination for the sea that made him particularly insensitive to the crisis now developing on the edge of the Kalahari Desert.

As Baring's entourage made its way to Serowe, Ruth and Phetu Sekgoma decided that Baring really had no right to address the tribe. Apart from promising his safe return, Sillery, the Resident Commissioner, had assured Seretse that no British government official would address a Kgotla in his absence. What was more, there was nothing that Baring could tell the Bamangwato that they didn't know already. At a meeting with senior tribesmen, it was agreed that the Bamangwato should boycott the Kgotla. If it were successful, Ruth was sure it would provide a tremendous boost to Seretse's morale. So that the British could not implicate her in the boycott, Ruth moved to Palapye to stay with Doris Bradshaw and Alan moved up to Serowe to help keep an eye on things.

Early on the morning of 13 March, Baring and his party arrived at the house of District Commissioner Sullivan. Down in the village, Serowe's whites were gathering, seating themselves on chairs specially provided to one side of the Kgotla ground. Next to them stood the press, there to report the High Commissioner's message to the tribe. Around the perimeter stood several dozen policemen under the command, as they had been the previous June, of Major Langley, now newly promoted to Colonel and the most senior policeman in the entire protectorate.

By 10.30 a.m., the time the Kgotla was due to start, no more than six Bamangwato had appeared. Since dawn Phetu Sekgoma had posted small groups around Serowe telling those arriving for the Kgotla that the meeting had not been called by their chief and that therefore they shouldn't go. Colonel Langley and his police had been watching them very closely for any signs of intimidation but had found none.

Back at the Kgotla ground, Phetu Sekgoma delivered a message to the press explaining that the tribe was boycotting the meeting. Only a chief had the authority to call a Kgotla and, anyway, Sir Evelyn had nothing to tell them that they didn't know already. Monsarrat, acting as Baring's Press Officer, also had a message for the journalists. Seretse's supporters were nothing better than thugs who had been going round the village violently threatening all those who dared to approach the Kgotla. It was a disgraceful affair, he said, and underlined why the British government had taken the action they had in banning Seretse from the place.

Throughout these press briefings, the fifty or so whites had been sitting bored under the climbing sun. For nearly an hour they had been waiting for the Kgotla to start and the red-faced mariner's rage provided welcome entertainment.

Baring then ordered policemen to deliver personal instructions to the twenty senior members of the tribe requesting their immediate attendance. The police could only find twelve of them who politely accepted the instructions and carried on sitting comfortably in the cool of their huts. Phetu had another message delivered to the press saying that the twelve tribesmen would attend the Kgotla 'only if we are handcuffed and dragged there'. Finally, Baring admitted defeat. Monsarrat was instructed to tell the white traders to go back to their shops and the reporters to come up the hill to Sullivan's house for a press conference.

Unlike the strident and fuming Monsarrat, Baring appeared urbane and suave, refusing to begin until he was sure everybody had a drink. He then began by explaining that the history of the Bamangwato was one of quarrels and feuds with continual disruptions to tribal life. 'We had to stop the development of one of the biggest and worst dynastic feuds that there had ever been. We want the tribe to have a chief who is responsible and wise.' The administration of the reserve would henceforward be carried out directly by the District Commissioner taking the place of the chief. He would be assisted by tribal leaders who had already been invited to form an advisory council.

One journalist then asked the High Commissioner if South Africa had had any part in the banishment. Baring replied: 'The Union Government has taken no action, except banning Seretse Khama from its territory. The Union Government has made no approaches to the British Government.'

John Redfern of the *Manchester Guardian* then asked Baring to comment on Monsarrat's allegations that the Kgotla boycott had been the result of widespread and violent intimidation. Baring said the Chief of Police was better qualified to answer that and Colonel Langley stepped forward. 'I have had no incidents and no violence reported to me, sir. There has been no intimidation apart from verbal persuasion.' Baring then declared the conference closed and Monsarrat, still red-faced, walked quickly into the District Commissioner's house.

As the reporters walked down the hill, Phetu Sekgoma sent a messenger to give them a statement issued on behalf of all the tribe. The Bamangwato, the statement said, would now follow a policy of non-cooperation with the British. The annual tax of £1.8s due from every male over 18 would no longer be paid. The British decision to impose direct rule contradicted the agreement between Khama and Queen Victoria when the protectorate had been first established. The tribe was angry that the District Commissioner had issued invitations for senior tribesmen to join an advisory council. 'The administration can rest assured that it will not find such quislings among the Bamangwato to accept such office.' The statement went on to appeal to 'the British public, the non-European races in the world and all men of good will to prevail upon the British government to let Seretse Khama return as chief of the tribe. Seretse Khama's marriage is a matter that only concerns the Bamangwato and to think the tribe might change its mind is midsummer madness'.

Baring had been shocked at the depth of the tribe's resentment. Before leaving Serowe for Pretoria he cabled Gordon-Walker in London. 'I regret to inform you that owing to successful action by Seretse's followers I was unable to hold Kgotla today. Considerable numbers of people were in Serowe from the Reserve but were dissuaded by peaceful picketing and argument from attending. I therefore cancelled meeting. I was unable to see Ruth as she left Serowe last night.'

He was now genuinely concerned for the first time about the

possibility of rioting in Serowe. Within twenty-four hours of his departure he was even more worried after gangs of youths in Serowe had tried to burn the house of Dr S. M. Molema, a friend and cousin of Tshekedi, threatening to kill him if he didn't leave the village. Baring ordered an immediate review of police forces in the protectorate. Normally, there were only twenty-five policemen in the Bamangwato Reserve, a number which in an emergency could be increased to ninety-seven, seventeen whites and eighty blacks. During the recent disturbances, 179 black policemen and forty whites had been brought into Serowe, having been transferred from Basutoland, Swaziland and Southern Rhodesia. Sillery, the Resident Commissioner, now told Baring he would need another fifty brought in to ensure peace and stability. In London, at Baring's request, Liesching organised Southern Rhodesian armoured cars to be driven down to the border and to wait in reserve. In Pretoria, Baring ordered his officials to draw up plans to accommodate an airlift of British troops into Serowe should they be needed. The High Commissioner's fear was that South Africa might take advantage of any breakdown in law and order in the protectorate to intervene herself. As Baring wrote to Liesching: 'Any means, including flying troops in, should be used to quell any disturbances. If they are not quelled immediately, South Africa will have no hesitation in sending troops herself.'

Baring felt a more experienced District Commissioner than Sullivan was needed in Serowe and he arranged for the transfer of the Resident Commissioner of Swaziland, Forbes McKenzie, to take over from Sullivan at the beginning of April.

Finally, Baring decided to act on the complaints he had heard from the local officials about Ruth's friend Alan Bradshaw. On his way back to Pretoria, he stopped off at the Chamber of Mines in Johannesburg and asked for Bradshaw's immediate transfer out of Bechuanaland. As he explained in a telegram to Liesching:

An unsavoury aspect of the affair is the participation of certain local Europeans. The most important is the representative of the native recruiting corporation. For several years the administration has made repeated complaints against him. On Seretse's arrival, he became very friendly with him and his wife and, more recently, I am told by officials and journalists, he has participated very actively in anti-Government activities including the organisation of the Kgotla boycott. When passing through Johannesburg, I asked formally for his transfer and was told that this would be arranged at once.

Indeed it was. On 16 March, two days after Baring's visit to the Chamber of Mines, Bradshaw received immediate transfer orders. Six days later, Labour MP Tom Driberg asked Gordon-Walker whether the government had had a hand in Bradshaw's sudden transfer. The Secretary of State cabled Baring for advice on how he should reply. The High Commissioner told him that since his request to the Chamber of Mines had been in the strictest confidence, he could safely deny any government involvement in the affair.

Baring's high spirits of just a few days ago had now entirely left him. The bitterness of the tribe was far more intense than he had ever imagined and the danger of riot far greater. As Baring sat in Pretoria, his officials in Serowe were performing the thankless task of walking round the village's streets handing out typed copies of the speech the High Commissioner would have delivered had the Kgotla been held. To a man, the tribesmen screwed the sheets of paper up into balls and threw them aside without reading them.

Even more ominously, Baring knew the government in London was starting to totter beneath the avalanche of hostile public opinion that had descended upon it. If Whitehall's policy were now to go into reverse, Baring believed the danger would be incalculable.

21
Shattered Faith

On the night before Baring arrived in Serowe to try to address the Kgotla, the Seretse Khama Fighting Committee held a mass meeting in central London. More than a thousand people crammed into a hall in Victoria. Some 300 were white and English, the rest, many of them students, were black and from every part of British colonial Africa and the Caribbean.

Seretse himself arrived late. The previous week had taken its toll and he was tired and depressed. The prospect of endless exile from his homeland and the tribe together with the separation from Ruth had sapped his resilience. What he regarded as the British government's treachery had saddened him as well as making him angry and he felt cold and lonely, lost in an English winter far from sunny Serowe.

As he entered the hall, the crowd stood, clapping and cheering him as he made his way to a small platform to sit next to the chairman, Leary Constantine. But even such exuberance could not lift his spirits. He raised his hand to quieten the cheers and said: 'I am happy that even though this action has been taken by the British government, the British people, with their sense of fair play, have not associated themselves with it.' As he tried to carry on, his voice broke and faltered and, unable to speak, he sat down. Leary Constantine broke the silence that followed. He told the audience that all the major political parties had been invited to send official representatives to the meeting. Only the Communist Party, however, had managed to send someone. At that, large sections of the crowd cheered.

Constantine continued that the Conservatives had said they would be glad to send a speaker to the next meeting (loud jeers and boos), the Liberal Party had said the notice had been too short to find someone (jeers and boos again) and the Labour Party had said it could not oppose a government decision (hoots of derision).

Seretse had now regained a little of his strength and once

175

more he climbed to his feet, the crowd, quiet now, watching him. 'The people back home will be very glad to know you have taken up the fight for them and for yourselves.' Before the applause had died down, Seretse had left the hall and was in a taxi on his way back to his Haymarket flat.

The Revd Sorensen, the Labour MP for Leyton who had attacked Gordon-Walker in the House of Commons debate the previous week, told the crowd that he was there in his personal capacity and not as a representative of the Labour Party. He said that many MPs in all parties were deeply shocked at what the government had done. He said no one was in any doubt that the government's real fear had been that recognition of Seretse would lead to serious repercussions from South Africa. 'What the government has done will intensify suspicions about the white man's real intentions throughout Africa.'

Mr Sorensen was to have the distinction of being the only speaker of the night to stick to the point. For everyone else there, but particularly the black people from Britain's colonies, the Seretse affair was the catalyst that allowed the smouldering resentment about the way they felt they were treated in their own territories to burst into flames. Speaker after speaker began by denouncing the government's treatment of Seretse and then moved on to what they described as the injustice in their own lands. The loudest cheers of the night came for references to the guerrilla movements fighting for independence in Malaya and for the victorious advances of the Communist forces in China and Vietnam. Many expressed their sadness that the injustice to Seretse had been committed by a Labour government, saying how Attlee's election victory in 1945 had given blacks great hope for a fairer future. Now, it appeared, the Labour Party was no better than the Tories.

At the same time, black organisations from all over the empire were protesting to the government. Black trade unions in Jamaica and Nigeria passed condemnatory resolutions. The Trades Union Council of British Guiana telegrammed the government: 'We consider disgraceful discriminatory conduct likely to shatter faith in concept of British justice and undermine unquestioned spirit of loyalty to British Crown.' One local paper in Calcutta commented: 'For every white man placated in South Africa, a hundred Indians and Pakistanis have been affronted. The Labour government has created for itself a situation for which Moscow might have prayed.'

The West African Students' Club at Oxford University wrote to Prime Minister Attlee:

British Africa is divided between an independent state which believes in the colour bar and a number of smaller states in which the colour bar is repudiated. We cannot overlook this issue. We are convinced it is very relevant to the present question and we deplore a decision which shirks this issue. Only a revelation of all the facts can allay our suspicions. We cannot see how action of this kind can inspire the confidence of Colonial peoples in Great Britain or help them to see any more clearly the essential difference between the methods of democracy and those of totalitarianism.

It was starting to look to many in the Commonwealth Office that the next generation of African leaders – then studying in England – were being soured irrevocably in their opinion of the mother country. If the action to ban Seretse had been taken, in part, to preserve the existing Commonwealth, it looked increasingly as if it was to be at the expense of any future one.

Even the London Missionary Society, until now a stalwart supporter of government policy in the affair, was now receiving so many complaints itself that Ronald Orchard, its director, wrote to Gordon-Walker.

Possibly it is too late now to check much of the rising tide of passion and prejudice, but a clear, factual and comprehensive statement from you which enabled the public to feel confident that all the factors leading to the decision had been made known, might at least enable responsible opinion to present a more balanced picture of the whole matter to those, both African and European, who are at present convinced only that Seretse has been victimised and a small African people sacrificed to political expediency.

That same day, Orchard set out his feeling to A. J. Haile, his African Regional Director in Bulawayo.

While I am prepared to accept the Government's assurance that its decision was not taken out of regard for the Union, most folk won't believe that and the general effect of it all makes me wonder how long the British Government can go on hunting with the Union hounds while running with the hare of the trust of Africans in Colonial territories. In many recent instances, we appear to lose African friendship without gaining that of the Union.

Haile himself was writing that same day to Orchard, furious with the 'shabby way Gordon-Walker has handled everything. Why hasn't the inquiry been published? Why won't they come clean? Why trick Seretse into going back? They are alienating black opinion around the world.'

As the pressure on the LMS increased, Orchard finally issued a statement condemning the government's handling of the affair and pointing out the widespread belief that Seretse's exile was because of his marriage to a white woman.

These suspicions, though possibly unwarranted, have had the worst possible effect on the Africans' trust in the integrity of the British administration and on racial relations throughout the Commonwealth. The LMS urges His Majesty's Government to declare it to be their policy to oppose such racial discrimination in any of the territories for which it is responsible.

Finally, the society called for Seretse to be returned to Serowe. 'The Government says there would be danger in that but wouldn't there be more danger in his non-return?' In an effort to turn back the tide of protest, the Colonial Office sent briefing papers trying to explain the government's position on Seretse Khama to officials throughout Britain's Colonies. One cable was circulated to the Bahamas, Barbados, Bermuda, British Guiana, British Honduras, Cyprus, Fiji and Western Pacific, Gambia, Gold Coast, Hong Kong, Jamaica, Kenya, Malaya, Mauritius, Nigeria, Northern Rhodesia, Nyasaland, Sierra Leone, Singapore, Tanganyika, Trinidad, Uganda, the Windward Islands and Zanzibar.

On 17 March, the Seretse Khama Fighting Committee met Gordon-Walker. Leary Constantine and three others representing black organisations in Africa and the West Indies began by telling the Secretary of State that he should be in no doubt about the great anger of black people in Britain and around the world. There had even been some extremists, they warned, who were urging the shooting down of British officials throughout the

Colonies. They continued that they had been deeply disappointed that the Labour government had done nothing to change what they felt was oppressive Colonial rule. At the same time, the government had appeared to support a whites-only Australia policy, racial segregation in South Africa and discrimination in the United Kingdom. When Gordon-Walker protested that there was no racial discrimination in Britain, Leary Constantine said that he and his wife had been racially insulted several times. Then he took out of his pocket a concise encyclopaedia published by Asprey and Co. Ltd, of New Bond Street, London W.1. which he had bought a few days before. He asked the Secretary of State to look up the definition of 'Negro' and read it out. Gordon-Walker read: 'Negro – breeds fast and is a growing menace'.

After the delegation had left, Gordon-Walker declared he would refuse to see them again. Most of his officials agreed, their view being that they were becoming increasingly 'abrasive' and 'anyway weren't of much importance.'

While, perhaps, the outrage of Colonial blacks came as no surprise to the government, the opposition of almost everybody else as well was starting to take its toll. The weekly magazine, *The Spectator*, wrote:

Is it a good thing that a young African chief should come to England to be educated? Having come, is he to be segregated from his British fellow-citizens, or mix with them and learn all he can from them? Is he to meet no English girls, make no friendships with them, never find a basis for a relationship transcending all differences of tradition and colour? A British Commonwealth that demanded that would have no justification for existing. Nor would a religion which held that, although in Christ there is neither Greek nor Jew, bond nor free, yet between black and white an impenetrable barrier must be permanently maintained. In this matter, the Government is wrong and public opinion right.

Almost every newspaper had by now come out against the government and constituency Labour parties up and down the country were passing motions of protest, putting pressure on their MPs who were in turn passing it on to the government. If that was worrying for the politicians, no less disturbing for the civil servants was the demoralising effect the affair was having on Colonial officials around the world. The Colonial Service Club in London's Tavistock Square was bombarded with letters from officers around the Empire. One of the club's supervisors, Hugh Elliot, bundled them all up and sent them to the Colonial Office. They made sorry reading. A Mr David Roberts, who worked in the Administration Service of Nigeria's Northern Province had written that he and many of his colleagues were deeply disturbed at what the government had done.

> The idea has got about that the deciding factor in forming government policy was not consideration of the welfare or wishes of the tribe concerned but a wish to maintain good relations with the Union of South Africa. This idea may be quite wrong, but it is still being spread by the more responsible part of the press and it is hard to controvert. If it should ever turn out to have much truth in it, it would, I believe, have a very depressing effect on the morale of the Colonial Service. Many officers, like myself, have found the trend of much of the government's recent policy, with so much stress laid on the gaining of confidence of colonial peoples, to be rather inspiring.
>
> The confidence of people cannot be gained if they are given reason to think that their interests are liable to be sacrificed to our good relations with other countries . . . If government were to go on and make a series of decisions on such grounds I do not think I exaggerate in saying that a number of us might feel inclined to look around for different work.

Peter Radcliffe, an Assistant District Officer in Nigeria's Western Province, wrote:

> If moral issues and obligations in the case of Seretse Khama are indeed to be sacrificed to political expediency – as at the moment appears possible – then Britain's prestige in the world as a whole will suffer irreparably, the tempers of colonial people will be difficult to control, and the morale and confidence of the European officers in the Colonial Service will vanish. This is the sort of thing that could make one's job in the Colonies quite distasteful.

Only one country was strangely silent in its criticism of the government. The United States establishment had rarely missed an opportunity since the war to criticise what it saw as Britain's outdated imperial policies. But in this affair, there had hardly been a word. Oliver Franks, the British Ambassador in Washington, offered an explanation in a cable to the Foreign Secretary, Ernest Bevin.

It is perhaps of interest to consider why those elements in this country who can generally be relied upon to seize any opportunity to attack 'British Imperialism' have not sought to exploit the present case more fully. The reason probably is that, however wrongly, the case has generally been regarded as turning on the question of mixed marriage. This is of course a subject of very considerable delicacy in this country so that, except for the Negroes, the majority of would-be critics were reluctant to rush into this particular field even if it meant forgoing a promising line of attack on colonialism.

From the Negro element reactions have been, as was inevitable, much more intense. For instance, during early March, my Education Officer visited the Virginia State College in Petersburg, which is a land grant college for Negroes. He reported to me that considerable feeling was evident on the subject of Seretse Khama. He formed the impression that the case had had a very bad effect on Negroes generally who felt much moved and almost personally affected by it. From the remarks addressed to him, he gathered that the two features which have impressed themselves upon the minds of Negroes are firstly the implication that Seretse Khama had got into trouble with the UK Government on account of his marriage with a white girl and, secondly, that he was enticed away from his homeland on false pretences and only told on arrival in the UK that he could not return home.

But if the White House withheld condemnation, then it was small comfort for Gordon-Walker. As criticism of the government mounted, it centred more and more on the immediate effect of the ban which was the separation of a man from his pregnant wife. On 13 March, Gordon-Walker telegrammed Baring asking him if there was not some way that Seretse could be allowed to stay in the protectorate. The political pressure to end the enforced separation was now almost irresistible, he said.

Baring, having just returned from Serowe with a vivid understanding of the high state of tension in the Bamangwato

Reserve, did all he could to stiffen his Secretary of State's backbone. He telegrammed London:

> If the United Kingdom Government alter their view and allow Seretse and his wife to remain in the protectorate not as a temporary expedient but as a more permanent arrangement, serious repercussions in the Union of South Africa may be anticipated. Government of the protectorate would be impossible if Seretse remained there. He is determined to make trouble, issuing instructions for people not to pay taxes or comply with Government orders. Similarly, while he is there, no one dare come forward to join the new advisory council.

The pressure to allow Seretse to return temporarily was, however, too much for Baring to resist. The Commonwealth Office turned to the legal dispute between Seretse and Tshekedi over who owned the chief's cattle. This, they decided, would be the reason they would choose for allowing Seretse back into the protectorate. Once there, it would not be unreasonable for him to be allowed to be with his wife when she went into labour. Late on 15 March, Seretse was told by Gordon-Walker's officials that the government would allow him to fly to Lobatsi very soon. His spirits immediately lifted, he sent a cable to Ruth: 'AWAITING GOVERNMENT OK TO GO HOME. EXPECTING IT SOON.' As a small sign of goodwill, the tribe announced it was suspending the non-payment of taxes for three months.

The next morning Gordon-Walker endured the stormiest Cabinet meeting of the entire crisis. He had prepared a memorandum which he proposed should serve as a draft of a White Paper to be published on the affair later in the month. In the paper, the government denied that their decision to ban Seretse had been influenced in any way by South Africa. Gordon-Walker listed the reasons for the ban as:

(1) the danger of serious disruption within the tribe if Seretse were recognised;
(2) Seretse's irresponsibility in contracting a marriage which 'he knew would be unpleasing to his people'. In so doing 'Seretse showed himself to be utterly unmindful of the interests of his tribe and to be setting his private feelings above public duty';
(3) The existence, according to Gordon-Walker, of 'a consider-

able body of responsible African opinion' opposed to the recognition of Seretse.

However, in deference to public opinion, the Commonwealth Secretary told the Cabinet that he intended that afternoon to announce to the House of Commons what he had told Seretse the previous afternoon. His statement would say that he had decided to allow him to go back to the protectorate to settle his legal affairs provided that he did not 'interfere with the good government' of the territory. 'Subject to good behaviour by him' he would also be allowed, if he asked for it, to visit his wife in the Bamangwato Reserve during the last stages of her pregnancy.

But the Commonwealth Secretary's proposals fell far short of what his Cabinet colleagues wanted. The ferocity of the attacks from the press, from their own backbench MPs and from their constituents made them anxious for some escape. There was no evidence, they said, that Seretse would stir up trouble if he were allowed to go back. It would create the wrong impression if Gordon-Walker should stress the conditions he was imposing upon him when he spoke to the House. Rather he should show himself to be acting out of generosity and humanity. Similarly, the Cabinet felt, the offer of permission to visit his wife should not be conditional on his asking for it. If the government was being forced to make concessions, the Cabinet felt, they should at least be seen as expressions of human kindness not grudging parsimony.

Furthermore, the Cabinet wondered, why should Seretse be banned from the whole protectorate? Wouldn't it be enough just to exile him from the Bamangwato Reserve as the government had done with Tshekedi? It seemed unreasonable to impose so much harsher a decision on Seretse and they could see no reason for it. In fact, it would help matters greatly if the Commonwealth Secretary could announce soon that the government was considering allowing Seretse to live permanently in the protectorate, though outside the reserve. Gordon-Walker promised to think about what they had said.

That afternoon he told the House that Seretse was being allowed to go back to Lobatsi in the protectorate to prepare for his civil case against his uncle. 'I have also told him that arrangements will be made for him and his wife to be together around the time of her confinement.'

That night, he cabled Baring in South Africa telling him that the public pressure was now so intense that the government was considering allowing Seretse to remain in the protectorate indefinitely so long as he didn't cause trouble.

Baring, compared with his high spirits of the previous week, was now in despair. His belief that the advice he had given the previous July was correct had never wavered. Indeed, as the months had gone by his conviction had hardened. On a more personal level, of course, he realised that were that advice to be overturned at this late stage, he would have little alternative but to resign. With all this in mind he went to see the Union's elder statesman, Field Marshal Jan Smuts. What the old man told him was almost word for word what Douglas Forsyth had said eight months earlier. In a cable that reached London on 20 March Baring described Smuts' belief that any recognition of Seretse as chief would lead to a general election in South Africa. Such an election, called on such an issue, would not only weaken the position of Smuts and his anti-apartheid party but would substantially increase the strength of Strydom and his hardline supporters inside the National Party. Smuts had no doubt that they would hold an immediate referendum to take South Africa out of the Commonwealth and would almost certainly attempt the military annexation of the Bechuanaland Protectorate.

Baring added that in his opinion if the government now decided to 'relent and allow Seretse to remain in the protectorate, I would feel that the consequences would be so dangerous for relations with South Africa that I should want to fly home to London for immediate consultations'.

On the same day, Seretse addressed a huge rally in Trafalgar Square organised by his supporters. The rally called for his immediate recognition as chief. He told the crowd that the British people had shown their opposition to the government's decision in a magnificent manner. He said he had received messages of support from all over the country. Several Labour MPs spoke. One, Fenner Brockway, told the rally that the majority of the Parliamentary Labour Party now opposed the ban.

While the rally was still in progress, at the other end of Whitehall the Cabinet was meeting again. Ministers said they were still very concerned about the level of protest and hoped that Gordon-Walker's White Paper would do much to take the pressure off them.

Gordon-Walker then told the Cabinet of his meeting with

Leary Constantine and the other members of the Seretse Khama
Fighting Committee. They had complained, he said, of the level of
racial discrimination in Britain and had wondered why nothing
was done about it. In the general discussion that followed,
ministers pointed out that many blacks found it difficult to get
jobs in this country and that 'serious difficulties would arise if
this immigration of coloured people from British Colonial
possessions were to continue or increase'. James Griffiths, the
new Colonial Secretary, was asked to look into the problem and
report back. When he did, several weeks later, it was to say that
the government's policy of assimilating black immigrants into
the community was running into difficulties because of the large
numbers involved. It was time, the Cabinet decided, to consider
'the question whether the time had come to restrict the existing
right of any British subject to enter the United Kingdom. In
almost all other Commonwealth countries power had been taken
to restrict the admission of British subjects from other parts of
the Commonwealth. Was it certain that the balance of advantage
still lay against taking this course in the United Kingdom itself?'
At the end of the meeting, the Cabinet agreed that Prime
Minister Attlee would 'arrange for a review to be made of the
further means which might be adopted to check the immigration
into this country of coloured people from British Colonial
territories'. It was a fine irony that the same black people who,
prompted by the government's treatment of Seretse, complained
to Ministers about the discrimination practised against them,
were the very ones to incite ministers to consider passing a law
discriminating against them.

For the rest of the week the government tried to dodge
discussing the Seretse affair in the House of Commons. Finally,
at 11.30 at night on 28 March, Labour MP Fenner Brockway
forced a debate. He began by saying that colour prejudice was
the cause of some of the most dangerous divisions in the world.
For him and for many people the marriage of Ruth and Seretse
Khama had become a symbol of how that division could be
healed. 'When, in these tribes in Bechuanaland, Seretse Khama
was endorsed as Chief by a vote of over 5,000 to fewer than 50,
that decision should have been welcomed by the House and by
the Government as a great stepping stone in the advance
towards racial equality in the world.' Turning to what he
believed was the secret pressure from South Africa he continued:
'I believe that the Government have started on a course of

appeasement with the South African Government, which stands for the principle of refusing to recognise those who belong to the black race as members of the human family at all.'

From the opposition benches, Quintin Hogg, Tory MP for Oxford and destined, as Lord Hailsham, to occupy some of the highest offices of state in his long life, rose to speak.

> The case of Seretse Khama symbolises the determination of this Government to override the decision of a native people to accept as their prince and their princess the person and his wife whom they would wish to see . . . The Government have been given an opportunity to justify the decision which they have come to. It is a grave decision and they have failed to justify it . . . It is perhaps fortunate that following this Debate tonight there can be no Division, because in such a Debate we can express our opinions freely without any fear of upsetting the Ministers opposite. But I hope they will understand that not merely honourable Members behind them, not merely honourable Members on the Liberal benches but many honourable Members on these benches, question, on the highest Imperial grounds, the wisdom, as well as the humanity, of the decision which they have taken.

When, at half past midnight, Gordon-Walker rose to reply, he refused to give an inch. The reasons he gave were the same: tribal disruption and the irresponsibility of Seretse. There would be no movement in the government's position.

On 24 March, Seretse boarded the BOAC Flying Boat for the first leg of his flight to Lobatsi. That morning's *Times* carried a letter from him.

> I have been banished from my people who have wanted me and also from the land to which I belong. For what? No crime, except that I have married an Englishwoman . . . The present [law in South Africa] forbids the marriage of a native to a European. There is no such prohibition anywhere in the Colonial Empire yet it was the policy of racial discrimination which influenced the Imperial Government in their decision regarding my succession to the Chieftainship . . . The questions which the British people have to ask themselves are: Is our conscience clear over the whole event? Have we allowed expediency to prevail over political integrity? Upon

these answers alone is greatly dependent morally and politically, Britain's future status as the mother country of the Commonwealth.

As Seretse's airliner lumbered into the air, the focus of attention switched back once more to Bechuanaland. Readers of that morning's *Daily Telegraph* would have been wise to read a small article on the affair by Colin Reid. In it he referred to the 'very unusual personality of Seretse's wife, whose fixity of purpose and determination have to be reckoned a major factor in every development'. His analysis could not have been more accurate.

22

Sleepless Nights

In Serowe Noel Monks was hatching a plan. For more than seven weeks Seretse had been separated from his wife and it looked as if it would be several weeks more before they were united. Meanwhile, Ruth, eight months into her first pregnancy, was still stubbornly refusing to leave the Bamangwato. Now, as a direct result of the pressure of public opinion, the British authorities were flying Seretse to Lobatsi so he would be near at hand for the birth.

Monks reasoned that while it was their separation that gave the story its poignancy, it was clearly their reunion that would be the next major event. If, somehow, such a reunion could be engineered, even if only briefly, under the very noses of the British, then he would have a scoop.

The quickest way from London to Lobatsi was to fly to Johannesburg and then catch the train. For Seretse that was impossible since he was a Prohibited Immigrant in South Africa. He was therefore flying to Victoria Falls where the government was planning to charter a light aircraft to fly him on to Lobatsi.

From the falls to Lobatsi was a trip of more than 400 miles. Monks learned that the 'plane the British were chartering was a De Havilland Rapide, a small bi-plane, and 400 miles was too far for it to fly in one stretch. The aircraft would therefore have to refuel somewhere en route. What better, thought Monks, than to make sure it refuelled in the Bamangwato Reserve at a place where Ruth would be waiting to snatch a few stolen moments with her husband? With a photographer on hand to record the meeting, he would have a story and a set of photographs that would go round the world.

To help organise everything he needed help and so he shared his plan with John Redfern of the *Daily Express*. Monks contacted the pilot of the charter plane, a Wing-Commander Pritchard, and it was arranged that he would land to refuel at Mahalapye, 350 miles from Victoria Falls and a bumpy three-hour drive from

Serowe. Redfern flew to the falls to make sure there were no hitches and Monks waited at Serowe.

At four o'clock on the afternoon of 27 March, Seretse disembarked from the Flying Boat at Victoria Falls to be met by British officials. He would be leaving very early the next morning, he was told, and was introduced to Wing-Commander Pritchard. In Serowe, Monks told Ruth of the plan and she, although with less than four weeks to go to the birth, agreed to meet him and his photographer at the airstrip in Mahalapye at dawn the following morning.

At 3 a.m., Ruth climbed into her car and began the long, dark drive through the desert.

Though cold and sleepy, she was filled with excitement at the hope of being with Seretse again if only for a few minutes. It would be a delicious moment and she savoured the anticipation as she bumped over the dirt roads towards Mahalapye. Many a pregnant woman would have refused to make such a journey. Indeed, when the British officials in Serowe had suggested to her that she might like to move to Lobatsi to be with her husband, she had told them she could not possibly travel over such roads at this late stage in her pregnancy. Even her doctor friend, Don Moikangoa, had said the British would have to accept full responsibility if they forced her to make such a journey. Now, as the car heaved itself across the rutted desert tracks, Ruth's baby clung on with all the tenacity of its mother. Ahead of her on the same road, Monks was also excited. What a story, what pictures, what a poke in the eye for the Brits! 'Stolen moments of love', 'Dawn kisses in the desert', 'Ruth's Kalahari Comfort', the headline possibilities were endless. As the eastern sky lightened, both cars swung on to the dirt road running parallel to the railway line and began the last stretch to Mahalapye.

But it was not to be. Even as Monks had been preparing for bed the previous night, the British had got wind of the plan. Pritchard was informed that he would be refused permission to land at Mahalapye and that arrangements had been made for him to refuel at Francistown instead. Redfern never did discover who had leaked the information. It seemed unlikely that Pritchard had done so since he seemed visibly upset by his new instructions. The best he could do, he said, was to fly over Mahalapye. At least Ruth and Seretse might then catch a glimpse of one another. As Ruth and Noel Monks drove into Mahalapye, Pritchard and Seretse took off for Francistown.

The airstrip at Mahalapye is some 500 yards from the railway line and is fringed by the mud huts of the village. Cold and tired, Monks and Ruth parked the truck and waited for Seretse's plane. But the first aircraft to arrive was Redfern's bringing news of the British discovery. Almost before the disappointment could sink in, they heard aircraft engines to the north-east. Stepping away from the truck, Ruth strained to see the approaching plane, her hand shading her eyes from the rising sun. The Rapide approached the airstrip, flying low above the scrubland. As he got closer, Pritchard throttled back and the plane sank even lower. At no more than fifty feet above the ground, the 'plane roared across the airstrip, the rush of wind from its propellers raising a cloud of dust which whirled around Ruth as she scanned the cabin windows for a glimpse of her husband. Aboard the 'plane, Seretse, his face pressed against the cabin window, fixed his eyes on the lonely figure, her hands raised to shield her eyes, almost lost in the swirl of dust. As Pritchard swung the 'plane hard around for another pass, Seretse saw the rush of wind from their passing whip Ruth's blonde hair and flatten her clothes against her pregnancy. On the ground, Ruth fancied she saw a shape in one cabin window but whether or not it was Seretse she couldn't tell. As the Rapide completed its second pass and set its course to the south-west she slowly walked back to the truck for the long, dusty ride home.

Forty-five minutes later, Seretse's Rapide landed at Gaberone, a small village half an hour's drive from Lobatsi. There to meet him was his uncle, Phetu Sekgoma and some 150 tribesmen. In his uncle's lorry, he drove to Lobatsi where the government had reserved a two-roomed house for him. Inside they had provided a metal bed, two unpainted chairs and an unpainted table, two tin mugs, two tin plates, two tin knives, forks and spoons. As Seretse would later remark, such furnishings were probably not intended as an insult but were rather regarded by the resident British officials as standard issue for 'native' accommodation. Phetu and the others immediately went out to buy proper furniture, crockery and cutlery and Seretse settled down to make the best he could of his new abode.

Seretse's return to the protectorate did nothing to calm things down. The Bamangwato were in increasingly belligerent mood and all were aware that events were moving towards some climax. Such restlessness worried not only the British administration but also the protectorate's white residents, many of whom were beginning to doubt the wisdom of robbing the tribe of its chief. 'The natives are getting out of hand without a leader,' the manageress of the Mahalapye Hotel confided to the *Sunday Express*. 'I can do nothing with my cook these last weeks.' Few, however, were prepared to accept that the troubles were the result of frustrating the Bamangwato's democratic will. As Sir Godfrey Huggins, the Prime Minister of Southern Rhodesia, said at a press conference in London on 4 April: 'It is irresponsible to place such a dangerous weapon as the vote in the hands of people who still seek solutions to their problems by studying the entrails of a goat.'

In Serowe itself tempers were flaring. When one of the former headmen who had opted for self-exile with Tshekedi tried to move some of his cattle from the village, groups of Seretse's supporters tried to stop him. When the police arrived, fighting started and the crowd was finally broken up by tear gas. Eleven tribesmen were arrested and imprisoned in one of the administration offices. More than a hundred Bamangwato immediately surrounded the building demanding to be arrested as well. Forbes McKenzie, the newly arrived District Commissioner, addressed a stormy meeting of more than 300 who insisted that all cattle movements must stop until the civil case between Tshekedi and Seretse over the ownership of the herds had been settled. McKenzie described the mood of the meeting as 'very hostile'. Immediately on arriving in Lobatsi, Seretse had begun officially to request permission to visit Ruth. This was refused and Seretse's lawyer, Percy Fraenkel, told the press. The newspapers also reported the restrictions being placed on Seretse's movements in Lobatsi and the government soon found that their concession in allowing him to go to Lobatsi had done nothing to placate public opinion.

On 12 April, Labour MP Fenner Brockway, one of the most outspoken opponents of the government's handling of the affair, sent a handwritten note to Gordon-Walker. He said that considering Ruth's illness the previous year and the government's refusal to allow Seretse to visit her, he was becoming worried about her health. He said he also felt that Seretse was being treated in an undignified manner, escorted everywhere by an official, obliged to give detailed accounts of his intended movements and generally being subjected to 'unnecessarily humiliating conditions'. 'I do beg of you,' he wrote, 'not only to

191

recognise the immediate human problem of his domestic circumstances but to remove all impression of an absence of human approach.'

Gordon-Walker, however, was not susceptible to such a plea. Seretse was lucky to be in the protectorate at all, he replied, and, given the potential for public disturbances, his movements must be monitored. 'The way has always been open – and is still open – for Mrs Khama to proceed to Lobatsi where she would be able to be with her husband until her confinement is over . . . If Mrs Khama has had to wait for a reunion with her husband, and if it is unlikely that they can remain together continuously, the real reason for this is that she has given her own determination to remain at Serowe a priority over her desire to be with her husband.'

Neither Ruth nor Seretse, however, was prepared to wait upon the Commonwealth Secretary's pleasure. Seretse, having had his request for permission to visit his wife turned down on 11 April, decided that he would visit her anyway that weekend. Through Phetu, he sent a message to Ruth saying that he would be arriving in the middle of the night, would spend a day secretly with her in the house, and would then drive back to Lobatsi the following night. Ruth felt there was next to no chance of his getting away with it. Luckily for both of them, she was working on a plan of her own.

Ever since Seretse's arrival in Lobatsi, she had been trying to put pressure on the British to allow him to visit her. She had asked her friend, Dr Don Moikangoa, if he would tell the British that he feared a recurrence of her nervous breakdown if Seretse were refused permission to visit her. He refused. Much though he supported Ruth and all she and Seretse stood for, he told her he could not lie in his professional advice. As far as he could see, she was hale and hearty and he could not, in any professional diagnosis, state anything but the truth.

Ruth decided to relieve her friend of this embarrassment. On 10 April, she took to bed an alarm clock and a thermos flask of tea. Throughout the night she sat up, constantly resetting the alarm clock, an hour at a time, to awake her every time she dozed off. With hot tea and magazines she made it through to dawn feeling exhausted.

The next night, 11 April, she repeated the process, staying awake until the morning. Again the next night she did the same. Every hour throughout the night the alarm clock rang, jerking her awake, depriving her of sleep. On the morning of 13 April, she dragged herself to Serowe hospital to see Don Moikangoa. She hadn't slept for three nights, she told him, and was feeling absolutely dreadful. She missed Seretse and knew she would sleep better if he was allowed to visit her.

Don Moikangoa was shocked and worried. He had treated her the previous year when she had collapsed from nervous exhaustion. He was well aware of the pressure she was under, coping with her first pregnancy, separated from her husband, unsure of the future. Now, just as last time, there had been a sudden deterioration in her condition. She looked completely exhausted again and, remembering how advanced her pregnancy was, he was deeply concerned for her safety and that of the baby. He immediately cabled Percy Fraenkel in Lobatsi instructing him to tell the British administration that Ruth's mental and physical well-being was now in jeopardy and he feared the consequences if Seretse's visit were long delayed.

Anthony Sillery, the Resident Commissioner in Mafeking, immediately dispatched Dr Freedman, the protectorate's Director of Medical Services, to Serowe to check on Ruth's condition. Sillery also cabled Baring in South Africa who sent a telegram to Gordon-Walker headed 'EMERGENCY' and 'TOP SECRET'. If the British government's action were now to lead to Ruth's nervous breakdown and the possible termination of her pregnancy it might well result, given the prevailing public mood, in the fall of the government. At the very least some very senior people – Baring and Gordon-Walker to name but two – might soon be looking for new jobs. Baring's cable read: 'Resident Commissioner has had reports from Ruth's African doctor that he is concerned about her health, both physical and mental. Protectorate Director of Medical Services left last night with Seretse's concurrence for consultation but it is clear that early visit by Seretse will help allay her anxieties. This may be bluff but Resident Commissioner thinks there may well be something in it.'

Later the next morning, Freedman arrived in Serowe only to find that Ruth refused to see him. In reply to his request, she sent a message saying that she had complete confidence in her own doctor, did not know Dr Freedman and had not sent for him. When Freedman asked that Dr Gemell, the white senior doctor, be allowed to examine her, she sent back a similar reply.

Don Moikangoa's reputation carried the day. Although they

could not personally confirm his diagnosis they knew him as a man of scrupulous professional honesty and Freedman cabled Sillery that if Moikangoa was concerned then there must be very good reason. That evening, with Baring's agreement, Sillery told Seretse he was going to Serowe that weekend. Seretse, his plan to visit Ruth illegally now firmly set in his mind, thought to himself: 'I know that, but how do they know?' The Resident Commissioner then explained that Ruth's health was causing concern and that the government had decided to grant him permission to visit Serowe from 16 to 20 April. The following conditions would apply:

(1) He would inform the District Commissioner immediately on his arrival in Serowe;
(2) He would do nothing to interfere with the good government of the Bamangwato Reserve;
(3) He would not hold or attend any public meetings.

He would be removed immediately from the reserve if he broke any of those conditions.

The next day, 15 April, Phetu Sekgoma filled his lorry up with petrol and he and Seretse prepared for the journey. Seretse's permit was valid from the following day so he planned to enter Serowe one minute after midnight on the 16th. To be there on time, he had to set out from Lobatsi that afternoon.

The British in Serowe, Mafeking, Pretoria and at the Commonwealth Office were by now in such a state of tension that credibility was given to the wildest tittle-tattle. On the morning of the 15th, Baring sent a telegram to Sir Percivale Liesching saying: 'I have heard two rumours recently that Ruth is busy urging her sister or a friend or both to join her in Serowe. The second report reached me through a correspondent of a Johannesburg newspaper who was in Serowe recently. He also had a story that Seretse's closest supporters hoped that Ruth would be successful in her efforts as this would give them the opportunity to emulate Seretse's successful wooing.'

Disinterested observers would have found it difficult to summarise the state of mind that could send such a telegram or, on receiving it, give it any credence. It was as if, in the dark night of their policy's moral failure, the British were being haunted by the ghosts of their own prejudices.

With a lighter heart than any belonging to those in authority above him, Seretse set out for Serowe in his uncle's lorry. He shared the driving with Phetu and in the back of the lorry sat John Redfern, the *Express* correspondent.

As the autumn sun dipped to the west, he drove towards the night, through Gaberone, following the railway line north-eastwards. Through the dust thrown up behind him he could see the headlights of a government official sent to follow and keep tags on him.

By the time he reached Mahalapye, 100 bone-jarring miles along the road, the headlights behind him had gone. The official, plagued by punctures, had fallen well behind. In Mahalapye, Seretse stopped to rest. John Redfern watched as he sat on a wall, smoking a cigarette. Soon the villagers began to gather around him. One held up a hurricane lantern which lit sharply one side of his face as he sat, smiling at his people. Women held up their small children for him to touch them. He then moved a little down the street and sat, talking quietly to some of the men, a chief again among his tribe. Further up the road, the British official, his tyres now fully inflated, roared into Mahalapye searching for Seretse. As he appeared, Seretse broke off from his talks and climbed into his truck. 'I cannot help people gathering around me,' he told the official who made a note in his report that at least one of the conditions already appeared to have been broken.

Seretse arrived outside Serowe about half an hour before midnight. Through a messenger earlier in the day he had told Ruth when he would be coming. She had been sitting on the verandah of her bungalow for the last three hours with Noel Monks and half a dozen other reporters and photographers. At the sound of every approaching car she hauled herself to her feet. Ruth was now very heavy with her baby and it was the end of a long day of waiting. Finally, a minute or so after midnight, she heard the deeper roar of Phetu's lorry. Clambering up once more she ran from the house towards the road, reporters and photographers hard behind her. Running through the night, down along the twisting track, she made it to the headlights growling towards her. As she reached the lorry, Seretse leaped out and swept her up into his arms. As flash bulbs popped around them they clung to one another, nearly two and half months of separation over at last. Then, with Seretse driving and she on the lorry's running board, her arm around his neck through the open window, they drove slowly to the house, the press swarming around them. In the garden, on the verandah and in the sitting room they posed for the newspapers, arms around each other, she chiding him for the stubble on his chin. He had promised himself that he would not shave again until they were together for good.

The next morning, Sunday, they woke to find several hundred tribesmen camped outside the house steps. Following the conditions of his visit, Seretse and Ruth then drove to District Commissioner McKenzie's house to announce his arrival. 'Prisoner reporting,' snapped Ruth as she and Seretse were shown into the house. Declining offers of tea and polite conversation they went back outside to find hundreds of other men, women and children flocking around them. For the rest of that day, sitting on two chairs on the verandah of their house, the chief and his wife held court as long lines of Bamangwato queued to pay their respects.

The next morning, some 300 men assembled at the Kgotla ground, waiting for their chief to address them. Seretse sent a message saying he could not talk to them because the government would not allow it. By noon about 400 men had gathered outside his house. Standing on his verandah, Seretse told them he had been exiled for a minimum of five years because his presence among them was 'disruptive'. He was not even allowed to talk to them and what he was doing now was against the law of the British. That evening McKenzie summoned him to his house to warn him that his speech had been against what had been agreed and if he addressed the tribe once more he would be removed from Serowe by force. Meanwhile, the crowds continued to gather outside the Khama's house. As news of his visit spread throughout the reserve, men walked from distant villages and cattle-posts to see him. On 19 April, the last day of his permit, teachers gathered choirs of schoolchildren in front of the house to sing songs for Seretse and his wife. As the songs ended and the crowd grew larger, Seretse rose to address them.

The British government did not want this to happen. They wanted me to sit by my house alone. This crowd will show the British that the Bamangwato love me.

The British have banned me from here for five years because they say there will be trouble if I stay here. My wife and I lived here for many months last year and there was no trouble. We have not fought with anyone. But, I have no choice in the matter. The government says I must go and I must leave Serowe before midnight tonight.

A loud rumble of discontent went up from the men, descanted by the shrill ululations from the women.

'Nevertheless, however much we disagree, we must obey the law. I want you all to go back to your homes now and cause no trouble.' As the crowds slowly drifted away, McKenzie, furious at first at Seretse's second illegal speech, had to admit that he had defused a tense situation.

That evening Ruth found it very difficult to be brave and fight back the tears. As midnight approached she clung to her husband trying to absorb some of his strength. The government had promised that when she went into labour, he would be brought to her bedside as quickly as possible. Until then, they must be apart. It all seemed so cruel, so lacking in sympathy and human warmth. Neither had done anything wrong. Two years before they had fallen in love, nothing more. Now they wanted to be together, to have children, and for Seretse to lead his people. None of that was anything to do with the British. Why didn't they get on with their own business and leave her alone? The very thought of what they were doing to her made her chin lift. It was always the bitter sense of injustice that gave Ruth the strength to carry on. Whenever she thought of Gordon-Walker and the rest, the tears of sadness turned to anger. She and Seretse would show them. From the start, their love had fed upon the opposition that it had provoked on every side. No one had given them a chance and whole governments had tried to break them up. The result had been that they were now closer than ever even if they must be separated physically. Their child would be born in Serowe, among its people and the British could not prevent that. She would find the strength to see it through. Shortly before midnight, Seretse climbed into Phetu's lorry, kissed her one final time, and drove off into the night. Ruth stood by the roadside until the lorry's rearlights finally flickered from view. Slowly she turned and walked back up the path she had run headlong down only four days before.

23

Together at Last

Forbes McKenzie, Serowe's District Commissioner, was furious about Seretse's visit. Instead of reporting to his immediate senior in Mafeking, he cabled direct to Baring in Pretoria.

It is quite clear that far from adopting the attitude one might have expected of him, seeing that he had been allowed to return on compassionate grounds for a purely private visit to his wife, his attitude has been one of making himself as much of a nuisance as he could without really overstepping the boundary. Experience of this visit has shown that if and when he is allowed to come back to the reserve again, the conditions of his visit must be stricter.

In London, the government was equally angry at the amount of press coverage the visit had attracted. Seretse's visit had been covered in every detail and British readers were left in no doubt as to the exiled chief's popularity. Stories reporting how the police reinforcements drafted into Serowe had been issued with rifles and steel helmets only added to the picture of a repressive government imposing its will by force.

Finally, the *Sunday Dispatch* began a serialisation of Ruth's 'own' story, further inciting sympathy for the pair.

It was quite a relief for everyone at the Commonwealth Office when *Picture Post*, the top selling news magazine, carried ten pages on the affair by their top correspondent Fyfe Robertson. Robertson, who would later go on to national fame as the querulous Scottish reporter on the BBC's *Tonight* programme, returned from the protectorate with a very unflattering report. While Seretse had impressed him – 'independent, strong-willed, likeable, courteous, quiet, reasonable' – he had not liked Ruth. He had found her cold, hostile, suspicious and easily offended. As far as he could see, she had no interest in the Bamangwato and cared only for herself. As his report appeared, the *Sunday*

Dispatch's serialisation of Ruth's story was carrying quotes from her pledging herself to the betterment of the tribe. 'I would be content to spend the rest of my life helping my husband bring his people to that state of development to which, as British subjects, they are entitled.'

On his return from Serowe, Fyfe Robertson had taken it upon himself to brief the government on what he had discovered. In a private interview at the Commonwealth Office with Sir Percivale Liesching he said that, having been to the protectorate, he didn't doubt for a minute that the government was fully justified in taking the decision that it had. In his opinion, he said, they should have acted earlier. He further believed that the importance of Ruth in the whole affair was much overrated. She showed no inclination to take an interest in 'the natives'. Forbes McKenzie, the District Commissioner, on the other hand, was very popular among the tribe and his arrival in Serowe had brought a sense of confidence to the leading Bamangwato. He concluded by saying that he was sure there was no serious threat to law and order.

Meanwhile, press speculation was turning towards the birth of Ruth's baby and the nature of 'mixed-race'. While most readers' hearts had gone out to the way the couple had been treated there remained widespread reservation about the practice of 'miscegnation', interbreeding between different races. The *Sunday Express* 'Empire Correspondent', Don Taylor, was moved to write a personal piece in the issue of 23 April.

> If you travel abroad – in the East, in Africa – you can see the products of mixed marriages. You can see them in the great ports of Britain itself. Often there is undoubted intelligence, but a fatal weakness of character, a lack of responsibility, of belief in themselves . . . I feel strongly that interracial marriage is not a particularly good thing . . . I believe too that the white man must provide leadership for a long time yet.

Indeed, the prospect of the birth not only sparked debate but revealed a certain ignorance among many of those apparently born to lead. So great was the confusion among *Sunday Express* readers, for example, that the newspaper commissioned an article by a professor from Edinburgh University to explain the racial facts of life to a bewildered audience. On 21 May, beneath the headline 'The Sun-tanned Baby', Professor F. A. E. Crew explained:

Let it be understood that the human species comprises ALL mankind, one and indivisible. It is a single species wherein individuals have the same basic constitution although there may be varied permutations on that foundation. Many ill-informed people are inclined to regard this much-discussed marriage as a union between two different animal species. It most certainly is not. Animals belonging to different species are commonly unattractive to one another sexually. Their reproductive habits can be utterly different. Mating can be impossible.

Many readers must have slept easier in their beds that night.

Meanwhile, one of the most famous pregnancies in the world was moving to its termination. During the early hours of 15 May, Ruth was woken by what she was convinced was indigestion. She was sure that she still had a month to go and did not recognise the first contractions of labour. For the rest of the night she remained certain it was a stomach upset. At seven o'clock she went to see Don Moikangoa who told her to come back in an hour. By 8.30 he was sure that labour had started and she was admitted to Serowe hospital soon after 9 a.m.

Thirty minutes later, McKenzie was informed that Ruth was about to have her baby and a message was sent to the British in Lobatsi to issue Seretse with a four-week pass to visit Serowe. By lunchtime a very surprised Seretse – he also thought the pregnancy had at least another three weeks to go – had been contacted and then a search instituted for uncle Phetu and his lorry.

At 1.30 p.m. Ruth gave birth to a baby girl, Jacqueline, who weighed 7lb 4oz. The new mother then propped herself up in bed to await her husband, refusing all requests to sleep until he came. By 2.30 p.m., Phetu's lorry was full of fuel. With Seretse at the wheel, uncle and nephew set out on the nine-hour drive to Serowe. After about five miles Seretse stopped and told his uncle to take over. So anxious was he to get to his wife's side that he had been driving wildly along the dangerous dirt roads and had convinced himself that if he carried on, neither he nor Phetu would ever make it.

At 5 p.m. Don Moikangoa came into Ruth's ward to see if she was resting peacefully. There, determinedly propped up against two pillows, Ruth stared back at him. 'Has Seretse come? What time did they get the news to him? What time did he leave Lobatsi?' Moikangoa was amazed that she still hadn't slept and told her he would wake her the moment Seretse arrived. Ruth said she refused to sleep until her husband was at her side, just as the British had promised he would be.

When Moikangoa came back at 8 p.m. to the same sight and when the nurses confirmed that she hadn't even closed her eyes, he spoke sternly to her for the first time.

'You have the responsibilities of a mother now. You have an infant to nurse and it's ridiculous that you haven't slept since the birth. If you are not asleep in an hour, I will give you something to make you sleep.'

His patient replied that she had no intention of sleeping until Seretse arrived. Then she would sleep, but not before.

An hour later, Moikangoa returned with the biggest syringe that Ruth had ever seen. Unable to resist, Ruth was given her injection and then doctor and nurses left her in peace.

Much later, at 11 p.m., Phetu's lorry arrived outside the hospital. Seretse jumped out and went immediately in search of Don Moikangoa.

The doctor quickly reassured him. The birth had been normal, the baby was perfectly healthy as was her mother.

'Can I see Ruth now?' Seretse asked. Taking him by the arm, Moikangoa walked him to Ruth's ward explaining that he wouldn't be able to speak to her until the next day since she was exhausted and heavily sedated.

As the two men opened the ward door, Serowe's Assistant Government Medical Officer's mouth fell open in amazement. There, still propped up against her pillows, fighting her sedation with every ounce of her will, Ruth shouted 'Seretse!' As he rushed towards her, he held out his arms. As he reached her bedside, the hospital lights fused, the ward was plunged into darkness and she fell asleep in her husband's arms.

24
Exile

The British administration gave Ruth, Seretse and baby Jacqueline four weeks to get out of Serowe. The authorities were not to be denied and everyone, the new parents and the tribe, sullenly accepted it.

The Bamangwato instead turned to a policy of passive non-cooperation. It now became impossible for the British to collect taxes in Serowe and the position was almost as bad in the outlying villages. McKenzie, now empowered with the responsibility of imposing direct rule on the Bamangwato, found himself blocked at every turn. Constant invitations to leading tribesmen to come forward to form an advisory council were ignored and when McKenzie summoned Kgotla meetings in order to announce important matters they were boycotted. On 31 May, he summoned a Kgotla meeting and only one person turned up. On 7 June, he called another and six people arrived. There had, at that time, been an outbreak of foot and mouth disease just outside the reserve and McKenzie was trying to distribute information telling the villagers how to protect their cattle. Finally, he had to tour Serowe with a loud hailer, shouting out the instructions at every street corner.

On 12 June, the date by which the British had told them they must leave Serowe, Ruth, her husband and baby quietly left their home and drove to the government house in Lobatsi previously allocated to Seretse. They had asked that there be no large-scale demonstrations, no crowds to see them off. In Britain, there was increasing speculation that they would be allowed to stay on in the protectorate, as Tshekedi had, and neither Ruth nor Seretse wanted to give the British any excuse for expelling them.

In London, Gordon-Walker was very aware that the mood of the Cabinet was to let Ruth and Seretse live on in Lobatsi. Since the baby had been born and the couple had been reunited, public opinion had been mollified and the government certainly didn't want to inflame matters all over again if it was possible to avoid it.

Throughout the latter half of May and into June, Gordon-Walker conferred with Baring about the possibility of letting them stay in Lobatsi. The High Commissioner was as adamant as ever that they must go. Finally, Gordon-Walker sat down with his officials to compose a memorandum to put before the Cabinet meeting of 29 June. In it he set out all the reasons for sticking to the original plan of expelling them both once the baby had been born. He began by explaining that it was impossible to set up any alternative method of governing the Bamangwato while Seretse was still in the protectorate. Everyone, he explained, was far too frightened to offer himself for government service in case he was branded a traitor by Seretse. No progress could be made in governing the Bamangwato until Seretse was removed. Gordon-Walker continued:

> Broadly speaking, the same arguments apply to the exclusion of Ruth from the protectorate. She has not, admittedly, the prestige of a claimant to the chieftainship; but she is astute and ruthless and has made it clear that she intends to cause as much mischief as she can. There is also a strong case to be made for removing husband and wife together and not exposing ourselves to the charge of inhumanly separating them. If she remained behind we should be constantly under pressure to let him return to visit her. She has already shown that she is ready to feign illness.

Gordon-Walker then turned to the real reason why he and Baring were insisting that the couple be removed. 'We must . . . do our utmost to keep the Union [of South Africa] solidly in the Commonwealth for strategic, economic and other reasons.' The original reason for the decision had been the fear that South Africa would invade and annexe the protectorate and walk out of the Commonwealth.

> If the Union got into a mood to defy us and the world, there is very little that we could do to hold the Territories. Quite apart from force, economic boycott (though it would hurt the Union) would render us helpless. The Seretse case represents perhaps the one set of circumstances that could unite – and inflame – all white opinion in the Union against us. It raises

the question of mixed marriages, which arouses the most highly charged emotion and can drive South Africa into completely irrational attitudes and actions . . . There is overwhelming evidence that if, as it would seem to the Union, the United Kingdom had set its official seal upon mixed marriages in the midst of South Africa by recognising Seretse, there would have been an outburst of uncontrollable emotion and anger in the Union, which would have thrown the whole of white opinion behind Dr Malan.

The rest of the memorandum concerned the mechanics of actually expelling them with the minimum of fuss. 'If Ruth and Seretse go quietly I do not think there will be too much of a stir. But if we have to use force, we must count on a fierce, but perhaps not very long, outburst of criticism. It should not be overlooked that if we left them in the protectorate they could attract as much public attention over there – maybe more – as if they were in England. Press men would be hanging around them eager for stories, and even (as has already happened) instigating them to create incidents.'

When the Cabinet read the memorandum and heard the Commonwealth Secretary speak in its support, they reluctantly agreed to what he proposed.

In July, Nettleton, the Acting Resident Commissioner, went to see Ruth and Seretse and suggested 11 or 18 August as suitable dates for their departure. Seretse replied that no date was suitable and if they left they would have to be ordered out. Nettleton left saying he would work on 11 August as the most probable date.

A few days later Seretse and Ruth were shopping in Lobatsi and went into a large general dealers. As they walked in, everybody in the shop suddenly fell silent, staring at Ruth. She was not surprised; she was used to being stared at wherever she went. But then Seretse took her arm and guided her towards a well-dressed, middle-aged African man examining some goods in the corner. Walking up to him, Seretse turned to Ruth and said: 'Meet my uncle.' As Ruth's eyes met those of the stranger, she knew exactly which uncle he was. 'How do you do?' said Tshekedi, shaking her hand. No one in the shop had moved or spoken since the couple entered and, in the complete silence, Ruth replied that she was pleased to meet him. Tshekedi then asked if he might come round to their house to see their baby.

They agreed and a short time later he arrived. It was the beginning of what would become a slow but, eventually, total reconciliation between uncle and nephew. Hardly more than a week after the meeting with Ruth, Tshekedi drove all the way to Pretoria to ask Baring not to enforce the banishment order. It was useless; Baring was immovable.

On 2 August, Baring sent his deputy, W. A. W. Clarke, to Lobatsi to serve Ruth and Seretse with their orders to quit. In the presence of Vivian Ellenberger, the man from the Resident Commissioner's office who had attended Seretse's triumphant Kgotla fourteen months earlier, they arrived outside the Khama's government house. They told Ruth and Seretse that since the reasons for Seretse's visit to the protectorate were now at an end, the British government would like them both to leave as soon as was convenient.

Inviting them in, Ruth offered them tea and walked into the kitchen to prepare it. Seretse explained to the two men that since he had done no wrong and felt he had every right to live in his own country, he could not agree to leave voluntarily. Leaving the two men for a moment, he went into the kitchen to help Ruth bring in the tea. He found that she had reached up into the cupboard to find the original two tin mugs that the government had supplied to Seretse when he had arrived from London at the end of March. Preparing Seretse's and her tea in the china cups that Phetu Sekgoma had bought for his nephew, she was preparing to serve tea to the British in the tin ones. 'You can't do that,' whispered Seretse in protest, taking the tin mugs off the tray and replacing them with china ones. 'Don't be silly,' said Ruth, putting the tin ones back on the tray, 'they obviously expect to drink tea from tin mugs or they wouldn't have supplied them to you.' In fits of giggles, both placing and replacing the two tin mugs, they finally settled for china and re-entered the living room. Their humour was shortlived. Standing up, Clarke served them both with papers ordering them to leave Bechuanaland within two weeks. Seretse accepted his, Ruth kept her hands at her side. 'This is the first direct step that the government has taken towards me,' she said. 'I find it surprising and ridiculous that a woman could be regarded as a danger to the peace.'

Accepting the inevitable, they then got down to discussing the details of shipping their possessions to England and even the inoculations necessary for the flight. When Clarke said that any passenger without a yellow fever certificate was likely to be detained in Egypt (they would be travelling home by Flying Boat), Ruth said, with a wry smile, that 'other distinguished exiles had lived there before'. Clarke later wrote to Baring in his report of the meeting: 'I was compelled to some admiration of Ruth whom I had not met before. She has obviously been through a lot including loneliness, but she was neat in appearance and composed in manner. She displays a quick intelligence and a ready wit. She undoubtedly has courage.'

When news got out that they were about to leave, John Redfern and some other journalists invited Ruth to a farewell lunch at the Lobatsi Hotel. When she walked into the hotel bar with the journalists for a drink before the meal, many of the local whites and even some of the British officials ostentatiously walked out. Sitting at a table in the now almost deserted bar, the party was approached by a member of the hotel staff. It was explained that since Mrs Khama was 'no longer a member of the European community' she was therefore 'not entitled to enjoy the facilities of the hotel'. As a concession, the staff member explained, she could have a drink in one of the bedrooms where she would not be seen by other Europeans in the hotel.

During the last two weeks, the preparations for their leaving took up all of Ruth's time. It had been decided that Naledi, Seretse's younger sister, should come with them to London. Naledi, now a trained nurse, would be able to help Ruth look after Jacqueline.

At the same time, Seretse and Tshekedi were moving towards full agreement. They agreed to drop their civil case and settle the ownership of the cattle herds amicably.

Meanwhile, the British secretly moved two white Southern Rhodesian policewomen into Lobatsi in case, at the last minute, Ruth had to be put on the aeroplane by force. But there was no point in further resistance and Seretse, Ruth and the tribe were resigned to the government's decision. In Serowe, the Bamangwato had sunk into a mood of sullen non-cooperation and Forbes McKenzie described the situation there as very 'difficult'. In Lobatsi, on the morning of 17 August, Ruth and Seretse, with baby Jacqueline and Naledi, drove to the airstrip at Gaberone to board the light aircraft chartered by the government to take them to the Flying Boat at Victoria Falls. There to see them off were more than 350 of the most senior Africans in the protectorate. Phetu Sekgoma and the leading Bamangwato were there as also were the leaders of the other main tribes. Tshekedi and Seretse had already issued a statement announcing their partial reconciliation and now Seretse stood in front of the crowd to say his final goodbye.

I want you all to know that I leave you unwillingly. I am going because I and my wife have been served with an order to leave the country. I had planned that with God's help and your cooperation I would have been able to introduce reforms for the advancement and happiness of my people. To be deprived of the opportunity to do so is a sad and bitter disappointment to me. While I am gone, I give you this advice. Pay your taxes and obey all lawful orders given to you by the government. Above all pay due homage and remain loyal to His Majesty, King George VI. To each one of you, my wife and I with sorrowful hearts express our deep appreciation of your loyalty and unlimited kindness. Your welfare and happiness will be our constant concern wherever we may be. May God bless each one of you and protect you.

In silence, he and his family turned and boarded the aircraft. With a roar of its twin engines, the 'plane bumped down the rough airstrip and lifted into the air. Behind them on the ground the crowd slowly moved away.

Postscript

The years that followed the exile of Ruth and Seretse were, in the end, kinder to them than to those who did them harm. In the immediate aftermath of their departure, the British government was delighted that it had managed to get them out of Bechuanaland without provoking wide-scale rioting. Congratulations flew between London, Pretoria, Mafeking and Serowe. Special praise was heaped on Baring including a personal note of approval from Attlee. Relations with South Africa warmed up considerably and Baring joked that 'Malan and I are now practically blood brothers'.

But the problem of the Bamangwato refused to go away. Ruth and Seretse waited out their banishment in a rented house in southern England, becoming a rallying point for the growing number of people both inside and outside politics who wanted Britain to move quickly away from its colonial heritage. In an effort to rid themselves of this troublesome couple, the government offered Seretse a senior diplomatic post in Jamaica. Ruth was shown glossy brochures of palm-fringed golden beaches and deep blue seas in the hope that she too might be persuaded. The offer was rejected, Seretse arguing that if he was unfit to lead his tribe then surely he must be unsuitable to be a diplomat.

In Serowe itself, the situation deteriorated rapidly. There was sporadic violence and property belonging to Tshekedi and his supporters was destroyed. The tribe sank into a state of sullen inactivity resisting all attempts by the British to create an alternative administration. In the years that followed, they refused either to form the advisory councils that the British wanted or to elect a new chief. In September 1954, they sent a telegram to the young Queen Elizabeth II. 'Great White Queen,' they wrote, 'we are desperate. The Bamangwato are sad. Over our land there is a great shadow blotting out the sun. Please put an end to our troubles. Send us our real Chief – the man born our Chief – Seretse.'

In October 1951, Attlee's tiny parliamentary majority forced him to call another general election. This time he lost. The electorate returned Winston Churchill and the Conservatives to government and an urgent review of the Seretse affair was ordered. Many people, remembering Churchill's reference to 'a very disreputable transaction' and the withering Conservative criticism of the Labour government's decision to exile the young chief, were hopeful that his banishment would soon end. However, when the new ministers looked at all the documents, they announced that, instead of Seretse and Ruth being exiled for 'a minimum of five years', it had been decided to banish them 'indefinitely'.

Sir Evelyn Baring left South Africa soon afterwards and in 1952 became Governor of Kenya. For the next seven years he presided over an increasingly terrible situation, wrestling with both the determined territorial ambitions of the white settlers and the horrific atrocities of the Mau Mau guerrilla movement. In the 1960s, he became chairman of the Colonial Development Corporation before retiring to his family estates in the north of England. There, in 1973, while out walking across rugged country, he fell heavily and died soon afterwards.

Sir Percivale Liesching continued as the Commonwealth Office's Permanent Secretary until 1955 when he was appointed to Baring's old job as High Commissioner to South Africa and the three protectorates.

Meanwhile, in England, the Labour Party was waiting out the thirteen years of Tory rule that followed Churchill's 1951 victory. Patrick Gordon-Walker remained in the front rank of the party and, at the 1964 general election, was the Labour Party's Shadow Foreign Secretary. The Tories lost and Harold Wilson formed a new government. Dramatically against the trend, Gordon-Walker suffered the embarrassment of losing his seat at Smethwick. Ironically, it was racial prejudice that ousted him although this time he was on the receiving end. Smethwick had seen a great influx of black immigrants in the previous ten years and the Conservative campaign in the constituency played on white fears of being 'swamped'. The Labour government was identified with a more liberal policy on immigration and 'If you want a nigger neighbour, vote Labour' became an unofficial campaign slogan. Labour voters abstained in large numbers and when the poll was declared, Gordon-Walker had lost the seat he had held for nineteen years.

Harold Wilson nevertheless named him as Foreign Secretary and a search was started for a constituency that would return him to Parliament. At the end of 1964 Harold Wilson elevated Reginald Sorensen to the House of Lords. Sorensen, one of Gordon-Walker's most vociferous critics in the days of the Seretse crisis, represented the poor, East End of London constituency of Leyton and had held a safe majority of nearly 8,000. But, in the bi-election, Gordon-Walker fought a poor campaign and when the votes were cast in January 1965 the Conservative candidate had pipped him again, this time by just 205 votes. He was left with no choice but to resign as Foreign Secretary and leave politics.

Meanwhile, in South Africa the National Party was increasing its majority at every election. In 1954, Johannes Strydom, the fierce Transvaaler, succeeded Malan and the pace of apartheid quickened. Within a very few years, segregation of the races had entered every aspect of South African life where it did not affect the social or economic convenience of the ruling whites. At the same time, the Nationalists used their political power to promote Afrikaner businessmen and industrialists and gradually began to shift the balance of economic control away from the English speakers.

By the time Strydom was replaced by Hendrik Verwoerd in 1958, the National Party leadership felt strong enough to make one last try for its ultimate goal – final freedom from the British. The urge that had sent the trekkers into the wilderness in the 1830s, that had spurred the farmers of the Transvaal and the Orange Free State to take on the mightiest army in the world in the 1890s, that had been secretly at the centre of Anglo-South African relations throughout the Seretse crisis, that urge, under Verwoerd, was not to be frustrated. Now, at last, they would take South Africa out of the Commonwealth, replace the British Queen as Head of State with an Afrikaner President and sever the last political link with the Empire of which they had been an unwilling part for 150 years.

As the National Party and the secret Broederbond organisation began preparing white public opinion for the referendum on continued Commonwealth membership, they received an unexpected boost from the British themselves. On 2 February 1960, the British Prime Minister, Harold Macmillan, delivered his famous 'Wind of Change' speech to the South African Parliament in which he spoke of the spirit of African nationalism sweeping the continent. 'It is our earnest desire,' Macmillan said, 'to give South Africa our support and encouragement but . . . there are some aspects of your policies which make it impossible for us to do this without being false to our own deep convictions about the political destinies of free men, to which, in our territories, we are trying to give effect.'

It was becoming clear to a majority of South African whites that if they wished to continue as they were, then they must continue alone. On 5 October 1960, South African whites queued up to vote either 'yes' or 'no' to staying within the Commonwealth. Fifty-two per cent voted to get out and the Afrikaner Nationalist triumph was complete. For John Vorster, soon to become Verwoerd's Minister of Justice and subsequently Prime Minister himself, it was 'the fulfilment of a lifetime's ambition. To become a Republic; that's what you fought for, that's what you hoped for, that's what you prayed for.'

Yet no sooner had they got rid of one enemy, than they realised that there was a larger and much stronger one in their very midst. As the inequities of apartheid increased, so did black resistance. The explosion of black resentment in the mid 1970s and again in the mid 1980s led some Afrikaners to a fundamental reassessment of apartheid and, subsequently, to the re-emergence of that old fault line in Afrikanerdom first opened up by the trekkers. At the end of the 1970s with the retirement of the old Transvaaler John Vorster, the leadership of the party passed, once more, to the Cape. The new Prime Minister, P. W. Botha, announced that apartheid was dead and that the country must move to a more equable form of government. In rapid succession a series of apartheid's most precious icons were smashed, including the Prohibition of Mixed Marriages Act. At the same time, a search was instituted for a political formula that would both preserve white interests yet satisfy sufficient black demands to prevent a tide of terrorism sweeping the country. While many outside South Africa felt this a wise, if overcautious, policy, an increasing number of Nationalists in the Transvaal, the traditional keepers, as they believed, of the true Afrikaner flame, had no stomach for it. A new party, the Conservative Party, was formed drawing almost all its support from the Transvaal and dedicated to the preservation of those institutions that had brought the Afrikaner to power and kept him there. By the end of the 1980s, this new party had won a string of election victories throughout the Transvaal. The reforms, which seemed to many outside the country as merely cosmetic, had split the Afrikaner nation more deeply than at any time since the Anglo-Boer War.

But what of Ruth and Seretse? As the vision of emerging independent Africa became clearer in the 1950s, so Seretse was among the first to realise that the continent's future lay not in the old tribal institutions of the Chief and the Royal Household, but in new political structures better able to cope with the challenges of imminent nationhood which lay ahead. In 1956, he renounced his claim to the chieftainship of the Bamangwato and the British government allowed him and Ruth back to Bechuanaland as 'private persons'. There, with like-minded people from all the tribes in the protectorate, he formed a political party. When, in 1966, the British granted Bechuanaland its independence, Seretse's Democratic Party won a landslide majority in the first election and he became Prime Minister of the Republic of Botswana. Soon afterwards he was knighted by the Queen. Fighting and winning three subsequent elections, Sir Seretse established a political and social framework in Botswana which serves as an example to every other country in Africa. A genuine multiparty democracy governed with a sense of public service under the rule of law, Botswana today has one of the soundest economies and currencies in Africa and the future for all its people is bright. Compared with the rest of the continent, corruption hardly exists and general levels of crime are extremely low. There has been no great rush to the cities or establishment of vast shanty towns as has happened elsewhere in post-independent Africa. The traditional social framework, based upon the village and its cattle, has held and been built upon. Through careful investment in cattle production and, more recently, mineral exploitation, the country has now the strongest economy of all the so-called 'Frontline' states, those black African countries bordering South Africa.

The economic and military power of Pretoria, however, still casts a long shadow over the whole of southern Africa and some states, Angola and Mozambique in particular, have been brought to the point of collapse. Botswana has also suffered regular armed incursions from South Africa. Armoured vehicles and helicopters have crossed the border to shoot and destroy what the South Africans have claimed are bases of the banned African National Congress, the black guerrilla movement fighting to end white rule. Botswana has consistently claimed that it does not allow such bases on its soil and although the international community has chided South Africa for its actions, Botswana remains in permanent fear of attack.

Politically, Botswana remains a multiparty democracy. So firmly rooted were the institutions that Sir Seretse Khama built, that they have survived his death from cancer in 1980. He was 59. In the obituaries that followed his funeral, he was praised as a pragmatic politician who skilfully nursed his impoverished country towards prosperity, always putting the welfare of his people before ideology and yet never compromising their independence in the face of South African threats. As a man, he is remembered by all who knew him as gentle, intelligent and warm. His sense of humour allowed him to see the ridiculous side to prejudice and discrimination. After independence, he told friends he was considering naming his official residence 'The Woodpile'.

Today, his widow, Lady Ruth, lives on in Botswana as a kind of unofficial Queen Mother, loved and respected by the nation. Her daughter Jacqueline was followed first by a son, and then by twins, both boys. Her life today is as full as ever. She established and still leads the Botswana Council of Women, an organisation dedicated to improving the knowledge of the nation's wives and mothers in nutrition, child welfare and medical hygiene. She is also president of the Botswana Red Cross and represents her country at international meetings of that organisation.

She has two homes, one a farm twenty miles to the north of Gaberone, the national capital, and another on the fringes of Serowe.

But how to place those dramatic events of forty years ago in their proper context? The marriage of Ruth and Seretse, simply because he was black and she was white, shook the foundations of his society. There was much bitterness and division before the tribe accepted the chief's wife. In doing so, many Bamangwato were forced to come to terms with the very racial prejudices that they criticised so vehemently across the border in South Africa. In the end they did overcome them and triumphantly so.

And what of South Africa and Great Britain? It has been difficult to find any villains in this secret, twisted tale. Many of the characters are unsympathetic, some callous and unfeeling, others weak and irresolute, and yet others passionately convinced of their duty. But, like all of us, they were the prisoners of history. The Afrikaners who had come to power in 1948 stood at the end of what they saw as 150 years of subjugation and injustice at the hands of an arrogant imperial power. So often had they appeared to stand on the brink of extinction that they had developed an obsession with self-preservation. In the policy of apartheid they had found the evil means to ensure just that and they would not be thwarted.

The British government found itself leading a country which still retained all the trappings of its former glory but with a shattered economy unable to pay any of the bills. It now faced the difficult task of adjusting to the new reality. It would take another fifteen years before Britain had granted independence to most of its colonies. Before it could do so, the British people and their leaders had to undergo almost a revolution in their attitudes to their black colonial subjects. The simple love story of Ruth and Seretse, a story that ordinary British people could take to their hearts, played a part in the developing awareness that the days of haughty, colonial dictat were drawing to a close.

As for uranium and the atomic bomb, it is still not possible to tell the whole story. The desire to remain a major power led Attlee, Bevin and others – and the governments which followed them – to make the development of nuclear weapons a priority. Atomic bombs seemed a cheap and attainable way of retaining a place at the centre of world affairs. The way to force the Americans to share their nuclear secrets was to offer them uranium and South Africa seemed to have that in abundance. But the whole history of uranium supply is bedevilled with secrecy and deceit. Even today, most of the British files dealing with uranium negotiations with South Africa remain closed. In reply to a request from me, the South African government considered opening their file on the issues surrounding their opposition to Ruth and Seretse's marriage. After a lengthy examination Pretoria informed me that on no account should the file be released. It is difficult to imagine how, forty years after the event, anything other than the uranium negotiations could provoke such a response. In the event, Britain failed to get exclusive rights to South African uranium. The power of the American dollar and the need for the South Africans to sell for the highest price saw to that.

And yet the ties between South Africa and Britain remain as close as ever. Every British government has vigorously condemned apartheid while remaining South Africa's most powerful diplomatic ally. At the time of the marriage of Ruth and Seretse, Britain's leaders found that national interest conflicted with their official, public position. The same may be true today.

In Serowe, meanwhile, the Bamangwato had overcome the last of their prejudices, a mixed-race chief. Ever since Seretse had given up the chieftainship to begin the political campaign which led to his leadership of the whole country, the tribe had felt the loss very keenly. Although in independent Botswana the chieftainships of the tribes had become largely ceremonial, the Bamangwato pleaded with Seretse's son, Ian, to assume the title. For years Ian, whose official name is Seretse Khama Ian Khama, resisted. Finally, in what was to prove the last year of his father's life, he gave in. At a huge ceremony in Serowe's Kgotla ground, his parents watched as he was installed as Paramount Chief and the traditional leopard skin was draped around his shoulders. The tribe roared its approval.

Above the Kgotla ground on the south-eastern slope of Serowe Hill, the Bamangwato bury their chiefs. Cut into the rock of a smooth plateau, one side looking down upon the huts of the village, the other out across the vastness of the African plain, are the tombs of Khama, Sekgoma, Tshekedi and Seretse. Ruth goes there frequently. Apart from the desert wind that roars across the plain, it is a quiet place to be alone with memories.

Bibliography

Interviews conducted by the author:

Lady Khama
Mrs Muriel Sanderson
Mr Goareng Mosinyi MP
The Hon. J. G. Haskins MP
Mr Radipophu Sekgoma
Mr Goaletsa Tsukudu
Mr Mokatcha Mokadi
Rt Revd Trevor Huddleston
Revd Alan Seager
Mr Michael Fairlie
Miss Eleanor Emery
Rt Hon. Tony Benn MP
Ms Mary Benson
Mr and Mrs Tommy Shaw
Mrs Maria Stoneham
Miss Audrey and Mrs Gwen Blackbeard
Mr Jack Tarr

Unpublished Sources

British Government papers lodged in the Public Record Office, Kew, Surrey:

Commonwealth Relations Office under the following Group, Class and (where
    relevant) Piece numbers: DO10; DO11; DO13; DO18/56; DO35/4113, /4114,
    /4115, /4116, /4117, /4118, /4120, /4121, /4122, /4123, /4124, /4125; DO64;
    DO102; DO117; DO118/56; DO119/1152, /1160; DO120; DO121/24, /25, /26,
    /27, /147, /148, /149, /150, /151; DO128/17, /18.
British Cabinet papers: CAB 129/38, /39, /40, /41.
Atomic files: AB16/394.

The archives of the London Missionary Society catalogued by the Council for
World Mission and lodged at the School of Oriental and African Studies,
London University: AF/37 Box 51, 52.

Bibliography

Published Sources

Newspapers and Periodicals

UK – *The Times, Manchester Guardian, Daily Mail, Daily Express, Daily Mirror, Daily Graphic, The Spectator, Evening News, Sunday Express, News of the World*.
Southern Africa – *Die Transvaler, Die Burger, Natal Witness, Bulawayo Chronicle*.

Articles and Essays

'The Statesman: Tshekedi Khama' by Michael Crowder.
'New Voices Before World War II' by T. Mooko.
'The Protectorate and World War II' by D. Kiyaga-Mulindwa.
'The Central District: The Bamangwato Crisis, 1948–1956' by Neil Parsons.

All the above were published in *The Birth of Botswana* by Longman (Botswana) 1987.

Books

Benson, Mary, *Tshekedi Khama*, London, 1960.
Douglas-Home, Charles, *Evelyn Baring: The Last Proconsul*, London, 1978.
Fisher, John, *The Afrikaners*, London, 1969.
Gowing, Margaret, *Independence and Deterrence*, London, 1974.
Harris, J. C., *Khama: The Great African Chief*, London, 1923.
Harrison, David, *The White Tribe of Africa*, London, 1981.
Judd, Denis, *The Boer War*, London, 1977.
Morris, Donald R., *The Washing of the Spears*, London, 1965.
Redfern, John, *Ruth and Seretse: A Very Disreputable Transaction*, London, 1955.
Rey, Charles, *Monarch of All I Survey* (edited by Neil Parsons and Michael Crowder), Gaberone, 1988.
Ritter, E. A., *Shaka Zulu*, London, 1958.
Serfontein, J. H. P., *Brotherhood of Power*, London, 1979.
Sillery, Anthony, *The Bechuanaland Protectorate*, Cape Town, 1952.

Index

Abrahams, Sir Sidney 146, 153
Addison, Viscount 122, 146, 153, 157
African National Congress 212
Afrikaans 79
Afrikaners 95–6, 79, 214: settlement in S.
    Africa 13; trek from Cape Colony,
    1830 14; defeat Zulus at Blood River,
    1838 14; found Natal 14; found Orange
    Free State and Transvaal 14; defeated
    in Boer War 18–19; poverty in 1920s
    80; develop 'apartheid' 81–2
Arden-Clarke, Commissioner 60
Asprey and Co.'s encyclopaedia: definition
    of 'Negro' 179
Attlee, Clement 88, 100, 101, 133, 134, 135,
    150, 151, 154, 161, 165, 176, 177, 185,
    208, 214

Badirwang Sekgoma 77
Bamangwato tribe 7, 215
  age regiments 47, 57
  history: foundation, eighteenth c. 11;
    growth, nineteenth c. 12; raided by
    Matabele, nineteenth c. 13; defeat
    Matabele 16; threats to, late
    nineteenth c. 16–17; life under British
    rule, twentieth c. 22–3; reactions to
    Seretse's marriage 46, 48–57; opinion
    sways towards Seretse 59, 61, 62–3;
    tribal conference accepts Seretse as
    chief 66–73; suspicious of British
    desire for 'talks' 141, 143; boycotts
    conference called by Baring re
    Seretse's banning 170–2; decides to
    withhold taxes from British 172; fears
    of rioting among 172–3; disturbances
    connected with Seretse/Tshekedi
    conflict 191; learns of Seretse's
    sentence of exile from him 196–7;
    adopts policy of non-cooperation with
    British 206, 208–9; wish for Seretse's
    return, 1954 208; makes Seretse's son
    Ian Paramount Chief, 1980 215
  method of government by discussion 52
  racial discrimination against in World
    Wars 60, 61
  serve British in wartime 47, 59–60, 61

technical school 61
Baring, Sir Evelyn 27, 28, 40, 42, 44, 62, 66,
    75–8 passim, 102, 104, 105, 106, 110,
    122, 123, 135, 137, 138, 142, 152, 166,
    181–2, 183, 193, 194, 203, 205, 208
  career in colonial service 90, 91, 209
  death, 1973 209
  part in Seretse affair: persuaded to
    oppose Seretse's appointment as
    Chief of Bamangwato 92–6; belief in
    Britain's duty to native populations
    91; learns of Britain's ban on Seretse's
    chieftainship 111–12; unable to
    assemble Bamangwato for conference
    170–2; fears Bamangwato will riot
    172–3, 174; sticks to belief in
    correctness of Seretse's banishment
    184; asks Smuts' opinion 184
Bathoen, Chief of Bangwaketse 50, 56, 62,
    66: opposition to Seretse's marriage
    54, 55, 72
Bechuanaland 46, 76: Stone Age
    inhabitants 10; conquered by Tswana
    tribe 10; early settlement 10–11;
    threats to, late nineteenth c. 16–17;
    comes under British protection 17;
    allowed to remain free of Rhodes'
    influence 18; ambiguous status in S.
    African Union, 1910 19; white
    prejudice against Seretse and his wife
    119. See also Botswana
Bevan, Aneurin 88
Bevin, Ernest 88, 100, 181
Beyers, Lt-Gen. Len 98
Blackbeard, Audrey and Gwen 26, 118,
    119, 168
Blackbeard, Colin 119, 168
Botha, Louis 79
Botha, P.W. 211
Botswana 212–13, 215
  Botswana Council of Women 213
  Botswana Red Cross 213
  fear of attack by S. Africa 213
  new republic of 212
Bourke-White, Margaret: photograph of
    Seretse and Ruth 139
Bradshaw, Alan 119, 120, 168, 170:

victimised for friendship with Seretse
and Ruth 173, 174
Bradshaw, Doris 168, 170
Britain
colonial blacks' disillusion with re
Seretse affair 176–9
first general election of 1951 150–1
formula for Commonwealth of Nations
99–100
history of connection with southern
Africa: annexes Cape Colony, early
nineteenth c. 14; annexes Natal 14;
defeats Boers 18; causes deaths of
Afrikaner women and children in
'concentration camps' 18–19, 79;
attempts to stop Seretse's marriage
28–34, 35; press coverage of Seretse
and Ruth 43–5, 58, 74–5; fears of S.
Africa leaving Commonwealth 100;
wish to buy S. African uranium 101–4,
214; House of Commons furore over
banning of Seretse from chieftainship
163–4; popular support for Seretse
165–6
loses US nuclear cooperation 100–1, 214
post-war problem of colonial settlers'
demands 90–1, 105, 147
second general election of 1951 209
ties with S. Africa 214–15
British South Africa Company 16, 17
Brockway, Fenner 164, 185: concern for
Ruth Khama 191–2
Buchanan, Douglas 26–9 *passim*, 40, 41, 47,
77: sees problems with Seretse's
marriage 42
Buchanan, John 27, 29–32 passim, 34, 35,
38, 40, 41: view of Seretse's marriage
36–7
Burger, Die 110
Burgess, Joe 26, 40, 118
Bushmen 10

Chamberlain, Joseph 18, 21
Churchill, Winston 101, 209: criticises
government action over Seretse 163–4
Clarke, W.A.W. 205, 206
Colonial Office 29, 29n
Commonwealth Relations Office 28, 29,
29n, 33, 34, 40, 108, 111, 145: has
problems setting up Inquiry into
Seretse's suitability for chieftainship
121–3
Constantine, Leary 165, 175, 178, 179, 184
Coupland, Sir Reginald 27, 40
Creech-Jones, Arthur 104, 121, 134
Crew, Prof. F.A.E. on miscegenation
199–200
Cromer, Lord 90

Daily Express 107, 108, 195
Daily Graphic 74, 99
Daily Mail 44, 58, 109, 114, 117, 160, 169
Daily Mirror 58, 74, 75, 108: reports
Seretse's marriage 43–4
Daily Telegraph 187
Dingaan, Chief of the Zulus 14
Dominions Office 97, 102
Driberg, Tom 164, 174

Eden, Anthony 161
Egeland, Leif 88, 89, 102, 104, 105, 111
Elizabeth II, Queen 208
Ellenberger, Vivian 66, 70, 73, 75, 205
Elliot, Hugh 180
Evans, Adm. 22
Ewing, Sgt 144

Forsyth, Douglas 87–8, 94, 95, 96, 102, 104:
explains S. African concern over
Bechuanaland to Baring 92
Fraenkel, Percy 143, 146, 148, 153, 154,
156, 157, 159, 191, 193
Franks, Oliver: on US opinion re Seretse
181
Freedman, Dr 193

Gemell, Dr 169, 193
George III, King 14
Goareng Mosinyi 48, 52, 56, 57, 71, 143,
168: first meeting with Ruth 115
Gordon-Walker, Patrick 138, 152, 166, 172,
174, 178, 179, 181, 192, 193, 202, 203
becomes Commonwealth Secretary, 1951
151
election defeats, 1964 and 1965 209–10
part in Seretse affair: role into Inquiry
into Seretse's suitability 122, 131; fails
to persuade Seretse to resign
chieftainship 153–5; informs Seretse
he is to be exiled from Bechuanaland
156–9; startled by Seretse's press
conference 161; meets Seretse once
more 161–2; mauled in House of
Commons over government decision
on Seretse 162–4, 185–6; faces stormy
Cabinet meeting 182–3, 184–5; gives
Seretse permission to return home
temporarily 182, 183
Gorewang Sekgoma 77
Grey, Edward 96
Griffiths, James 185

Haggard, Rider 45, 7̣
Haile, Revd A.J. 30, 31, 32, 62, 128, 129,
177, 178
Hamilton, A.A.M. 99
Harragin, Sir Walter 125, 129, 132, 133:

leads Inquiry into Seretse's suitability
for chieftainship 122, 123
Hertzog, Gen. Barry 79–82 *passim*
Hogg, Quintin (later Lord Hailsham) 186
Huddleston, Father Trevor, 91, 93
Hudson, R.S. 123
Huggins, Sir Godfrey 191

Ink Spots 1, 2, 3
Inquiry into Seretse's suitability for
chieftainship: setting up 121–3; terms
of reference 123–4; team members 122,
123; progress 124–9; necessity for
attributed to Tshekedi 124, 125;
character analysis of Seretse 130–1;
commissioners' report 130–3; names
South Africa as obstacle to retaining
Seretse 131–2

Jacobs, George 114–15
Jameson, Dr L.S. 18
Jowitt, Viscount 143

Keikameng, George 71
Keith, John 29–32 *passim*, 34, 35, 37, 38, 41,
44, 108, 144, 148, 149
Kgari, Chief of the Bakwena 50, 62
Khama, Chief of the Bamangwato 15, 19,
51, 52, 53, 65, 66, 215: converted to
Christianity 15–16; defeats Matabele
16; Christian rule of Bamangwato 16;
successful appeal to Queen Victoria
for protection against Rhodes 17–18;
death, 1923 20
Khama, Jacqueline (daughter) 202, 206,
213: birth 200
Khama, Naledi (sister) 49, 50, 72, 206
Khama, Ruth, Lady xv, xvi, 58, 215
children 213
life after marriage: reconciled with
parents 59, 108; hears Seretse has
been accepted by Bamangwato 107;
pursued by press 107, 108–9; flies to
Bechuanaland 113–14; meets Seretse
115; driven to Palapye, Bechuanaland
115–16; harassed by press 116–17, 118;
sees Seretse's house in Serowe 117–18;
welcomed by Bamangwato 118–19;
suffers nervous collapse 120; declared
Prohibited Immigrant in S. Africa 124,
131; pregnancy 134–5, 137; suspicious
of British desire for 'talks' 140, 141–2;
learns of British decision to exile
Seretse 159, 160; support for 168,
169–70; friends in Bechuanaland
168–9; enlists aid of press 169;
prevents Baring addressing
Bamangwato 170; misses meeting with

returning Seretse 188–90; problems
with pregnancy 193–4; eventually
reunited with Seretse 195–6; forced to
part from husband 197; gives birth to
daughter 200; welcomes husband 201;
sent to Lobatsi with husband 202–7;
meets Tshekedi 204–5; exile in
England 208; life as widow in
Botswana 213
See also Williams, Ruth
Khama, Seretse Khama Ian (son): installed
as Paramount Chief of Bamangwato,
1980 215
Kipling, Rudyard 45
Kitchener, Lord 18, 79

Langley, Major (later Col) 66, 68, 70, 170,
171
Lawrenson, District Commissioner 65, 66,
75
League of Coloured Peoples: support for
Seretse 165
League of Nations 80, 89
Lekhutile, Simon 71
Liesching, Sir Percivale 93, 95, 97, 102,
105, 106, 108, 138, 143–6 *passim*, 148,
153, 154, 155, 157, 158, 173, 194, 199:
opposition to Seretse's chieftainship
97–9, 149–50, 152; appointed High
Commissioner to S. Africa, 1955 209
Livingstone, David 3, 15
London Missionary Society (LMS) 3, 15,
20, 21, 24, 27, 30–3 *passim*, 40, 41, 42,
49, 50, 53, 62: comes out in support of
Seretse 177–8
Louw, E.H. 103

Machtig, Sir Eric 28, 29, 40, 93
McIntosh, Phineas 21–2, 97, 119
McKenzie, Forbes 173, 191, 196–9 *passim*,
202
Mackenzie, John 3, 15
Macmillan, Harold: 'Wind of Change'
speech, 1960 210–11
Malan, Daniel 81, 82, 83, 85, 86, 88, 92–6
passim, 102, 137, 147, 160, 204, 208:
conflict with Strydom 87, 92;
fulminates against Seretse's marriage
119, 124
Manchester Guardian 74, 172
Manhattan Project 100–1
Manyaphiri Ikitseng 67
Mathodi, Ramarula 68
Mathware Kefhalotse 71
Milner, Baron 79
Miscegenation 199–200
Mitchell, Joseph 165
Moffat, David 3, 15

Moikangoa, Dr Don 168–9, 189, 192, 193, 200, 201
Mokadi, Mokatcha 51–2
Molema, Dr S.M. 173
Monks, Noel 109, 160: interviews Tshekedi in Serowe 109–10; pursues Seretse and Ruth 117; reports Ruth's reaction to British banning of Seretse 169; failure of plan to reunite Seretse and Ruth 188–90
Monsarrat, Nicholas 170, 171, 172: novels 170
Morrison, Herbert 88
Murcott, Brian 117
Mzilakasi, Chief of the Matabele 12–13, 15, 16

Natal: Boer republic annexed by British 14
Natal Witness 90
National Council for Civil Liberties: condemns British treatment of Seretse 165
Nettleton, Mr 123, 204
News Chronicle 118, 160
News of the World 116
Noel-Baker, Philip 88–9, 102, 103, 104, 121, 123, 130, 133, 135, 141, 143, 150: confronted with S. African objections to Seretse's chieftainship 89–90, 99; recommends British refusal to recognise Seretse's chieftainship 110–11; reaction to Committee of Inquiry report 133–4; decides to talk Seretse into resigning 135–8; puts plan before Cabinet 137; attempts to get Seretse to resign 146–7; leaves Commonwealth Office, 1951 151
Ntsaga, Olweleng 68

Orange Free State 15
Orchard, Ronald 27, 29–33 *passim*, 37, 38, 40, 41, 42, 49, 62, 120, 128
  misgivings over British handling of Seretse affair 177–8
  on strength of Seretse's marriage 43
Oxford University: West African Students' Club 177

Patterson, Revd Dr Leonard 9, 29, 30, 31–2, 33, 34, 37
Phetu Mphoeng 67, 76
Phetu Sekgoma 64, 71, 143, 168, 170, 171, 172, 190, 192, 194, 195, 200, 205
Picture Post 198
Pilkington, Dr Roger 29–32 *passim*, 35: view of Ruth Williams 35, 36
Platt-Mills, Mr 131
Pritchard, Wing-Commander 188, 189, 190

Radcliffe, Peter 180
Radipophu Sekgoma 46–7, 48, 52, 60, 71, 168
Rathcreedan, Lord 146, 148, 156, 158, 162
Redfern, John 172, 188, 189, 195, 206
Reid, Colin 187
Rey, Lt-Col Charles 21, 22
Rhodes, Cecil 18: ambitions in S. Africa 16–17
Roberts, David 180
Robertson, Fyfe: unflattering report on Seretse and Ruth 198–9
Roosevelt, Pres. Franklin D. 101
Royal Air Force: racial prejudice in 4–5

Seager, Revd Alan 53, 66: puts up Seretse and Ruth in Serowe 118, 120
Sekgoma I, Chief of the Bamangwato 13, 51, 215: friction with Christian son 15, 16
Sekgoma II, Chief of the Bamangwato 20, 52, 53, 215
Senzangakona, Chief of the Zulus 11–12
Seretse Khama xv, xvi, xvii, 20, 30, 56, 215: early meetings with Ruth Williams 1–5; proposes to Ruth 7; position as chief in Bechuanaland 6, 20; tells regent of decision to marry 9; first attempt to marry frustrated 31–4; applies for licence at Register Office 37; marriage 38–9; plans to return home and explain marriage to Bamangwato 43–4; besieged by press 44; flies to Johannesburg 49–50; reaches Bechuanaland 50; welcomed home by tribe 51–2; puts case before tribe 53, 54–5; returns to England 57, 58; continues law studies, 1949 59; meets regent in Mafeking 64; returns to Serowe 64; puts case for chieftainship to tribal conference 66–7, 68–9, 70–1; accepted as chief by Bamangwato 72–3; learns of British Inquiry into chieftainship 111; receives wife in Bechuanaland 115–18; recognised as Chief of Bamangwato 120; declared Prohibited Immigrant in S. Africa 124, 131; evidence to Harragin Inquiry 127–8; invited to talks with British government 139–41; travels to London for talks 141–5 *passim*; resists British pressure to resign 146–8, 153–4; offered allowance but barred from chieftainship 156–9; explains British decision to press conference 159–60; depressed at prospect of exile 175; addresses Seretse Khama Fighting Committee

175–6; popular support for 165–6, 176–9; addresses rally in Trafalgar Square 184; temporary return to Bechuanaland 186–90 *passim*; plan to visit wife 192, 194, 195; reunited with wife 195–6; tells tribe about his exile 196–7; forced to leave wife 197; given leave to visit wife on eve of daughter's birth 200; sees wife and new-born daughter 201; moves to Lobatsi with wife and daughter 202–7; reconciled with his uncle, the regent 204–5, 206, 207; exile in England 208; renounces claim to chieftainship, 1956 212; allowed to return to Bechuanaland 212; becomes prime minister of new republic of Botswana 212; knighted 212; death, 1980 213; tomb 215. *See also* Inquiry into Seretse's suitability for chieftainship

Seretse Khama Fighting Committee 165, 184

mass meeting in support of Seretse 175–6

meets Gordon-Walker 178–9

Serowe, Bechuanaland (now Botswana) 2, 20, 110, 135, 170, 174, 191

post office 26, 40

welcomes Ruth Khama 118–19

Shaw, Barbara 116, 117, 119, 134–5, 168

Shaw, Mrs 'Ma' 115–16, 118, 119, 168

Shaw, Tommy 116, 117, 119, 168

Shaka, Chief of the Zulus 12–13, 14

Sillery, Anthony 75, 77, 111, 123, 135, 138–41 *passim*, 173, 193, 194

Smuts, FM Jan 80, 82, 83, 87, 97, 101, 102, 184

Sorenson, Revd R.W. 162, 176: elevated to House of Lords 210

South Africa

Act of Union, 1910 19, 75, 79

Afrikaner take-over of Civil Service 84

'apartheid' 59, 82, 83, 86, 210: black resistance to 211; Citizenship Bill 95; Group Areas Act 83; Prohibition of Mixed Marriages Act 83, 211

'Broederbond' 81, 82, 84, 210

Conservative Party 211–12

development, 1910–49 81–4

Dutch Reformed Church 81, 82, 84, 85, 90

effect of Seretse's marriage on: outrage at Seretse's appointment as Chief of Bamangato 85–8, 90; protests to British at Seretse's appointment 88–90; threats to invade Bechuanaland 86, 92; threat to leave Commonwealth 86, 92–3; sales of uranium to UK and

Seretse affair 103–4

leaves Commonwealth, 1960 210–11

National Party 80–5 *passim*, 91, 92, 95, 184, 210

South African Indian Congress 165

United Party 95

Voortrekker Monument 95

World Wars – support for Britain 80, 82

Spectator, The: support for Seretse 179

Stoneham, Maria and John 119

Strydom, Johannes 82, 83, 86, 87, 92, 95, 165, 167, 184, 210

Sullivan, Richard 75, 117, 140, 170, 173

Sunday Dispatch: serialisation of Ruth's 'own' story 198–9

Sunday Express 74, 110, 191, 199

Tarr, Len 23–4

Taylor, Don: views on miscegenation 199

Times, The

condemns British treatment of Seretse 165

publishes letter from Seretse 186–7

Transvaal 15: Jameson Raid, 1895 18

Transvaler, Die 110, 166: on treatment of Seretse by British 165

Truman, Pres. Harry S. 101

Tshekedi, Regent of Bamangwato 6, 9, 43, 46, 47, 76, 77, 94, 97, 121, 158, 162, 215

dictatorial side 59

life and career: becomes regent, 1923 20, 59; conflicts with British 21–2; rule under the British 22–3; sends Seretse to Oxford to be educated, 1945 24; learns of Seretse's intention to marry, 1947 24, 25; consternation over marriage plan 25–6, 27–8; early moves to prevent marriage 26–8, 39; reactions to marriage 40–1, 48, 49; stops Seretse's allowance 41; organises tribal conference to discuss marriage 50–1, 54; states opposition to marriage 55–6, 57; tries to get Ruth banned from Serowe 61–2; loses fight over chieftainship to Seretse 65–6, 68–73; leaves Serowe 76–7; tells *Daily Mail* of opposition to Seretse's chieftainship 109–10; delighted at British delaying tactics 111; renounces claims to chieftainship 124; falsely used by British as instigator of Inquiry into Seretse's suitability 124, 125; gives evidence to Inquiry 125–7; views rejected by Inquiry 130, 131, 132; meets Ruth Khama 204; reconciled with Seretse 204–5, 206, 207

recruiting methods in Second World War 60

technical school project 61
  tomb 215
Tshukudu, Goaletsa 56, 57, 67–8, 71

United Nations 87, 89

Verwoerd, Hendrik 210, 211
Victoria, Queen 16, 18, 65, 66
Vorster, John 211

Wand, Right Revd William, Bishop of
  London 33, 35, 36, 37
Williams, Dorothy (mother) 5–6, 8, 59, 113
Williams, George (father) 5, 6, 13:
  opposition to daughter's marriage 8;
  reconciled with daughter 59, 108
Williams, Muriel (sister) 2, 3, 4, 6, 31, 33,
  38, 39, 40
Williams, Ruth

contempt for racial prejudice 4–5
courtship and marriage: early meetings
  with Seretse 1–5; agrees to marry
  Seretse 7; family opposition to
  marriage 8; loses job becauses of
  marriage plans 8; preparations for
  wedding 29; first attempt to marry
  frustrated 31–4; marriage at Register
  Office 38–9
family 2, 3, 5–6
wartime service 2–3
work at Lloyd's post-war 3
See also Khama, Ruth, Lady
Wilson, Harold 88, 209, 210
Woodfords, the 168

Zimmerman, John 31, 32, 38
Zulus 12: defeated by Boers at Blood River,
  1838 14; subjugated by British 16